MUSLIM COOL

Muslim Cool

Race, Religion, and Hip Hop in the United States

Su'ad Abdul Khabeer

NEW YORK UNIVERSITY PRESS
New York

NEW YORK UNIVERSITY PRESS
New York
www.nyupress.org

References to Internet websites (URLs) were accurate at the time of writing. Neither the author nor New York University Press is responsible for URLs that may have expired or changed since the manuscript was prepared.

ISBN: 978-1-4798-7215-2 (hardback)
ISBN: 978-1-4798-9450-5 (paperback)

For Library of Congress Cataloging-in-Publication data, please contact the Library of Congress.

New York University Press books are printed on acid-free paper, and their binding materials are chosen for strength and durability. We strive to use environmentally responsible suppliers and materials to the greatest extent possible in publishing our books.

Manufactured in the United States of America

10 9 8 7 6 5 4 3 2 1

Also available as an ebook

In the name of Allah
For the love of Muhammad
To honor the Ancestors
In celebration of my People

CONTENTS

ACKNOWLEDGMENTS

Like a hip hop awardee at the Grammys, first and foremost I would like to thank God. I thank Allah for making all things possible and ask Allah to purify my intentions and accept my efforts. I thank my mother, Amina Amatul Haqq, for her many sacrifices and my grandmother, Carmen Weeks, for her many gifts. I am grateful for Sharifa, for my Abuela Gertrude, and for Kareem, Faatima, and Nafiisah (for cover ideas!), for Anika Sabree, and Saleemah Abdul-Ghafur who always answer my calls, and for Majida Abdul-Karim, Aisha Touré, Sajdah Sabree, Azizah Kahera, Maisha Aziz, Saudah Saleem, Jannah Abdur-Rahman, Sameera Fazili, Kamilah Munir, Siddeeqah Sharif, Tannaz Haddadi, Adnan Zulfiqar, and Kendric Nixon for always holding me down. I am forever in awe of and inspired by all the bold, brilliant, beautiful, Black believing women who built this thing, Al-Islam in America, with their bare hands, like my aunties Jameelah Jalal Uddin, Aaliyah Abdul-Karim, Kareemah Abdul Kareem, Jamillah Adeeb, Sadiyah Abdul-Hakim, Adele Saleem, Umilta Al-Uqdah, and Mama Rakiah Abdur-Rahim. I also offer deep thanks to other family and friends, far too many to name here, for always believing in me and teaching me the importance of this kind of work. I also thank Amir Al-Hajj Tahir Umar Abdullah, my loving accomplice in this beautiful struggle.

There are many folks in the academy who helped move this project from idea to reality. I am certain that without Carolyn Rouse's support, this book would not be in our hands today. She always challenged me to think more deeply, describe more richly, and locate myself in this discipline. I thank Lawrence Rosen for "keeping it real," Carol Greenhouse for listening and guidance, and John J. Jackson, Jr., for always making time for my ideas and taking them seriously. I also must acknowledge the rest of the faculty and staff in the Department of Anthropology and the now renamed Department of African American Studies (Go 'head!) at Princeton University for intellectual community. Alf Shukr to Charis

Boutieri, Sami Hermez, and Erica Weiss for their intellectual fellowship and compassionate friendship, which included reviewing chapter drafts and fielding my writing anxieties. Special thanks also to John Voll at Georgetown University for support early on in my career. Furthermore, I owe great thanks to Amina Wadud, Aminah McCloud, Halimah Touré, Sulayman Nyang, Jon Yasin, Sherman Jackson, Amir Al-Islam, Zain Abdullah, and Jamillah Karim for modeling what it means to be Black, Muslim, and an engaged scholar.

I also want to give a special shout out to an amazing group of colleague-mentor-friends including my gurus Faedah Totah and Junaid Rana as well as Intisar Rabb, Zaheer Ali, Zareena Grewal, Hisham Aidi, Arshad Ali, Sohail Daulatzai, Maryam Kashani, Nitasha Sharma, Hussein Rashid, Edward Curtis, IV, Maurita Poole, Angela Ards, Jennifer Maytorena Taylor, Dawn-Elissa Fischer, H. Samy Alim, Sylvia Chan-Malik, Julianne Hammer, Rabiah Muhammad, James Braxton Peterson, Margari Azizah Hill, Maryam Griffin, and Tomiko Ballantyne.

My research and writing were supported by the Graduate School, the Center for African American Studies, and the Center for Arts and Policy Studies at Princeton University, the Department of Black Studies at the University of California, Santa Barbara, and the College of Liberal Arts at Purdue University. I am deeply appreciative of Ellen Gruenbaum, Venetria Patton, Evelyn Blackwood, Cornelius Bynum, and all the faculty and staff in Anthropology and African American Studies at Purdue for their mentoring and support of my work. I also would like to extend sincere thanks to Jennifer Hammer, Constance Grady, and everyone at NYU Press for recognizing the merits of my project and for a supportive publication process. Also, thank you Hanna Siurua for making copyediting painless and helping me sound good!

Of course, none of this would have been possible without the generosity of each of my teachers in Chicago and beyond. I have changed most of your real names in these pages yet whether I use your real name or a pseudonym I refer to you all as *teacher*. You are my teachers because I only know what I know because you allowed me to listen, to ask questions, to share my thoughts (even when we disagreed) and to be around you and yours (even when you thought the whole participant-observation thing was a bit weird). You are my teachers because you taught me and because I continue to learn from you.

I will be forever indebted to all of you, the amazing individuals I encountered in and through IMAN and in the U.S. Muslim community and the *ummah*, worldwide.

Jazakum Allahu Khairan

Introduction

ESPERANZA: *Stuff is kind of mashed up, and now [Arab and South Asian U.S. American][1] sisters are wanting to dress like the [U.S. Black American] sisters they see on stage. . . . It's girls that are probably first generation here, trying to find the aesthetic that fits them that is not their mother's or from their mother's land, which I can sort of understand since I come from an immigrant [Dominican] background, but what happens is that they start picking from the people that are around them, like the magazine White culture, and then they want to add an urban element cause it's a cool thing, cool to be from an urban environment, right? (Laughs)*

SU'AD: *What is urban? (Laughs) Is that a euphemism?*

ESPERANZA: *I don't even know what it is. (Laughs) You wanna wear cargo pants? . . . See, I have a camouflage scarf, I've worn it only once because this Pakistani girl walked up to me like (mimics a voice) "This is so cool" and I was like [to myself] I can't even pretend like that's OK with me (Laughter). And it's a girl that I love! Now I want to back this up by saying I have been wearing camouflage my whole life, I'm the camouflage queen! . . . I wear it a lot because I like it but also I feel like I can, it's appropriate for me to wear it because my brother was in war, people! (Laughs) Like geez, this is my actual surname on my jacket. Anyway so this sister comes just really sincerely, "I really like your scarf, where can I get it from?" and I was kind of like, "Like, thank you," but I don't know really what else to say.*

It's a compliment but in another way it's really a thievery because we don't have much, right? Like where does culture come from? It comes from people who don't have much. That's where hip hop comes from, that's where house music came from. That's where tying your hair up [in a scarf], wearing fatigues, because you ain't got no other clothes, right? So you got to make do with what you have, and when someone is taking that, you don't have anything left because you don't have much to begin with. You going home to your mansions—how many mansions did I visit in the last week, right?! You going home to silverware that's really silver but you taking my scarf?! Just let me have something. (Laughter)

And I get it; you can't really tell people what they can put on their body. I get that; but there is a certain level you can at least give due to where it's done and at least try to do it authentically yourself. You have to know your boundaries and give knowledge and respect.

Esperanza is a single mother in her early thirties. She is a multimedia artist who loves to teach but also teaches to pay the bills. I met up with her at her home in Humboldt Park in Chicago, and after she let her kids know "we handling important business here," we lounged and she shared her reflections on being raced, gendered, classed, and Muslim. Although Esperanza is a convert to Islam and was born and raised in Chicago and I was born to Muslim parents and raised in Brooklyn, we hit it off right away. This was because of the other things we had in common: Latinidad, being part of the hip hop generation, and having intimate knowledge of the joys and the frustrations of growing up working class in the 'hood. Indeed, our respective experiences of race, class, and gender as Muslim women were often parallel.

I had seen Esperanza at hip hop cultural events around the city, always observing folks, as artists are apt to do, before we formally met at an event at the Inner-City Muslim Action Network, IMAN. IMAN is a Muslim-run nonprofit that provides services, community organizing, and arts-based activism on the southwest side of Chicago. IMAN was a key site for me in the field just as it was a place of central importance for many of my interlocutors, who I refer to as my "teachers" because I drew on their generous sharing of their knowledge and experiences. These "teachers,"[2] such as Esperanza, are the progenitors of a discourse, an epistemology, an aesthetic, and an embodiment that I call Muslim Cool.[3] Forged at the intersection of Islam and hip hop, Muslim Cool is a way of being Muslim that draws on Blackness to contest two overlapping systems of racial norms: the hegemonic ethnoreligious norms of Arab and South Asian U.S. American Muslim communities on the one hand, and White American normativity on the other. For my teachers—U.S. Black, Latin@, Arab, and South Asian American Muslims engaged in hip hop–based activism—IMAN was a place where their intersecting identities, often rendered invisible by these hegemonic racial and religious norms, were visible and valid.

> ESPERANZA: When it first started I was so excited to find IMAN. I was excited mostly because I came from an artist background and I came from a church background and since I became Muslim I never found that type of community and that type of outlet. Progress Theater was the first group I saw [and] I literally cried, I had no idea Muslims could even do this. I was like freaking out, I mean I didn't just go to church, I was in *church*, it was for *real*! It was like people in the aisles, jumping up and down, so it just made me so happy!

When Esperanza saw Progress Theater perform at IMAN, she saw herself. The specific event was Community Café, which showcased performers who were generally Muslim, usually extremely talented, and predominantly working with hip hop and a sonic landscape that was charged with Blackness as a radical political perspective and expressive culture. Although not a hip hop group, Progress Theater, an ensemble founded by two U.S. Black Muslim women, fit right in: its storytelling exhibited a Black feminist aesthetic and its performances, which mixed theater, poetry, and song, were deeply grounded in Black expressive cultures, particularly those of the U.S. South. The ethnoreligious hegemonies of Arab and South Asian U.S. American communities would prescribe that Muslims could not "do that"; they could not engage Black expressive cultures as Muslims. Yet with Progress Theater and at IMAN, Esperanza found, the opposite was true: they could and they did.

IMAN is a site of Muslim Cool because it privileged Blackness as a politics and as an expressive culture of resistance and did so with a diverse constituency. Like my teachers, IMAN's events and work include Muslims (as well as non-Muslims) who are U.S. Black, Latin@, Arab, and South Asian American from a range of socioeconomic backgrounds. Accordingly, race and class tensions are also part of Muslim Cool, and Esperanza's subsequent experiences of cultural appropriation dampened her initial euphoria. IMAN, as a Muslim space, was affirming for Esperanza, but it was also a source of frustration. Esperanza wore camouflage because she liked it but also because racialized systemic inequalities had shut her family out of economic opportunity and shuttled her brother into "the service." In contrast, the "Pakistani girl" who thought the camouflage was cool had access to a set of class-based and cultural privileges—she was educated and suburban and had more cultural authenticity as a Muslim. Accordingly, the Pakistani girl's potential appropriation of camouflage was embedded in unequal power relations: Esperanza loved the girl and the girl loved her scarf but, as Esperanza put it, all that love was fraught, "no matter how much Islam we have in common."

The camouflage-loving Pakistani girl was not merely a cultural interloper; she was also a racialized and gendered Muslim subject navigating her identity at the crossroads of hip hop and Islam. The Pakistani girl in Esperanza's story reminded me of Rabia, a young Pakistani U.S. American woman who was one of my key teachers in the field. I could imagine Rabia admiring Esperanza's scarf with the same kind of unbridled enthusiasm, but in contrast to the first "Pakistani girl," Rabia was an activist who worked in Englewood, a predominately Black neighborhood in Chicago.[4] I asked Esperanza whether this made a difference:

SU'AD: Is there a difference, you think, with Rabia?
ESPERANZA: It is a really weird balance because a lot of these sisters are darker than me, are darker than my children, but they have such a suburban White mentality, and they are trying to figure out the crossroads, but yeah, there is a difference for Rabia, now that she is going to work in Englewood every day, she is not as naive about the struggle, but she had to fight for that and she is still fighting for it because she is still that educated Pakistani girl from the suburbs, at the end of the day. But it's the same on the other end: I could never really escape this no matter how much Islam we have in common. Even if I escaped this, even if I married a Pakistani man, even if I married Muslim and I married up and got real silverware, right? [Laughs] That camouflage would still be mine.

For Esperanza, Rabia was different because "the struggle" was not just a fashion accessory for her. However, she noted insightfully that this did not mean that Rabia, she, or any of us could escape the complex realities of race, identity, and power in the fight to contest hegemonies and overcome inequality. This insight is critical to understanding Muslim Cool: at the meeting of Islam and hip hop, intersecting notions of Muslimness and Blackness challenge *and* reconstitute the racial order of the United States.

I developed the concept of Muslim Cool through my long-term ethnographic research with young multiethnic Muslims primarily in Chicago, Illinois. I argue that by establishing connections to specific notions of Blackness, my teachers configure a sense of U.S. American Muslim identity that stands as a counterpoint to the hegemonic norms of Whiteness as well as to Arab and South Asian U.S. American communities. These connections are critical and contested interventions: critical because they push back against the pervasive phenomenon of anti-Blackness, and contested because questions of race, class, gender, and nationality complicate and trouble Muslim Cool's relationship to Black identities and cultures.

I make three central arguments in this book. First, I argue that Blackness is central to the histories, engagements, entanglements, and experiences of U.S. American Islam. The term "Blackness" in my work refers both to the histories, traditions, and customs of Black peoples and to the circulating ideas and beliefs about people of African descent. My rendering of Blackness is Diasporic (Hall 1990) and polycultural (Kelley 1999) and as such conceptualizes Blackness as culture and discourse, which relies on and exceeds the body, Black and otherwise.[5] I contend that Blackness shapes the individual Muslim experience in the United States and interethnic Muslim relationships as well as the terms of U.S. Muslim engagement with the state. Second, I make a case for the continuing significance of race and Blackness in the contemporary United States. The book focuses on interminority relationships to articulate a narrative of race and racism in the United States that transcends the Black-White binary but also the fallacy of postracialism, which holds that racism, particularly anti-Black racism, is over and that any talk of race is actually counterproductive to the work of antiracism. I identify the ways in which race, and specifically Blackness, is marshaled in the work of antiracism. For Muslim Cool Blackness is a point of opposition to white supremacy that creates solidarities among differently racialized and marginalized groups in order to dismantle overarching racial hierarchies. Yet as the stories in this book illustrate, these solidarities are necessarily entangled in the contradictions inherent in Blackness as something that is both desired and devalued. The engagement with Blackness by young U.S. Muslims, Black and non-Black, is informed by long-standing discourses of anti-Blackness as well as the more current cooptation of Blackness in the narratives of U.S. multiculturalism and American exceptionalism. Accordingly, my third central argument is that any analysis of contemporary Blackness must contend both with the ways in which it is used to resist the logics of white supremacy and with its complicity in that supremacy.

A light-skinned Latina, Esperanza hesitated to consider herself Black. She explained by example, "I didn't grow up eating those foods, I had to learn how to make macaroni and cheese as an adult." Nevertheless, Progress Theater's performance was still deeply meaningful to her. This was because Black expressive cultures, both U.S.-based and in the broader African diaspora, shaped her own experiences as a Latina who did not know how to make macaroni and cheese but who grew up on ecstatic evangelical church culture as well as house music and hip hop. Esperanza's macaroni and cheese learning curve is reflective of the Chicago context in which Black is defined as having roots in the U.S. South. However, Blackness, in the discourse and practice of Muslim Cool, and as I use the term in this book, is not limited to Black traditions originating in the continental United States.

For example, as I describe in chapter 2, my teachers contest claims that "music is *haram*" (forbidden) by placing hip hop in an Afrodiasporic Islamic genealogy. This genealogy is constructed through historic Africa and its transatlantic diaspora to assert the religious permissibility of Black music. Likewise, the style of head wrapping that I describe in chapter 3 is a practice found outside the United States. Yet Muslim Cool's relationship to place, specifically the United States, is not inconsequential. When multiethnic U.S. American Muslim women take up the Afrodiasporic head wrap tradition, this practice must also be interpreted with attention to the specificities of Blackness in the United States. Similarly, when U.S. Muslim hip hop artists travel abroad on the state-sponsored cultural diplomacy trips described in chapter 5, Blackness is entangled in its relationship to U.S. empire. Accordingly, the Blackness engaged in Muslim Cool is Diasporic—linked to the particulars of the Black experience in the United States as well as to questions of Black culture and politics that are in conversation with those of other Blacks elsewhere, particularly in other parts of the Americas.[6]

Muslim Cool is a way of thinking and a way of being Muslim that resists and reconstitutes U.S. racial hierarchies. This push and pull at the core of Muslim Cool is grounded in its relationship to hip hop. Hip hop, as an artistic form—expressed in DJing, emceeing, dance, and graffiti— and as a form of knowledge and cultural production—from ideas and language to fashion and style—is a site of critical contradiction and contestation. Perceptions of hip hop music and culture range wildly: hip hop is seen variously as deeply mass mediated and commodified and as a quintessential example of an expressive culture of resistance. The "hip hop wars" (Rose 2008) in the mainstream media and within the hip hop community reflect this kind of binary framework, with each side claiming to know what hip hop really is. However, hip hop is a traded commodity and an oppositional culture *at the same time*. Hip hop epitomizes what Stuart Hall described as the contradictory nature of Black popular culture: it is simultaneously rooted in the lived experience of the African diaspora and appropriated in ways that are unrecognizable to that lived experience (1998). Importantly, my claim for hip hop's rootedness in the African Diaspora is not a move to mark hip hop as "Black" in an essentializing way that erases, most specifically, the Latin@s, Black and non-Black, who were central to hip hop's development (Flores 2000; Rivera 2003). Rather it acknowledges hip hop's grounding in a Diasporic and polycultural Blackness (in which Latinidad is always an interlocutor, if not a participant) forged by involuntary and subsequent migrations and manifest in the aesthetics privileged in the music and culture (Rose 1994). Moreover, the contestation identified by Hall is not unique to Black popular culture, but it is a defining characteristic of the mass production of Blackness: the proliferation of Black expressive forms devalues Black life as often as it celebrates it.

The contradictions and contestations of hip hop are often depicted through the homonyms "roots" and "routes": hip hop is rooted in Afrodiasporic expressive cultures and has traveled on routes far beyond its origins (Gilroy 1993; Peterson 2014).[7] To the pair of roots and routes, I add the loop. I take "loop" from the hip hop sampling technique in which a selected piece of music is looped to play over and over as part of the creation of a new piece of music. Whereas roots and routes extend and splinter into multiple pathways, the loop extends and returns, not in a closure but in a cypher, the communal and competitive space in which hip hop culture regenerates and develops.[8] The loop is a metaphor for the linkages between Islam, hip hop, and Blackness in the twenty-first century that create Muslim Cool: Islam, as practiced in U.S. Black American communities, shaped hip hop, which in turn shapes young twenty-first-century Black and non-Black U.S. Muslims who return to Blackness and Islam as a way of thinking and a way of being Muslim—as Muslim Cool. Like a looped musical sample defined by sonic repetition and variation, Muslim Cool is a site of critical continuity and change.

"My Mic Sounds Nice": Interventions

This book is an intervention in several existing literatures. Anthropological research has a long history of studying Muslim communities. The Muslim body (as well as Black and Black Muslim bodies) has served as material and conceptual territory, as labor, and as a specimen for the construction of Euro-American colonial projects—projects that made and were made by anthropology. Today, the anthropology of Islam has moved away from a primarily orientalist narrative and attempts to offer more complex pictures of Muslim life. This is a critical challenge to the post–9/11 narrative of the "Muslim" as singularly backward and barbaric (Mamdani 2005; Mahmood 2005; Deeb 2006; Hirschkind 2009). However, although this work is important, much of it continues to focus on Muslims *outside* the United States and Europe, and this disciplinary emphasis on non-Western Muslims has an unintended effect: it reproduces the notion of Muslim as "other," which ends up reifying the static notions of "us versus them" that this research intends to undo.[9]

These unintended consequences also resonate outside anthropology. Early scholarship on Islam in the United States told a diaspora narrative in which Muslims emigrated from an "Islamic homeland" to the "West." The narrative centered on a bicultural clash between "American" and "Muslim" identities. Muslims were seen as analogous to other "ethnic" immigrants who face the challenges of integration and assimilation into the (White) American mainstream. This ethnicity-assimilation paradigm not only marginalizes nonimmigrants, replicating internal ethnoreligious hegemonies, but it can also elide the distinctions between different groups of immigrants.[10] Moreover, it locates Blackness and critical race studies at the fringes of the study of U.S. American Islam.

In the field of hip hop studies, scholars have tended to study hip hop as a text. The most common methodologies include lyric analysis (i.e., what does the music say; Cobb 2007; Dyson and Daulatzai 2009; Neal and Forman 2012), critical examinations of representation (i.e., what sorts of images are produced and reproduced in hip hop; Morgan 2000; Hopkinson and Moore 2006), and hip hop as a discourse linked to narratives of race, class, gender, and sexuality under material conditions of inequality (Rose 1994; Rose 2008; Morgan 2009). The contributions these studies have made are significant and unquestionable; yet, as others have noted (Dimitriadis 2009) they have left a critical area of inquiry underexplored. When researchers venture outside studios, stages, and street corner cyphers to different sites of inquiry, such as family rooms and friendships, what does hip hop look like there?

This question can be extended to the site of religion, which has also, until recently, received inadequate attention within hip hop scholarship. The social, cultural, economic, and political landscape of 1970s New York City and the expressive cultures of the African diaspora are common themes in retellings of hip hop's birth story. Yet these histories typically fail to account sufficiently for questions of faith, ethics, and spirituality in hip hop's birth narrative (Pinn and Miller 2009). Building on earlier work (Pinn 1999, 2003), a new body of research is emerging around these questions (Miller 2012; Utley 2012; Miller, Pinn, and Freeman 2015). This scholarship successfully challenges narrow notions of religion and spirituality that would disqualify the "religious" in hip hop, but has yet to fully attend to Islam's theoretical significance to the ways in which hip hop music and culture engage religion and spirituality.

In response to all these trends, *Muslim Cool* is an ethnographic study of Muslim life *within* the United States. It identifies the U.S. American Muslim experience as entangled in the workings of race, religion, and gender in the contemporary United States. It avoids reifying Islam/West dichotomies because it does not cast Muslims as peripheral or as outsiders who navigate assimilation but rather as actors whose lives and experiences are critical to the production and reproduction of the contemporary United States and the "West" more broadly. Further, while the ethnicity-assimilation paradigm continues to dominate some interdisciplinary approaches to the study of Muslims in the United States, this book joins a parallel body of scholarship in the study of Islam in U.S. America that pushes back against this tendency (McCloud 1995; Nuruddin 1998; Nyang 1999; Curtis 2002, 2006; Aidi 2009; Rouse 2004; Jackson 2005; Karim 2008; GhaneaBassiri 2010; Chan-Malik 2011; Grewal 2013). Like other contributions to this body of work, *Muslim Cool* offers an analysis that sees questions of race and Blackness as central to the U.S. American Muslim narrative.

Muslim Cool is a study of the relationship between race, religion, and popular culture. It also joins a growing body of work that has begun to explore Islam's relationship to hip hop in the United States. These scholarly and artistic contributions analyze the role of Islamic theologies in the development of hip hop along with examining the role of hip hop in individual pathways toward conversion to Islam (Spady and Eure 1991; Swedenburg 1997; Floyd-Thomas 2003; Banjoko 2004; Aidi 2004, 2009; Alim 2005, 2006a, 2006b; Miyakawa 2005; Knight 2008; Taylor 2009; Davis 2010). Like these studies, *Muslim Cool* traces the ways religious identity is constructed through hip hop, but it also documents the particular epistemological impact of Islam and Muslim practice on hip hop music and culture. This impact, I contend, was fundamental to the development of hip hop ethics and activism. *Muslim Cool* advances hip hop scholarship by bringing ethnography to hip hop research which has historically privileged textual analysis and explores the hip hop narratives of young men *and* women, in a genre that typically privileges males.[11]

"People's Instinctive Travels and Paths of Rhythm": Muslims in Chicago and the United States

Precise demographics about Chicago's Muslim community are scarce. The most extensive survey was done in 1997 by East-West University. This report estimated the total Muslim population of Chicagoland, which includes the city of Chicago and surrounding counties, to be 285,126 (Ba-Yunus 1997, 12). Nearly ten years later the Chicago chapter of the advocacy organization Council on American-Islamic Relations put the total population at approximately 400,000 (Inskeep 2006). The hundreds of thousands of Muslims who live in the Chicago metropolitan area come from a variety of backgrounds. Chicago's Muslim community is U.S. Black American, AfroLatin@, Latin@, White, South Asian, and Palestinian American. Chicago Muslims also hail from Nigeria and the Balkans (Bosnia-Herzegovina, Albania, and Kosovo). They represent a variety of Muslim experiences and Islamic perspectives, including converts and those born to Muslim families, Sunni and Shi'a Islam, Sufism, the Nation of Islam, and the Ahmadiyya Muslim Community. These communities, some of whom have had a presence in the area since the early twentieth century, live throughout Chicago's north, south, and west sides as well as in its northern, southern, and western suburbs.

The diversity of this metropolitan Muslim community maps onto the Chicagoland landscape in fragments, mimicking the racial and ethnic segregation for which the city continues to be known (Massey and Denton 1998; Pattillo-McCoy 2000; De Genova and Ramos-Zayas 2003; Bogira 2011). Today, as depicted in classic sociological texts—*Black Metropolis* (Drake and Cayton [1945] 1993), *The Ghetto* (Wirth 1929), *Gold Coast and Slum* (Zorbaugh [1929] 1976), and others—Chicagoans live in neighborhoods segregated by race and class. According to the 2010 census, African American communities remain concentrated in the traditional "Black Belts" on the South Side and West Side of Chicago, while Latin@ neighborhoods are found squarely within the near northwest and southwest sections of the city. Furthermore, as White families continued to move to the outer suburbs over the last decade of the twentieth century, communities of color with U.S. and foreign-born residents made their homes in the abandoned inner suburbs. Urban patterns of residential segregation were thus replicated in the suburbs. Muslim immigrants and their U.S.-born children reside in immigrant enclaves within the city, such as the West Ridge neighborhood that is home to the commercial and cultural district of Devon Avenue, or within ethnic enclaves in the suburbs, such as the Harlem Avenue community in Bridgeview. Immigrant and second-generation U.S. American Muslims also live in wealthy, majority-White suburbs. In comparison, most U.S. Black American, AfroLatin@, and Latin@ Muslims continue to live in predominantly Black and Latin@ neighborhoods. These same neighborhoods are often located within or near areas of concentrated poverty (Brookings Institution 2003).

Even with their slightly higher levels of education and income,[12] U.S. Black American Muslims live in segregated urban and suburban neighborhoods and are blocked from accessing the kind of advantages experienced by their South Asian and Arab U.S. American Muslim counterparts who live in White majority suburbs (Karim 2008). As a result of these residential patterns, racial segregation has become a fact of Muslim life in Chicago. From who runs the *masjid* (mosque) to whom parents consider suitable marriage partners for their children, institutional and community life is divided along lines of race and ethnicity.

Like the Chicagoland Muslim community, the U.S. American Muslim community is diverse. It represents more than eighty different countries and has origins in the African Muslim populations of the transatlantic slave trade as well as Ottoman-era Muslim immigration to the United States. Likewise, divisions within the Chicagoland *ummah* (Muslim community)[13] are a microcosm of broader divisions of race, class, and power that shape the national U.S. Muslim community. Tensions around race, class, and power in the U.S. Muslim community play themselves out across what community members call an "indigenous-immigrant" divide. The indigenous-immigrant divide describes a fissure between the three largest ethnic groups among U.S. American Muslims: U.S. Black Americans on the one side, and U.S. American Muslims of Arab and South Asian descent on the other. U.S. Black Americans are configured as "indigenous" or "more native" to the United States in comparison with their Arab and South Asian U.S. American counterparts, who are seen as "immigrants" to the country. The use of the term "indigenous," which was first appropriated by U.S. Black American Muslims in the 1960s (Nyang 1999), is meant as a critical inversion of an ethnocentric prejudice that privileges "immigrant" Muslims over "indigenous" ones.

This prejudice links race, ethnicity, class, and religion into an ideological framework that marks "immigrant" Muslims as more religiously legitimate and authoritative than Black U.S. American Muslims, a phenomenon that Sherman Jackson identifies as "Immigrant Islam." Jackson defines Immigrant Islam as the monopoly asserted by Muslim immigrants over the power to define Muslim identity and practice in the United States (Jackson 2005, 4). This claim to monopoly is based on the possession of ancestral ties to the "Muslim world," and it "enshrines the historically informed expressions of Islam in the modern Muslim world as the standard of normativeness for Muslims everywhere" (Jackson 2005, 12).

Under these ideological guidelines, a Muslim of Arab descent, for example, is presumed to have proximity to the Islamic tradition, and her religious practices and perspectives are endowed with authenticity simply because she is Arab. By contrast, a Muslim who cannot claim immediate descent from the "Muslim world," such as a U.S. Black American, is presumed to be new to the Islamic tradition, and her religious practices and perspectives have to be authenticated. Claims to proximity are a powerful form of cultural capital for Muslims in the United States who are geographically distant from traditional centers of Islamic learning yet entrenched in an ummah-wide crisis of the nature of Islamic authority today (Grewal 2013, 34). Immigrant Islam is an ethnoreligious hegemony grounded in this cultural capital, which makes the Muslim immigrant a religious and cultural normative ideal in the United States. This hegemonic norm holds internally within the U.S. American Muslim community as well as in certain state policies and popular narratives on Islam in the United States that rely on the Muslim-as-immigrant type. This state and media engagement endows further legitimacy on "immigrant" Muslims as Muslims over their "indigenous" sisters and brothers.

Muslims have a long history in the United States, beginning with the involuntary migration of enslaved African Muslims.[14] So it is important to note that the rise of the ethnoreligious hegemony of Immigrant Islam is tied to the arrival of a particular cohort of émigrés: Muslims from the Middle East and South Asia who arrived in the United States in larger numbers after the loosening of racialized immigration quotas in 1965. Muslims from those regions had immigrated to the United States prior to 1965, but their communities did not yet represent the face of Islam in the popular imagination as they do today. Rather, in the mid-twentieth century U.S. Black American Muslims were the prototypical Muslims on the domestic front. This was due to the convergence of a number of factors, such as the powerful and visible organizational presence of Black Muslims in the antiracism movements of the twentieth century, the ability of certain Muslim communities to "integrate" racially and culturally into broader U.S. society, and the relatively small size of these Muslim immigrant communities and their institutional life in comparison to contemporary numbers.[15]

Moreover, as American Studies scholar Sylvia Chan-Malik argues, the post-1965 demographic shift in the U.S. Muslim population precipitated diverging "and in many cases mutually opposed visions of Islam and the [U.S.] nation" (Chan-Malik 2011, 12) For U.S. Black Americans Islam was a spiritual tradition of resistance that was critical of the United States and designed to undo the racial logics of white supremacy, whereas South Asian and Arab U.S. American Muslims "saw Islam as a religious and cultural inheritance . . . [and] America as a land of prosperity and opportunity" (Chan-Malik 2011, 12). Critically, these perspectives, coming out of particular raced and classed positions, wield differential power and influence.

Classic U.S. American logics of anti-Blackness collide with these claims to religious authority and legitimacy. Ideologies of anti-Blackness that fuel anti-Black racism—the ideology in action—are grounded in the racial taxonomies of white supremacy. White supremacy advances notions of racial superiority and inferiority that privilege those identified as White as ideal—the culmination of human potential—and normative—the standard against which all other sentient beings are judged. White supremacy produces a racial logic that sets up a grid of associations in which Blackness, in relation to Whiteness, is always and already less-than, in terms of value, history and, most importantly, humanity. Blackness is also configured as morally deviant when juxtaposed against the idealized standard of normative Whiteness. Paradoxically this "deviance" is also positively valued as a site of the pleasures repressed by the standards of Whiteness. Accordingly Blackness marks leisure instead of hard work, erotic liberty in lieu of sexual restraint, a womanhood that is super heroic, and a Christianity, free from the strictures of the Protestant ethic, that talks loud and long to God. This is "an age-old image of blackness: a foreign, sexually charged, and criminal underworld against which the norms of White society are defined, and by extension, through which they may be defied" (Samuels 2004, 147–48).

Like all immigrants to the United States, Arab and South Asian migrants are encouraged to adopt ideologies of anti-Blackness as an immigrant rite of passage. They are primed to see U.S. Black Americans as less-than and deviant—a pathological and downwardly mobile population that is best avoided. Yet as non-Whites, Arab and South Asian U.S. American Muslims have their own complex relationships to Whiteness. Arabs and South Asians are racialized, as perpetually foreign and as alternately model minorities or enemies of the state (Jamal and Naber 2007;

Sharma 2010). The racial logics of white supremacy in the United States discriminates against Arab and South Asian U.S. Americans while simultaneously incentivizing the adoption of anti-Blackness by yielding limited kinds of privilege and access when these non-White U.S. Americans successfully avoid Blackness. Since one-third of all U.S. Muslims are Black a consequence of this distancing has been to render Blackness necessarily "un-Islamic": lacking religious authority and authenticity. Accordingly, the assertion of ethnoreligious hegemonies can work *within* the racial hierarchies of U.S. society to maintain the logic of white supremacy. This alignment with white supremacy has made the ethnoreligious hegemony of Arab and South Asian U.S. American Muslims one of Muslim Cool's primary interlocutors. Instead of avoiding Blackness, Muslim Cool is a move toward Blackness in the construction of a U.S.-based Muslim identity.

The racial and ethnic bifurcation of the American Muslim community into "indigenous" and "immigrant" Muslims reveals critical tensions, but the terms themselves are imperfect designations. They elide the history and lived experience of, for example, third-generation Arab American Muslims or U.S. Black American Muslims with Caribbean immigrant parents. The terms also render U.S. American Muslims who are indigenous to the Americas invisible, which reinscribes the erasure and violence of U.S. settler colonialism. I find value in Jackson's overall theorization and acknowledge that these terms are efficient in writing and have become common in everyday U.S. American Muslim discourse. However, I do not use the terms "indigenous," "immigrant," or "Immigrant Islam" in this book. I find that they tend to obfuscate rather than illuminate the significant raced and classed power dynamics that lie at the core of the tensions between Black U.S. American Muslims and Arab and South Asian U.S American Muslims. Accordingly, in lieu of Immigrant Islam I employ the much more clunky phrase "ethnoreligious hegemony" of South Asian and Arab U.S. American Muslims and use "indigenous" and "immigrant" only in quotation marks when necessary to communicate how my interlocutors use those terms.

"Don't Sweat the Technique": Methodologies and the Field

This book is based on more than ten years of research on Islam and hip hop, which I began before even considering a graduate education.

I attended the first (and thus far the last) Islamic Family Reunion and Muslims in Hip Hop concert in 2003 which ignited my interest in the topic.[16] My formal research includes twenty months of anthropology fieldwork in Chicago (from early 2007 to late 2008) and subsequent participant-observation research and interviews in Chicago, New York City, the California Bay Area, and the United Kingdom (2010–2015).

I went to Chicago at the invitation of Dr. Rami Nashashibi, executive director of IMAN. I met Nashashibi in the fall of 2006 at a meeting of young American Muslim activists and nonprofit leaders. We discussed our mutual projects: his (then) dissertation project on "ghetto cosmopolitanism" (Nashashibi 2009) and my interest in hip hop among young Muslims. At that time I had my sights set on conducting fieldwork in Morocco, but Nashashibi invited me to spend some time in Chicago, suggesting that IMAN's work was directly related to my interests. I accepted the invitation and began fieldwork in January 2007 as the event coordinator for "Takin' It to the Streets." This event, known as "Streets," is IMAN's biennial community festival. It has become one of the largest community festivals in Chicago and features a wide range of activities, including speeches by local and nationally renowned Muslim and non-Muslim leaders, community service projects, children's activities, sports tournaments, and musical performances. In 2007, the year I worked on the event, an estimated crowd of ten thousand people from just about all walks of life gathered from different parts of the city and the country to participate in the festival. Streets takes place in Marquette Park, where in 1966 Dr. Martin Luther King Jr. was greeted with rocks, bottles, and firecrackers during a march to protest residential segregation in the exclusively White neighborhood (James 1966).

The neighborhood surrounding Marquette Park is no longer predominantly White but rather U.S. Black American and Mexican American; however, the same issues of residential segregation and racialized inequalities continue to prevail in the neighborhood and throughout the city. Continuities between the past and the present made this site a symbolically meaningful location for the work that Streets was designed to do. With a goal to use art and education for community mobilization, IMAN's staff and volunteers often described Streets as the embodiment of the organization's vision of an American Muslim community that is *critically engaged* (Nashashibi 2005). This vision is defined by a commitment to "heal the 'hood."[17]

IMAN's commitment to heal the 'hood is a committment to antiracist work. This work includes projects on the ground in the South Side of Chicago that seek to counter the material effects of anti-Black racism, such as the organization's work on mass incarceration through a reentry program that provides skills and jobs for the formerly incarcerated. This work also included countering the ideologies of anti-Blackness as they circulate among U.S. American Muslims by centering the U.S. Black American experience as a critical site to critique the staus quo, within and outside the U.S. American Muslim community. Most specifically, by its support of arts-based activism through hip hop, Blackness became the means through which young Muslims, Black and non-Black, came to learn and incorporate that critique in their own self-making as Muslims.

I worked at IMAN for six of the twenty months I conducted fieldwork, but I continued to attend the organization's events, specifically programming geared toward youth, after the end of my employment. I was also allowed to use the IMAN offices to conduct interviews with local Chicago Muslims whom I met in the field. This was possible because IMAN served as a central location of Muslim life in Chicago, even though it was not in the center of the city. I consider IMAN a central site of Muslim Cool, given that many of my teachers began their journeys of Muslim self-making through IMAN. But my research interests and the relationships I built with young Muslim women and men also took me all over Chicagoland, which includes the city as well as its northern, western, and southern suburbs.

In the field I had two core groups of teachers. The first group comprised 18- to 22-year-old youth leaders in arts-based social activism, primarily at IMAN.[18] They were primarily Black and South Asian U.S. American Sunni Muslims. Almost all were born in the United States to Muslim parents. With this cohort of teachers, I conducted participant observation, structured interviews, unstructured interviews, and focus groups. I also spent time with key teachers at home and at school, at youth organizing meetings, and at a range of other activities. The second group was a slightly older cohort of young adults in their late twenties and early thirties, whom I also engaged through participant observation, interviews, and a focus group. Alongside my interactions with these two groups of teachers, I interviewed parents and older community figures who played important leadership roles in the Chicagoland Muslim community. I also attended a broad range of events, including banquets, fund-raisers, fashion shows, rallies, lectures, conferences, and *jummah* (weekly Friday congregational prayers), in the Black, South Asian, and Arab U.S. American Muslim communities of Chicago.

Muslim Cool results from an innovative methodological approach that brings performance studies as method and representation to anthropology. Performance ethnography consists of "staged, cultural performances . . . based on ethnographic data from the specific spheres of (a) the subjects, whose lives and words are being performed; (b) the audience, who witnesses the performance; and (c) the performers, who embody and enact the data" (Madison 2005, 172). The elements of performance ethnography are identical to those of more common ethnographic inscription: fieldwork, ethics, data collection and analysis, and thinking with, through, and *without* theory. However, as an embodied ethnography it is distinct from more common ethnographic practice because of the ways performance communicates "a sense of immediacy as well as the breadth and complexity" of the issues (Batiste 2005). Performance is visceral, *in* the moment, and—of particular import to those interested in public anthropology—accessible both within and outside the academy.

My use of performance ethnography as a methodological tool falls within the anthropological tradition of embodied knowledge. The practice of embodied knowledge resists the logocentrism that dominates the Euro-American intellectual tradition (Gilroy 1993). Instead of privileging the word, this practice identifies the body as a site of knowing. As Gina Ulysse reminds us, "the research process is an embodied endeavor, one in which lived and felt experience, through all the senses, is integral to both the data collection process and the knowledge produced" (Ulysse 2008, 128–29). In anthropology, this tradition is vibrantly illustrated in the work of Zora Neale Hurston and Katherine Dunham. Both Hurston and Dunham were authors of artistic work that contributed to public discourse by challenging popular and academic narratives about Black people. These works were based on ethnographic fieldwork and bridged the gap between art and the academy.

Despite their groundbreaking contributions, Hurston and Dunham remain marginal figures in the anthropological canon (McClaurin 2001; Chin 2014). Their marginality is a result of anxieties about anthropology's status as an "objective" science and the discipline's failure to decolonize itself fully (Harrison 1997). Nevertheless, their practices of embodied knowledge are central to one of the discipline's key methods, namely, participant observation. To do participant observation "you have to be *there*," sharing time and space—even when confounding these categories through technology—with your interlocutors. This "being there" is not disembodied but rather requires the anthropologist to *participate*—to speak with, dance with, eat with, Gmail chat with, feel with (Hage 2009)—her interlocutors; through shared experience, knowledge is produced intersubjectively.

I enter this tradition with my performance ethnography piece entitled *Sampled: Beats of Muslim Life*. *Sampled* is a one-woman show composed of a series of movements or vignettes, akin to scenes in a play but without a linear narrative structure. The piece uses movement, theater, and poetry to ethnographically (re)present my research and findings. The title, *Sampled*, is a reference to the practice of citation found in both hip hop and the academy. Hip hop artists "sample" or take excerpts from previously recorded songs in the composition of their own music. Similarly, academic scholars are also expected to "sample" the ideas of other intellectuals in the process of constructing their own original contributions. Likewise, the narratives in my performance ethnography are samples—excerpts and examples—of multiple stories I encountered in the course of my fieldwork. The characters I play do not embody specific interlocutors; rather, they are embodied (re)presentations of the many young U.S. American Muslims I encountered and learned from in the field.

My performance ethnography, like this book, does not presume to speak for my teachers or assert possession of indisputable knowledge. *Sampled* is a performance ethnography constructed in my own words, yet drawn from an intersubjective production of knowledge. Its vignettes document, explore, and interrogate the key themes of Muslim Cool. Chapter 3 describes how I used performance ethnography as a method of data collection and analysis. Chapters 2 and 4 use *Sampled* as a means of representing the complex of contradictions and contestations that make up Muslim Cool.

"Where I'm From": An Ethnographer with a Point of View

Like hip hop, Muslim Cool also has roots and routes; it is both tied to place and deterritorialized. The places of Chicago and the spaces created by IMAN were critical locations in the construction of Muslim Cool as a way of being Muslim in the contemporary United States. At the same time, these ideas have taken routes far beyond Chicago and IMAN. The movement of Muslim Cool documented in this book has crossed boundaries of race and class, gender and nation. Likewise, following the pattern of Muslim Cool and my multiethnic activist teachers, I have also moved across multiple boundaries.

I moved across boundaries as an anthropologist who was born and raised Muslim in the United States, a status I shared with most of my teachers. To some, this shared demographic fact makes me a "native anthropologist," and with this title might come the assumption that I had unfettered access to my teachers and their community and perhaps "natural" insight as well as a lack of critical distance due to the ways in which my own identity and those of my teachers overlap. However, as many others have argued, these assumptions, which essentialize the "native" ethnographer, elide the complexities of position and power that shape the research experiences of all anthropologists (Narayan 1993; Ulysse 2008).

In the field, simply being Muslim was never enough. In fact, my race and ethnicity (Black and Latina), my gender (female), and my regional identity (reppin' Brooklyn, New York!) as well as my religious community affiliations and my performance of Muslimness mediated my access—how I was seen in the field, what was said to me, and what was kept from me—as well as my own interpretations of my field site. For example, when I arrived in Chicago I was initially known as "the sister from New York," and therefore it was not that I was a Muslim but my relationship to IMAN that afforded me entrée into some local communities.[19] In other instances, when my IMAN affiliation showed its limitations, it was my relationship with congregations and prominent leaders in Brooklyn, New York, where I was raised that opened doors for me.

Taking my Black Muslim body into non-Black Muslim spaces also shaped the research process. The ethnoreligious hegemony described earlier marks the U.S. Black American Muslim as a Muslim with a lack of religious and socioeconomic pedigree. I confounded many of these assumptions because I did not convert to Islam, I spoke Arabic, I had studied Islam in the Middle East, and at the time I was pursuing a Princeton Ph.D. with a degree from Georgetown University in hand. While my non-U.S. Black American teachers were often engaged in activism in multiethnic Muslim and non-Muslim spaces, their home communities were much more segregated. Therefore, when I went home with them and met their parents, some of these assumptions about U.S. Black Muslims were circulating along with the expected range of parental concerns about a stranger spending time with one's child.

In these situations, my different forms of "pedigree" were useful. For example, during a visit with one Pakistani American immigrant mother, my familiarity with a specific Sufi saint and the time I had spent in the Middle East not only made her more comfortable with her daughter spending time with me but in fact seemed to make her think I might be a good influence on her daughter. Had I lacked this pedigree, would the mother have eventually warmed up to me, despite my Blackness? Probably. But what was clear, in this situation and others, was that my Ivy League "pedigree" and my performance of a particular kind of Muslimness—through speaking Arabic, having studied in the Middle East, and wearing a headscarf (though not all were comfortable with my headscarf style)—mattered.

I also moved across boundaries as a hip hop head. In the hip hop community a "head" is someone who loves and is invested in hip hop. My love for and investment in hip hop comes from my relationship to the music and the culture. As a member of the hip hop generation, hip hop is the soundtrack to my life—there is a hip hop song to mark almost every significant moment in it. Moreover, growing up in Brooklyn and particularly being a teenager during the golden era of hip hop made my connection with it even more meaningful. I was Black and Muslim, being raised in a household with cultural nationalist leanings, and the music and culture of hip hop were replete with Islamic references and pro-Black and pan-African messages.

The kinds of linkages between Islam, Blackness, and hip hop that invigorate my teachers' sense of Muslimness also shaped my own. In my pre–9/11 Brooklyn, to be a Muslim meant being known as righteous and seen as someone to respect, a reverence that was reproduced in hip hop music and culture. This admiration for Islam and Muslims persists in most hip hop communities today, although beyond the borders of those communities the meaning of being a Muslim has shifted in critical ways. In the post–9/11 United States, to be a Muslim is to be known as a target of suspicion and seen as a threat. To be a Muslim also means to be racialized as "Brown" and not Black. Accordingly, the links between Islam and hip hop that were so paramount in my own upbringing have faded for many. Now, hip hop and Islam are often imagined as "worlds far apart," and in the cases in which they come together the most popular narrative is one of hip hop as a tool of the so-called radicalization of young Muslims.

What I share with my teachers as well as where my knowledge diverges from theirs are what have motivated my interest and passion for this project. My analysis reflects the insights gained from firsthand on-the-ground ethnographic fieldwork, as well as forms of embodied knowledge I have gained by following the routes of Muslim Cool and drawing on the roots of "where I'm from."

"The Blueprint": Outline of *Muslim Cool*

Chapter 1, "The Loop of Muslim Cool: Black Islam, Hip Hop, and Knowledge of Self," begins by tracing the loop of Muslim Cool: Islam, as practiced in U.S. Black American communities, shaped hip hop, which in turn shapes young twenty-first-century U.S. Muslims who return to Blackness and Islam as a way of thinking and a way of being Muslim. I illustrate the ways in which hip hop, Black Islam, and the history of Black subjection in the United States serve as prisms through which they interpret their own racialized locations as U.S. American Muslims. Chapter 2, "Policing Music and the Facts of Blackness," examines the meanings of race and Blackness within U.S. Muslim communities by exploring the often fraught musical context of U.S. American Islam. In this chapter, I argue that Black music is targeted for two parallel tracks of regulation: disavowal and instrumentalization. I use these U.S. American Muslim debates around music to illustrate both the complexities of interethnic intra-Muslim relations and the ways in which these internal Muslim debates reflect primary engagements with Blackness in the United States today.

Chapters 3 and 4 explore Muslim Cool as racial-religious self-making that occurs at the complex intersections of race, class, gender, and style. Chapter 3, "Blackness as a Blueprint for the Muslim Self," begins the discussion by investigating a specific headscarf style, the "'hoodjab," to uncover how Blackness, interpolated through the 'hood, gives meaning, that is contested, to the female practice of Muslim Cool. Chapter 4, "Cool Muslim Dandies: Signifyin' Race, Religion, Masculinity, and Nation," explores the sartorial interventions of men I call Muslim dandies. I ask: how do Muslim men use dress to claim a U.S. American identity that directly confronts white supremacist ideas of Black pathology and likewise, hegemonic ethnoreligious aesthetics that render U.S. Black American Muslim men marginal in many U.S. American Muslim contexts?

Chapter 5, "The Limits of Muslim Cool," moves the discussion from interracial and gender dynamics to the dynamics of Muslim Cool's relationship to the state. It explores the ways Muslim Cool is entangled in neoliberal regimes of knowledge and power as well as U.S. imperialism. I trace the constraints that engagement in twenty-first-century arts and civic engagement culture places on my Muslim teachers' aspirations to reproduce a Black radical alterity to reveal the limits of Muslim Cool's resistance to hegemony. *Muslim Cool* concludes by reflecting on the relevance of the concept to contemporary struggles against anti-Blackness.

"Stakes Is High": Why Muslim Cool Matters

At its core, this book offers an examination of the critical cultural reverberations that arise at the meeting of Blackness and Muslimness in the twenty-first century. This meeting articulates a far from postracial reality in which race and Blackness continue to be significant terms of engagement in the United States, shaping how individuals and communities understand themselves and position themselves vis-à-vis each other and the state. The convergence of Muslimness and Blackness influences how individual Muslims in the United States experience, articulate, and perform their religious identities. But this intersection has a meaningful impact on inter-Muslim relationships as well. *Muslim Cool* illustrates the critical importance of Blackness to *all* U.S. Muslim self-making, including those who move away from Blackness as well those who, like my teachers, move toward Blackness as a way of being Muslim. These cultural reverberations that shape individual and community self-making are critical markers of change and continuity into the ways U.S. Muslims are positioned and position themselves as racial subjects and racialized citizens.

For many, the categories "Muslim" and "American" are not racial categories: Muslim is a religious designation and American is a national identity. Yet paradoxically, many non-Muslim U.S. Americans' understanding of who Muslims are in relation to the United States is framed by the question, "Why do they hate us?" The question is an indicator that these categories function as "racial projects" (Omi and Winant 1994, 56). "Muslim" is not simply a label of faith but rather a racialized designation, which mediates access to and restrictions on the privileges of being an American, itself also a racialized category.

In the late twentieth century, "Muslim" emerged as a racial category through historically specific processes of racial formation: older orientalist fantasies of the "exotic" east and white supremacist logics that privilege White and Christian citizens in the United States merged with the U.S. pursuit of economic and political dominance in resource-rich Muslim-majority nations. The convergence of these forces gave rise to what scholars call the "racialization of the Muslim" (Volpp 2002; Razack 2008; Jamal and Naber 2008; Maira 2009; Rana 2011). As a racial type, the Muslim is known through specific bodies—those with brown skin and "Middle Eastern" looks—and behaviors, such as prayer and the wearing of beards and headscarves. Importantly, these bodies and behaviors are not just markers of racial difference but also signals of the Muslim as a threat that have been used particularly since 9/11 to regulate and control Muslim bodies (Rana 2011). These signs of Muslim threat have come to serve as a shorthand justification for a regime of state surveillance in which U.S. American Muslims are monitored in their prayer spaces, charities, schools, homes, and even their intimate lives (Khera 2010; Cainkar 2011; Aaronson 2011).

In the United States, the category "Muslim" is racially triangulated against normative ideas of Whiteness *and* Blackness. Although U.S. American Muslims are racially and ethnically diverse, the Muslim as a racial type is non-White, "immutably foreign, and unassimilable" (Kim 1999) as well as non-Black, "mostly moderate and mainstream" (PEW 2007). This relationship to Whiteness and Blackness facilitates the further typing of the Muslim into the immutably foreign and unassimi-lable "Bad Muslim" on the one hand, and the moderate and mainstream "Good Muslim" on the other (Mamdani 2005; Maira 2009). The latter ideal type performs a middle-class respectability that is valued in main-stream U.S. America, yet the "Good Muslim" is also routinely "Brown" and thus never quite escapes the tendency to conflate "Muslim" with "foreigner." Accordingly, while U.S. American Muslims may experience the intersection of race and Muslimness in varied ways, the category "Muslim" continues to occupy a subordinate social position.

The racialization of the Muslim as Brown and foreign is a depar-ture from the mid-twentieth century, when the "Black Muslim" was the dominant face of Islam in America (Curtis 2006). The Black Muslim designation was shorthand for the Nation of Islam and for a practice of Islam that was considered heterodox and seen as a dangerous form of Black protest. Like the "Muslim" of today, the Black Muslim was known by specific bodies and behaviors: black skin, bow ties, and preaching "hate." Likewise, the Black Muslim was also under intense state surveil-lance under the COINTELPRO program (an FBI Counter Intelligence Program), which included the use of agent provocateurs to destabilize Black Muslim communities. Therefore, although the racial type associ-ated with Muslimness has changed from Black to Brown, there is also continuity: the Muslim continues to be seen as a threat to the state that is managed not only through state surveillance but also through notions of multiculturalism.

Muslim Cool poses a direct challenge to this racialization of Muslims as foreign and as perpetual threats to the United States. It confronts the idea of a break with the past that is implied in readings of the contem-porary moment as "postracial" and offers a more complex narrative of both the U.S. Muslim experience and the meanings and performance of Blackness today. Accordingly, *Muslim Cool* is not a portrayal of a mul-tiethnic postracial utopia built through hip hop music. Rather, it prob-lematizes the ways Blackness is used in U.S. American self-making as both a threat to America's progress and a symbol of it. *Muslim Cool* is neither the story of a complete break with the past nor an easy tale of resistance but rather a charting of the powerful and dynamic ways in which Blackness and Muslimness merge to challenge and reconstitute U.S. racial hierarchies.

1

The Loop of Muslim Cool

Black Islam, Hip Hop, and Knowledge of Self

Three pairs of Adidas sneakers and a pair of black combat boots lined the doorway of my apartment. The first pair of sneakers was chocolate brown with beige stripes, and the second was white and black underneath scuffmarks. The last was a pair of shell tops with emerald green trim and hot pink stripes. The shoes' owners were a small but diverse group of U.S. American Muslim grassroots activists—three men and one woman, of U.S. Black, South Asian, Arab, and mixed race heritage— whom I had invited to my home, then on the North Side of Chicago. As activists, they worked at the intersection of art and social justice through Chicago-based nonprofit organizations whose agendas for social change were characterized by the centrality of hip hop.

I had invited the group over for what I was calling a "head discussion," "head" being shorthand for *hip hop head*. In hip hop communities, a hip hop head is someone who knows hip hop, loves hip hop, and takes hip hop seriously, whether as an artist, an activist, an artist-activist, or a fan. At this point I had spent several months in Chicago, primarily on the South Side, exploring questions of hip hop and identity with college-aged Muslims. Since, as the hip hop saying goes, "real heads know," I was eager to pick the brains of some heads who were also Muslims equally dedicated to the future of young people and to the future of hip hop.

My Muslim hip hop head teachers had been raised in the city of Chicago or the surrounding suburbs; some had been born into Muslim families, while others had converted to Islam. Their trajectories to hip hop were likewise varied and included international migration and grade-school graffiti writing. For Tyesha, a Chicago native and a convert to Islam, that variation was what linked hip hop and Islam:

That's the beauty in it to me, to see someone who just came here, that immigrated, that is Muslim, and is attracted to hip hop, and a shorty [young
person] who hip hop's all they know, and it's a different kind of hip hop,
a ghetto hip hop is obviously different because it has a different purpose
and different means for coping, but I think the beauty of it is that this one
thing, hip hop, it serves all of our needs for really healing and dealing
with living in these times wherever we are. That's why [hip hop], it's Islam;
it's the costume for Islam.

Tyesha's comment points to the way in which hip hop could be relevant to a "shorty" and to "someone who immigrated," given its transcendent quality, which it shares with Islam. Tyesha made this claim
based on her years of experience as a Muslim and a Chicago activist
who uses hip hop to empower young U.S. Black Americans and Latin@s.
In fact, because hip hop "serves all our needs," it is so strongly aligned
with Islam that Tyesha equated the two: hip hop, she said, is Islam. She
further claimed that hip hop is "the costume for Islam." Although the
term "costume" is often associated with artifice or exaggeration, I read
her intended meaning as "hip hop is Islam in a different outfit." Hip hop
is Islam because of the long-standing dialogic relationship between hip
hop and Islam as practiced in urban Black communities in the United
States.

This is a relationship that begins with hip hop artists taking up ideals of self-determination, self-knowledge, and political consciousness as
poor and working-class Blacks and Latin@s from the antiracist Muslim cosmologies of Black Islam. It is a relationship that takes shape in a
number of ways, including representations of Islamic beliefs in hip hop
music, adoptions of specific Muslim practices and ethical stances within
hip hop communities, and stylistic choices such as *kufiya* scarves and
knitted *kufi* caps. It is a relationship that has constructed an epistemology through which the distinct yet historically rooted set of understand-
ings, self-making practices, and ways of meaning making give shape to
what I call Muslim Cool.

In *Development Arrested: The Blues and Plantation Power in the Mississippi Delta*, Clyde Woods theorizes the blues as epistemology. He argues that U.S. Black American conflict with "plantation powers," namely,
the White American moneyed elite, is "one of the defining features of

African American social thought" (Woods 2000, 29). Blues music as an epistemology emerges out of this conflict as a "self-referential classificatory grid" that produces "a distinct and evolving complex of social explanation and social action [that provides] support for the myriad of traditions of resistance, affirmation and confirmation" (Woods 2000, 29).

Woods's theory of the blues as epistemology is grounded in the roots of blues music in working-class Black life in the Mississippi Delta. Hip hop emerges from a similar milieu, though not (immediately) from the Delta but out of the convergence of the African diaspora—from the U.S. South and from the Spanish- and English-speaking Caribbean—in poor and working-class communities in New York City. And, like Woods's Delta Blues, hip hop is shaped by the conflict with "plantation powers" in the "North" who, like their southern counterparts, are participants in global economic, political, and cultural forces of domination, what hooks aptly terms the "white supremacist imperialist capitalist patriarchy."

Following Woods, Nitasha Sharma argues that "like the blues, hip hop provides epistemology" (Sharma 2010, 208). Marc Lamont Hill calls this epistemology "the pedagogy of hip hop," arguing that the consumption and production of hip hop culture "reorganize conceptions" of the self and the world in ways that "radically challenge sanctioned forms of knowledge" (Hill 2009, 121). Furthermore, H. Samy Alim identifies this epistemology as having the potential to "create a counterhegemonic discourse that 'threatens' the ruling class and their ideas" (Alim 2006b, 22). I follow Woods, Sharma, Hill, and Alim by likewise theorizing hip hop as epistemology. Like the blues, hip hop is committed to "social and personal investigation, description and criticism" (Woods 1998, 30). For my teachers, hip hop disrupts dominant theories of knowledge by offering alternative ways of reckoning history and interpreting and acting upon the world. Importantly, hip hop worked this way for my teachers because Black Islam played a central role in the development of hip hop's epistemology. As Alim notes, many hip hop artists cite their introduction to Black Islam as key to "regaining a 'knowledge of self'" that reoriented their perspective from being "merely 'artists'" to being actively engaged in acting upon the world (2006b, 38). Likewise, my teachers "show and prove" the ways in which Black Islam, through knowledge of self, has been and continues to be central to hip hop as epistemology and as a lived experience. Furthermore, they "show and prove" the centrality of Black Islam to the religious self-making of U.S. American Muslims.

In what follows, I chart knowledge of self as an epistemological route that leads to Muslim Cool. This route is composed through the loop of Muslim Cool: Black Islam gave knowledge of self to hip hop, which in turn confers knowledge of self to young twenty-first-century U.S. Muslims, who then return to Black Islam as Muslim Cool. I trace the first bend in the loop—how Black Islam gave hip hop knowledge of self—from a historical perspective and illustrate ethnographically the journeys of two of my teachers from knowledge of self to Muslim Cool. By looping back to this root—Black Islam—*through* hip hop, I show how my teachers chart their own routes to remake Muslim identity in the United States.

The Topography of Muslim Cool

I had been in the field for a few months when I met up with Tasleem and Man-O-Wax at a café in Hyde Park. Hyde Park is a historic South Side neighborhood that is home to the University of Chicago, Minister Louis Farrakhan, and President Barack Obama. It is a twenty- to thirty-minute eastward drive down 63rd Street from IMAN (and from where I lived at the time). The drive passes through predominantly U.S. Black and working-class neighborhoods such as Woodlawn, which borders Hyde Park and has a tenuous relationship with what some residents see as its land-grabbing neighbor, the University of Chicago. Driving through Woodlawn into Hyde Park, one cannot but be struck by the latter's historic architecture, tree-lined streets, and resources such as restaurants, health food and grocery stores, and independent bookstores. Meeting in Hyde Park was convenient for Tasleem, who lived further south at the time, but Man-O-Wax and Tasleem chose Hyde Park as a meeting location because there were few, if any, cafés in other neighborhoods on the South Side. As a result, Hyde Park was a common meeting, dining and hang out alternative for folks at IMAN seeking to avoid the long haul to White North Side neighborhoods such as Lincoln Park, Wicker Park, Logan Square, and Lakeview where café culture in Chicago was concentrated.

I had met both Man-O-Wax and Tasleem at IMAN. Man-O-Wax had just begun to work at IMAN full-time, and Tasleem was a frequent volunteer—what the organization calls an "IMAN leader." Beyond their work with IMAN, I saw them as key actors in the Muslim hip hop scene in Chicago; indeed, Man-O-Wax was one of my key teachers in the field. A hip hop DJ, Man-O-Wax worked as IMAN's youth director and later its Director of Arts and Culture. Man-O-Wax was a South Asian U.S. American in his late twenties, raised in an upper-middle-class Muslim family that had immigrated to the United States from Kuwait when he had been a child. He belonged to the older cohort of my teachers and was a teacher also in a broader sense: he had taught hip hop, as art and epistemology, to most of the other young Muslims whose stories I narrate. Tasleem was a U.S. Black American spoken word artist and fashion designer. A convert to Islam, raised between the city of Chicago and the southern suburbs, Tasleem also coordinated arts after-school programming and online courses on natural healing.

Given their different perspectives, I hoped that talking with them together would give me a fuller sense of the Muslim hip hop scene in Chicago. Man-O-Wax hesitated to call it a Chicago "scene." He explained, "It is more a mentality that has no geography. It is not big enough to be a geographic thing. There is a hip hop scene outside [the Chicago Muslim community]," but "until [IMAN's] Community Café there was a disconnect between some parts of the Muslim community and hip hop culture, aside from ISNA and the masjid rapper."[1] The "masjid rapper type" was a euphemistic way of describing a specific type of amateur Muslim musician, described by Tasleem as follows: "A person can't even sing but just because they said Allah, or throw *Alhamdulillah* in a [rap] song," they are allowed to perform at masjid or community events such as the annual convention of the Islamic Society of North America (ISNA).

As an artist himself, Man-O-Wax seemed to feel that there was no "scene" because there was no space. He knew the importance of venues, physical spaces in which community is built around music culture. Such spaces have been key to hip hop's development from the first hip hop jam planned by DJ Kool Herc and his sister, Cindy Campbell, to street corner ciphers. Because of the dearth of venues like IMAN's periodic Community Café, that took hip hop seriously as an art form, Muslim artists with more professional skills and ambitions tended, according

Community Café, February 2012. Courtesy of Eve Rivera.

Stage Crowders. Courtesy of Eve Rivera.

Community Café, April 2012. Courtesy of Eve Rivera.

to Man-O-Wax, to gravitate toward the larger Chicago hip hop scene "outside" the Muslim community.

Man-O-Wax saw an obstacle to the creation of a Muslim hip hop scene in the many "divisions within the [Chicago] Muslim community: ISNA, The Mosque Cares [community associated with Imam W. D. Mohammed], the NOI [Nation of Islam]," and even the Blackstone Rangers, "who read Quran and pray to the East," and the "Vice Lords," who have been influenced by Islam. As Chicago street organizations, the Blackstone Rangers (also known as the Black P. Stone Nation) and the Vice Lords are not typically included in descriptions of the Chicagoland ummah and do not always define themselves as Muslim. However, the point Man-O-Wax seemed to be making was that there are many different interpretations of "Muslim" in Chicago, which poses a challenge to establishing one scene in which all Muslims can equally participate.

Tasleem's assessment came from a slightly different angle. She noted that in the late 1980s and 1990s, when Chicago hip hop was taking off, Muslims were "inside" hip hop because of the influence of the Nation of Islam and the Five Percenters[2] on the hip hop generation. However, the Muslims inside the hip hop scene fell "outside" many orthodox Sunni

Muslim communities in Chicagoland. Tasleem explained, "no one rapping at the time, or very few, were calling themselves Sunni Muslims." This situation, Tasleem argued, differed from the contemporary moment, when many hip hop emcees explicitly refer to themselves as Sunni Muslims. She clarified that at that earlier stage, Black Islam had been part of the Chicago hip hop milieu, but the kinds of divisions identified by Man-O-Wax had been less salient. An artist may have been Muslim or a Five Percenter or just selectively practicing certain aspects of Black Islam, such as diet or dress. However, she argued, "people are more defined now" as they move to embrace Sunni orthodoxy, a move that she believed was prompted by artists feeling a responsibility to respond to misconceptions about Islam since 9/11.

Like Man-O-Wax, I see the Muslim hip hop scene as a mentality, a way of thinking, and an epistemology—as Muslim Cool. Therefore, the question whether the scene is big enough is immaterial; what matters is the existence of a network of Muslim hip hop artists that is not bound by city limits, state lines, or national borders. Man-O-Wax and Tasleem were part of a network of Muslim artists and activists connected to each other through shared music, faith, and hip hop–based activism. This network encompasses a long list of artists, both converts and those raised Muslim, including hip hop legends such as Jorge "Popmaster Fabel" Pabon of the Rock Steady Crew, as well as artists who have achieved significant commercial success, such as Yasiin Bey and Lupe Fiasco. Many others are stars of underground hip hop and up-and-coming artists, such as Brother Ali (Minnesota), The Reminders (Colorado), Omar Offendum (LA/DC), Ms. Latifah (Atlanta), Amir Sulaiman (Atlanta), Tyson (Oakland), Cap D (Chicago), Maimouna Youssef (Baltimore), Khalil Ismail (Baltimore), Miss Undastood (NYC), and Quadeer Lateef (Buffalo).

Many of these Muslim artists were involved in IMAN's work. Their artistry and activism predated their affiliation with IMAN, but their network formed an imaginary community whose "scene" was made by and through the spaces, physical and conceptual, enabled by IMAN as an organization.[3] Thanks to its vision of arts-based activism, IMAN had become the epicenter of the Muslim hip hop scene in Chicago, the wider United States, and even globally, and thus IMAN was central to my teachers' journeys through the loop of Muslim Cool.

My first visit to IMAN took place in the fall of 2006, before I officially began conducting fieldwork. IMAN had been established in 1997 by a group of undergraduate students from DePaul University; the group included Dr. Rami Nashashibi, who is currently the organization's executive director. During its early years IMAN served elementary school students, many of whom were Palestinian U.S. Americans, who would visit IMAN daily for after-school tutoring. At the time of my visit, IMAN's current office space was still in the process of being converted from its former use as a bank. IMAN was moving from its first and much smaller home further west along 63rd Street, affectionately called the *Markaz* (center) by the neighborhood's Arab U.S. American community.

According to Garbi Schmidt, who wrote one of the first academic studies on IMAN, "gathering in the Markaz everyday created a sense of community among the children" and a rare environment in the United States in which "being Muslim and Arab involved no risks" (Schmidt 2004, 49). Since its incorporation, IMAN has grown beyond the local Palestinian community to become a thriving nonprofit organization that has a budget of almost two million dollars and serves as a center for Muslim life in Chicago and a model for Muslims around the country. This success was due to IMAN's efforts to create spaces within and outside its walls where being Muslim and American "involved no risk."

One part of IMAN's new building had been completed by the time of my first visit in 2006: the mural that covers the building's entire eastern wall. This mural, which can easily be seen from a distance, announces IMAN's presence and priorities even before a visitor or volunteer walks through its doors. The mural was realized as a joint project between IMAN, the Greater Southwest Development Corporation (GSDC), and the Chicago Public Arts Group (CPAG), an organization that manages public art projects through collaboration, youth mentoring, and community development (CPAG 2010). The mural is named "Reflections of Good" and features mirrors shaped like tear drops along with arabesque motifs, spray-painted Arabic calligraphy, and pieces of broken dishes collected by the fifteen young people from the neighborhood who worked on the project with Juan Chavez, the lead artist.

The production of the mural is emblematic of IMAN's style of community engagement. IMAN, a Muslim-run organization, partnered with local non-Muslim nonprofits and community institutions, GSDC and CPAG, and local non-Muslim master artists, Juan Chavez and Zor, on a project that bridges art and activism. In the project, Chavez and Zor, the artists, acted as mentors to the neighborhood youth who assisted in producing the piece of public art. As part of this process of community engagement, nonprofits, neighbors, artists, and youth together determined the mural's design, which is infused with IMAN's Muslim identity—symbolized by the Arabic calligraphy of Qur'anic verses, written by Zor—while espousing values that are universal in their appeal. More than a neighborhood beautification project, the mirrors that adorn the wall were meant to reflect the good that already existed in the surrounding community. This point was important, because many outside the neighborhood, including many Chicagoland (the Chicago metropolitan area) Muslims, saw this area of the city as a place of fear and danger rather than as a space of good.

Revising this dominant perception of the 'hood is central to how IMAN positions itself and is positioned within the Chicago and national Muslim community. Explicitly committed to antiracist work, IMAN privileges the U.S. Black American experience as a critical site of critique for U.S. Muslims. As the *Inner-City* Muslim Action network, IMAN identifies the locus of its work as the economically resource-poor community of color on Chicago's Southwest Side, where the organization is located. IMAN's work in the 'hood includes not only the provision of services to its poor and working-class neighbors but community organizing with residents around the social and economic justice issues that most affect the neighborhood.

While I was in the field, Nashashibi was often called on to speak publicly, and when he did—whether giving a speech at a volunteer meeting or delivering a lecture at a local university—he would always come back to the social, economic, and political disadvantages faced by Black and Latin@ urban communities and trace how systemic inequality determined the ways in which U.S. Americans live, from residential patterns, schooling, and policing to modes of consumption (Massey and Denton 1998; Gregory 1999; Woods 2000; Pattillo-McCoy 2000). Critically, the often implicit associations with Blackness and the 'hood—how material conditions of disadvantage become material for conceptions of the 'hood as a space inextricably tied to Blackness—were not lost on IMAN's leadership. Accordingly, the "inner city" in IMAN's discourse reflected a hip hop remix on the 'hood in which working-class Black and Latin@ residential areas were conceived as culturally rich communities rather than as inner-city wastelands (Forman 2002). This point is particularly salient because racism and ethnocentrism continue to beleaguer American Muslim communities in Chicago and beyond.

As described in the Introduction, ethnic prejudices often drive tensions over religious authority and legitimacy within the U.S. American Muslim community, and they also shape the representation of this community vis-à-vis the state. These prejudices preclude the possibility of U.S. Black American Muslim leadership over the broader U.S. American Muslim community (McCloud 1995; Jackson 2005; Karim 2008). IMAN's operation within the context of the 'hood and its privileging of Blackness make it unique among U.S. Muslim nonprofits. The majority of such associations tend to focus on the concerns of middle-class immigrants from South Asia and the Middle East. A growing number of nonprofits address the needs of poor immigrants from the same regions, particularly around issues of immigration and civil rights. Yet very few make the concerns, the tensions, and the fortunes of the 'hood the focus of their work.

Moreover, like their constituencies, these other organizations are relatively homogeneous. By contrast, IMAN's staff, volunteers, and clientele are ethnically and socioeconomically heterogeneous. To be clear, IMAN is no racial utopia and maintaining a culturally diverse space is always a work in progress. But in comparison to its peer organizations in Chicago, the ethnic diversity among Muslims at IMAN events and activities is remarkable. As Jamillah Karim described in her work on U.S. Black-South Asian American Muslim relations, "[few Muslim] organizations demonstrate substantial inter-ethnic relations, but one group that comes close to this ideal is the Inner-city Muslim Action Network" (Karim 2008, 15).

I had come to IMAN in 2006 to participate in its first Artist Retreat. I was invited by Nashashibi as an academic scholar (most of the other scholars invited were religious scholars) and thus as one part of the scholar-artist-activist tripartite whose synergy, he believed, was critical to shaping a U.S. Muslim identity that was critically engaged in the broader U.S. society. The retreat was designed to be a safe and private space, and I will thus not go into much ethnographic detail about it here. However, a description on IMAN's website of its third Artist Retreat, which I also attended, aptly describes the purpose of these events: "These Retreats have not just been a deliberative space for the exchange of ideas over the meaning of art and the role of artists in the American Muslim community, but they have also been a creative space where artists collaborate during cipher sessions that are intimate and spontaneous, and a spiritual space where artists and scholars explore the connections between creativity and spirituality" (Najam 2011).

The retreat, which represented one of the two ways in which the Muslims I knew in the field engaged with IMAN, was critical to my understanding of Muslim Cool. Intimate events such as the Artist Retreat and public venues such as the Community Café and Takin' It to the Streets were all structured similarly in that they provided a space for the "Muslim and hip hop focus" that Man-O-Wax identified as having been missing before IMAN's founding. For my older teachers, such as Man-O-Wax and Tasleem, this space provided an important sense of community among established Muslim artists as Muslims and supported the cultivation of their artistic expression and professional lives as artists.

The other role that IMAN played, and the primary focus of this chapter, was enabling a discourse and creating spaces through which hip hop as Muslim Cool was introduced to young Muslims:

> TASLEEM: One thing I like about IMAN is, it is a kind of center for introducing that kind of music to young Muslims; where else would they find it? Cap D, The Reminders, these are people they probably would not have heard. We need more of that around the country. I think it breeds pride; young people can be, "I can still be cool, I can still be hip." And there is quality [in the music]. IMAN is putting on concerts at professional venues and a young person is like, "Wow, I am proud to be a Muslim, it's cool." Even if they go to a non-Muslim school they have music they can share with their friends and feel really included in society. Teens face a lot of peer pressure; they are bombarded with MTV, BET. . . . The thing people like about Lil Wayne is his tight beats and good production, so in order to compete a Muslim has to do both and have even tighter lyrics. IMAN plays a key role in that.

Tasleem's comments underscore the challenges of context for young Muslims in the United States. Like other youth of color, Muslim youth do not often see themselves represented or elevated in mainstream media or the broader mainstream popular imagination *as Muslims* in ways that ascend to the level of "cool"—a category of value coveted not just by the young. The artists mentioned by Tasleem—Cap D, a Muslim emcee from Chicago who is well known locally and a member of IMAN's board, and The Reminders, a Colorado-based husband-and-wife rap duo—do not have Lil Wayne's fame; you won't find them on mainstream radio or music television, where many young people have the easiest access to music. Yet they are not "masjid rappers." Rather, as Tasleem described it, they are quality artists who model how to be Muslim and "still be cool."

Yet the religious self-making IMAN facilitated went a level beyond the provision of role models. IMAN was a key stop for my younger teachers' journeys through the loop of Muslim Cool.

> MAN-O-WAX: To me, the trajectory usually goes: you get into hip hop for whatever reason it speaks to you, and that usually leads you to something beyond hip hop. Either you get into the elements [rapping, b-boying and b-girling, DJing, and graffiti], you start learning about them, you learn how this all goes back to indigenous culture, the drummers, the DJ . . . or just in the music itself, you like hip hop and you start hearing samples and you realize, "Oh, I like soul and funk, too," or you may like jazz or blues or something, and it [hip hop] becomes an entryway into appreciating a larger culture, Black culture in general, African music for some.

The trajectory Man-O-Wax traced was not meant to be Muslim-specific; rather, it described hip hop as epistemology. The key element of this trajectory, namely, hip hop leading somewhere beyond hip hop to Black culture in general, is precisely the loop of Muslim Cool. My younger teachers' interest in hip hop typically arose before they started to volunteer at IMAN. They knew hip hop as the preeminent soundtrack of urban Black youth culture and a significant part of mainstream popular culture. Yet it was through their relationship with IMAN that they turned to Black Islam and traveled the loop of Muslim Cool, reorienting what it meant for them to be Muslim and American in the contemporary United States.

OmarMukhtar

OmarMukhtar[4] was a twenty-something Libyan American engineer and visual artist who had been a volunteer at IMAN for a few years by the time I began my fieldwork. He grew up in Bridgeview, Illinois, a southwest suburb of Chicago, and belonged to the older cohort of my teachers. He had first heard of IMAN as a teenager but could not get involved until he had more autonomy and mobility as a college student in the city of Chicago:

> [I] tried to get involved with IMAN, but it was hard to get in touch. Shahidah Jackson [an IMAN organizer] reached out to me to do a logo; a buddy of mine did a lot of events around the community, he asked me to do some design work, he was on the steering committee for Streets, and Rami was like, "I need a graphic designer," and so he called my guy, Adnan, and Adnan was like, "Try my guy OmarMukhtar." And Rami, and this describes [how] IMAN [works], called me real late at night, like, "Ok, I need you to do this, it's for tomorrow, can you do this for us?" And I was enthralled by the fact that Rami called me direct. [I was] hungry and eager to put art into the world and didn't sleep for two days straight, went to class all tired [the next day].

OmarMukhtar's IMAN initiation story was typical: a call from Rami Nashashibi, asking for help on a project that had to be finished "yesterday." Like all the young Muslims I encountered at IMAN, OmarMukhtar was enthusiastic about IMAN's work and eager to get involved. Since that first phone call, he had volunteered as IMAN's go-to graphic artist, designing all sorts of materials from flyers to T-shirts. During the long days and late nights when I worked at IMAN on Streets, OmarMukhtar and I shared grievances over Rami's "deadlines." We also shared a love of all things hip hop—although OmarMukhtar liked to test me by quizzing me on my knowledge of rap music. Working with OmarMukhtar (and answering his quizzes), I found him to be a very reflective individual with strong opinions and very little filter.

OmarMukhtar shared his IMAN initiation story with me during the second of two formal life history interviews I conducted with him. For the first interview, which had lasted four and a half hours, we had jumped into my now dearly departed Corolla for a tour of his old and current "stomping grounds" in Bridgeview and on his college campus. For this second interview, we met at a café near the West Loop; I wanted to follow up on some of the stories he had shared earlier, including his disappointment with his local community, which had led him to IMAN:

> You had people who were just as young as me at IMAN who were contributing in ways that you didn't see in Bridgeview. At the time, Rami was a very "bring it to your face" kind of guy. I remember him going up to ISNA and just chewing out the people for not building with the Warith Deen community, who had a convention the same week, just on a different side of town: "How do you guys not at least acknowledge them? . . . You are not the only Muslim game in town." And I saw him doing these things, and in my college angst . . . I was like, "That's the truth right there; that's what's going on."

OmarMukhtar described being attracted to IMAN because he saw that young people were being active in ways that mattered; namely, like Rami they were pushing back against anti-Black racism within the Muslim community. The "Warith Deen community" OmarMukhtar referenced was the primarily U.S. Black American Muslim community guided by the teachings and leadership of Imam W. D. (Warith Deen) Mohammed.[5] This Sunni Muslim community, with affiliated masjids across the country, has been known by a number of names during its history: Bilalian, the World Community of Islam in the West, the Muslim American Society, and currently The Mosque Cares. Like The Mosque Cares, ISNA is a national association of Sunni Muslims, but ISNA's primary demographic is South Asian U.S. American Muslims, with a strong Arab U. S. American contingent.

For most of the first decade of the twenty-first century, the yearly conventions of the community of Imam W. D. Mohammed and ISNA were held in two different parts of the Chicago metropolitan area during the Labor Day weekend. The tens of thousands of Muslims attracted by each convention were segregated along an ethnic divide, with the primarily U.S. Black American Muslim "Warith Deen community" inhabiting hotels in the Loop or the south suburbs and the primarily South Asian U.S. American Muslims of ISNA, along with some Arab U.S. American Muslims, filling a convention center in Rosemont, a northern suburb. While The Mosque Cares and ISNA's leadership publicly endorsed each other, OmarMukhtar voiced the common perception that ISNA would not "build" with the community of Imam Mohammed because South Asian and Arab U.S. American Muslims implicitly believed that their Black coreligionists were ill-equipped to offer the authoritative religious education and religiously sanctioned social environment both conventions promised. Accordingly, Rami was "chewing out people" at ISNA to call them to account for what he and many others perceived as anti-Black racism.

For OmarMukhtar, IMAN stood in stark contrast to his primarily Palestinian U.S. American community in Bridgeview, where "unless you meet three very basic requirements—you have a beard, you are married with children, you have a stable job and speak very good Arabic—your voice and opinion are ignored." Young people in the community, he observed, were particularly likely to be ignored. During our first stop on the life history interview tour, we parked in the lot of the local youth center near the Bridgeview mosque. It was a two-story square brick building that matched the industrial feel of most of the surrounding area. We tried to go inside, but the use of the center alternated between "sisters' days" (restricted to women) and "brothers' days," and the day we arrived was a sisters' day. It was a breezy yet sunny March morning, so we walked around the neighborhood. As we drew closer to the mosque, the neighborhood changed, becoming less industrial and more suburban, with both garden apartments and more sprawling homes.

The Bridgeview Mosque was built in 1982, and by the time of the interview my teachers could point out the few homes that were still owned by non-Muslim families in the Arab section of Bridgeview. The sociologist Louise Cainkar describes White flight from this suburban neighborhood thus: "The Arabs . . . were viewed by many of the majority White suburbanites as 'non-White' invaders. As their numbers grew (to ten percent in some southwest suburbs), they were increasingly seen as undesirable and unwelcome neighbors whose presence would lower a neighborhood's property values" (Cainkar 2005, 183). Like most immigrants, the first wave of Muslim immigrants to Chicago lived in the city, and the move to the suburbs fell in step with the national ethos, emergent in the 1950s, of the suburban subdivision rather than the city as the home of the American dream.

Yet in a deeply segregated metropolitan area and nation, the American dream remains a racialized one; so when Muslim immigrants moved to the suburbs, they also moved away from Chicago's Black belt and away from a certain kind of Blackness, the undisciplined and un-middle-class Blackness that is, incidentally, most commonly associated with hip hop. Moreover, the suburban homes of many Muslim immigrants and their families are equally distant from the Black middle class.[6] Although entangled in, and often reproducing, the logics of anti-Black racism, this suburban movement of immigrant Muslim parents was also part of an overall strategy to create Muslim spaces that would enable these new immigrants to live a Muslim life until they could return to their nations of origin. Speaking specifically of the Palestinian U.S. American Muslim community in Bridgeview, Cainkar explains: "The dream of most early Palestinian immigrants was to work hard, save money, and retire under their grape arbors in Palestine. Many never saw this earthly dream fulfilled. They were instead buried in the Muslim section of Evergreen Cemetery at 8700 South Kedzie Avenue" (Cainkar 2005, 188).

As the immigrants realized that the return "back home" was increasingly unlikely—for reasons including denial of the right of return to Palestine as well as the wish to ensure that their children benefited from the U.S. education system—establishing community life in the suburbs came to be motivated by the desire to stem the loss of culture and religion within the second generation. The Muslim youth center in Bridgeview was established as part of this effort, but, OmarMukhtar noted, there was a constant struggle over control of the center between the young men who ran the center "on a shoestring budget" and the older men who ran the masjid community. Nevertheless, according to OmarMukhtar, young people were not ignored within the walls of the center and the space proved to be significant in his developing sense of his Muslim identity:

I was an active participant. They had a weight room, half basketball court, foosball table. Every day after 'isha [night prayer] there would be a thirty-minute conversation about something relevant to what was going on, 'cause the guys [who ran the center] were a little bit older than us, but they were still plugged into the neighborhood. So they would be, "I heard this and that from my brother" . . . "You guys shouldn't be fighting the Latinos" or "getting into beefs [disagreements] over girl-friends," and they would tie it in with an Islamic lesson. At that point, for such a long time, before high school, Islam was this abstract thing that my parents practiced and they tell us to practice and that made us different in one way or another, but moving into high school, my iden-tity, being a part of the center, kind of changed. Now it was practical, now it's relevant.

As a teen, OmarMukhtar learned what it meant to be Muslim in a more "practical" way at the youth center, yet it was his exposure to the Black radical tradition through hip hop that pushed him to look for a way to understand his identity as a Muslim in the context of the broader struggle for racial equality in the United States. In high school, he began reading writings from the Black radical tradition, "a lot of Black Pan-ther literature, Eldridge Cleaver, Mumia [Abu Jamal]," through which he began to see that "you just swap the word 'Black' with 'Muslim' or 'Palestinian' [and] it all becomes very relevant. You start to attach the struggles together, the civil rights struggle and at the time I was really into the Palestinian thing, and you start to identify the two and under-stand the two together."

The Black radical tradition challenges systemic anti-Blackness through intellectual analysis and creative exposition informed by Black consciousness, and it asserts a political agenda that transcends national boundaries and links Blacks across the diaspora (Robinson 2000; Shakur and Davis 2001; Moten 2003; Kelley 2003). In OmarMukhtar's narra-tion of his trajectory, the Black radical tradition and its analysis of anti-Black racism in the United States resonated with his own experience as an Arab U.S. American Muslim. He used the metaphor of "swapping" to describe how he found Blackness to be relevant to his own experi-ence as a Muslim. However, he did not merely "swap Black for Muslim," which would imply exchanging one distinct identity—"Muslim"—for another—"Black." OmarMukhtar did not swap Blackness out but rather linked himself to it as a racialized Muslim subject.

Further, IMAN's approach to anti-Black racism within the U.S. Muslim community drew him to the organization. OmarMukhtar's movement from the youth center to the literature of the Black radical tradition and then to IMAN shifted his perspective—he linked justice within his local Muslim community to justice on a national and international scale. This made him challenge the Muslim status quo on race in his local community: "They had this 'honorary White' sort of understanding. They were like, 'Oh, we're exempt because we are here and they like us,' and so people try to lay low, and I am like, 'If they are coming for us, they are coming for all of us.'" OmarMukhtar's evolution also underscores how anti-Black ideologies circulating in the wider United States are paralleled within the U.S. Muslim community, which encourages Muslim complicity in the society's structures of dominance. Thus, linking Blackness to his Arab Muslim identity became a means for OmarMukhtar to critique his position as a member of a racial minority in the United States and a means of intervention in interminority relations among U.S. Muslims.

It was through such critiques that young Muslims such as Omar-Mukhtar articulated Muslim Cool as an alternative to the dominant discourses in their local Muslim communities. OmarMukhtar had been a hip hop head since early adolescence. Listening to hip hop emcees "using Muslim language" over low-fi hip hop radio shows way into the night and devouring hip hop manifestos such as the 1994 book *Bomb the Suburbs* (Wimsatt 2008), he found that hip hop helped him interpret his own Muslim experience:

Through hip hop I did validate my own Islam, it no longer felt like I was, you know, apart from something greater. 'Cause through hip hop it was like you always heard Nas, The Fugees, mentioning Islamic references in their rhymes and it was like, OK, word, so I am not just like this minority group offshoot, sort of like sect almost, it's like I am recognized. . . . I guess through hip hop, listening to a lot of music about being conscious, about being aware of what's going on, it kind of, like, simplified Islam for me. Islam is a simple religion if you really think about it, and the prophetic tradition is very simple as well. If you look at him, his attributes were not how long his beard was or how short his *thobe* [gown] was, that's all irrelevant. What's really relevant is that he was a compassionate, truthful, honest human being, and if Muslims understood that then it would turn our understanding of the world upside down. We would no longer be bound to these things: you have to say these things, pray in this order; your *wudu'* [ritual ablution] is invalid if you do it this way. No; what matters is that if you can focus on these things—being compassionate, truthful, honest, sincere, just—then your whole well-being is transformed and your whole understanding of the world is transformed. And it's the same thing with hip hop. What they are really looking for is for people to be understanding, compassionate, truthful and just, merciful. It's like the RZA[7] said—[this statement is] a Five Percent thing I like to carry around—"You need knowledge, wisdom, understanding, justice, freedom, equality, love, peace, and happiness." And in that order. And that makes perfect sense, to have the understanding of how to get justice, freedom and equality is fundamental for you to be happy . . . successful, to have love, peace, and happiness.

It was precisely the interconnections and intersections, rather than disconnections and divisions, that he saw between the "Black" and the "Muslim" that enabled OmarMukhtar to find himself as a Muslim in hip hop. In his narrative, hip hop as epistemology is central. Islamic references in hip hop music made him feel like he belonged and they cultivated his understanding of Islam itself. The relationship he described between a growing awareness of his Muslimness and hip hop is not coincidental: OmarMukhtar was able to find himself as a Muslim in hip hop because, as Tyesha argued, hip hop is Islam. In fact, despite some omissions of Islam in academic treatments of hip hop, as described in the Introduction, Islam, and specifically Black Islam, has had a significant presence in hip hop's origins, and this genealogy roots the loop of Muslim Cool.

Black Islam and Hip Hop

POPMASTER FABEL: DJ Afrika Islam, they call him the son of Bambaataa[8] because he was similar to Bam in playing rare selections and he had a similar DJ style. He would dj on the radio, on WHBI, and he would play break beats, and [he] was the radio show [Zulu Beats Show] host, and he would play excerpts from El-Hajj Malik Shabazz's speeches, . . . Elijah Muhammad, [Louis] Farrakhan. [DJ Afrika Islam would] take little sound bites . . . you would hear a break beat and over it [someone saying the greeting] "As Salaamu Alaikum" [and the response] "Wa Alaikum as Salaam," . . . [and] The Supreme Team with Just Allah the Superstar and Se'Divine the Mastermind and they were on the radio, part of a show in '82, maybe with Mr. Magic.[9] They would make references to the Five Percent and always end their show with words of wisdom for life, which is cool, and would have some Islamic ideas.

In my interview with Jorge "Popmaster Fabel" Pabon, he described some of his earliest recollections of Islam in hip hop, years before his own conversion to Islam. Popmaster Fabel is a legendary hip hop figure. He is the senior vice president of the Rock Steady Crew, the first hip hop b-boy collective, and a longtime member of the Universal Zulu Nation, the first hip hop organization. I had first met Popmaster Fabel as a preteen, long before I formally began my research on Islam and hip hop. I had attended a performance of his off-Broadway hip hop musical "Jam on the Groove" even further off Broadway—at a public school in Brooklyn, where I grew up. I would later cross paths with Popmaster Fabel as an adult at cultural festivals and events within and outside the NYC Muslim community and also, thanks to my research, at IMAN events in Chicago. Then as now, I found Popmaster Fabel, true to hip hop epistemology, to be a *teacher*.

During our conversation, Popmaster Fabel identified early links between Islam and hip hop in DJ Afrika Islam's radio play list, which included speeches by NOI leaders Elijah Muhammad and Minister Louis Farrakhan and the 1983 song "Malcolm X No Sell Out" by a European DJ, a track in which selections from the speeches of the late El-Hajj Malik El-Shabazz (Malcolm X) are mixed over break beats. In addition to the Nation of Islam, Popmaster Fabel also referenced the Five Percent Nation of Gods and Earths in his historical narration of the relationship between Islam and hip hop and listed what he called "warning songs" that he described, later in the interview, as "an extension of the proper Islamic tradition." These early tracks included "It's Life" by Rock Master Scott and the Dynamic 3, "Get Tough" by CD III, and "Problems of the World Today" by the Fearless Four. His turn of phrase "warning songs" is a clear allusion to the Qur'anic assertion that the Prophet Muhammad was sent to warn humanity.[10] Accordingly, the songs Popmaster Fabel identified narrate social ills in order to warn of their negative effects and to promote more ethical life choices.

In marking these songs as "an extension of the *proper* Islamic tradition," Popmaster Fabel underscored how Muslim Cool and its ties to Blackness are implicated in tensions over orthodoxy in the history and experience of Islam in the United States. Yet he also identified the songs as "an *extension* of the proper Islamic tradition," thus also emphasizing the reach and influence of Black Islam beyond Black Muslim communities. He highlighted key hip hop technologies—vinyl records, tape cassettes, the radio, and sampling techniques—as essential mediums that introduced and reintroduced Black Islam to non-Muslim audiences, and he located these songs within the ethical and spiritual Muslim tradition, whether or not the artists who wrote and performed them were Muslims themselves.[11]

"Black Islam" is a big tent term I use to describe the range of articulations of Muslim beliefs and practices among U.S. Black Americans. Under this big tent I include the Ahmadiyya Muslim Community, the Moorish Science Temple, the Nation of Islam (NOI), and the Five Percent Nation of Gods and Earths as well as Sunni and Shi'i orthodoxies (which include Sufi traditions). The wide breadth of the term is undoubtedly controversial to some. Many orthodox Sunni and Shi'i Muslims identify the Ahmadiyya, the NOI, the Moorish Science Temple, and the Five Percenters as unorthodox or even as non-Muslims because of these groups' approaches to the Qur'an and *hadith*.[12] Further, according to the ethnoreligious hegemonies of Arab and South Asian U.S. American Muslims, the fezzes and turbans of the Black Moors, the bow ties of the NOI, and even the Geles (head wraps) worn by many U.S. Black Sunni women symbolically distinguish Black Islam as falling outside "true" Islam.

However, following the critical work of scholars Aminah McCloud, Sulayman Nyang, Yusuf Nuruddin, and Edward Curtis IV, I am less interested in claims of heterodoxy than in what links these articulations of Islam to the broader Islamic tradition, to each other, to U.S. Black American history and contemporary life, and consequently to hip hop. These traditions of Black Islam share a pointed concern with the realities of

Black communities living in conditions of systemic inequality. They respond to conditions of injustice by articulating alternative cosmologies, politics, and social norms geared toward individual and community empowerment. Moreover, through the construction of what Curtis (2006) terms African American Islamic history narratives, these traditions assert genealogies that connect present-day U.S. Black Americans to a past that predates the transatlantic slave trade and to a transnational Black identity as well.

These varied engagements with Islam have related but diverging relationships to the intellectual and spiritual traditions that have developed throughout global Muslim history, yet I bring them together under the banner of Black Islam, because within U.S. Black communities they speak the same language of Black consciousness, which is an important part of Black vernacular culture. By Black vernacular culture I am referring to the everydayness of the Black experience in the United States. Black Islam is not only part of the extraordinary moments of Black life, embodied by larger-than-life figures such as Malcolm X, but also part of the grammar of everyday practices from language and dress to food.

Speaking to me over tea during my interview with her and Man-O-Wax, Tasleem gave the following detailed account of Chicago during the 1990s:

> [Chicago hip hop artist] Common was like that: when he first came out, he would use words in his lyrics, he and other artists [said] things like "God" and "Earths." They were influenced by God-consciousness; it was knowledge. Because I knew their crew personally, I know their diet and consciousness were influenced by Islam, whether it was the Nation of Islam or the Five Percenters. X Chromosome was [another] artist in the early 90s, a female, and she rapped about Black consciousness. She was in the Nation of Islam and the two guys with her were registered members, so they got their knowledge and their influences from the Nation of Islam. The Nation of Islam at that time was very visible and even the Hebrew Israelites were everywhere. They all had street credibility. You saw brothers selling *The Final Call* [the NOI newspaper], and even if you weren't going to the mosque [as a Muslim], we all went to Saviours' Day or went to listen to Khalid Muhammad; it was everywhere. Even the Sunni Muslims were visible and Muslims got much respect, people wouldn't mess with

a Muslim. People used to call the *adhan* [call to prayer] out the windows at this one masjid, and the whole neighborhood knew. Even Jeff Fort and the El Rukn, they were calling themselves Muslim then, and the women would wear scarves and *jilbabs*.[13]

Tasleem's account describes a Chicago in which Black Islam was Black vernacular culture: "it was everywhere," she said, underscoring the significance of the relationship between hip hop and Black Islam that Popmaster Fabel described beyond New York City and the 1970s. Like Popmaster Fabel, Tasleem traced Islam's influence on hip hop not solely through Sunni orthodoxy, but through the NOI and the Five Percenters as well.

Tasleem identified the influence of Black Islam in a diverse collection of people, places, activities, and material cultures. She mentioned the Chicago emcee Common, who is now a mainstream household name. Common's hip hop reputation, like that of the less known emcee Tasleem also named, X Chromosome, is tied to his lyrics, which reflect "Black consciousness." X Chromosome and her crew were members of the NOI, whose presence was palpable at that time. Male members sold the organization's newspaper, *The Final Call*—likely at 79th Street and Stony Island Avenue near the NOI national headquarters—and NOI ministers were extremely popular; a prominent example is Khalid Muhammad, a controversial, now deceased NOI minister, who was (and continues to be) cited by artists of the hip hop generation.[14] Further, Tasleem described an NOI whose influence was so great that even non-NOI members attended the NOI annual convention, Saviours' Day, which celebrates the organization's founding.

In Tasleem's recollection, the Sunni Black Muslims whose call to prayer echoed throughout their neighborhoods, and the "literal, symbolic, and transnational connections to Muslim culture and identity" made by the Chicago street organization the Black P. Stone Nation also represented Black Islam (Nashashibi 2009, 271–72). The Black P. Stone Nation was led by Jeff Fort, who upon his release from prison in the 1970s, renamed the organization the El Rukn, a word that means "corner" or "pillar" in Arabic. Sunni Muslim culture was also evident in the female dress Tasleem described.

The terms Tasleem used to describe the influence and widespread proliferation of Muslim practices, "God-consciousness," "knowledge," "[healthy] diet," "street credibility," and "respect," point to the central motivation of Black Islam: reshaping the way in which Black people see themselves, take care of themselves and each other, and remake the world. Importantly, Tasleem also included an explicitly non-Muslim group, the "Hebrew Israelites" or the community of Ben Ammi Ben Israel,[15] not because she misidentified them as Muslim but rather because they spoke the same language as their Black Muslim counterparts. Her references, from Black Jews to Black Muslim newspapers, reflect the rhizome-like travel of Black Islam through many different yet connected actors to become Black vernacular culture.

Tasleem's narrative demarcates the centrality of hip hop in this milieu in which Black Islam was easily recognized and always "got much respect." The Chicago context that it describes reflects what many call the "golden era" of hip hop. In contrast to the period that follows it and that is dominated by "Gangsta rap," the golden era is defined by "the sheer number of stylistic innovations that came into existence," innovations made by male as well as a growing number of female emcees that were lyrical, sonic, and thematic (Cobb 2007, 47).[16] Critically, as Tasleem described it, in addition to innovations in style, the golden era was also defined by a renewed and powerful interest in Afrocentricity and Black Nationalism.

The video for Queen Latifah's 1989 Black feminist anthem "Ladies First" opens with slides of five women: Harriet Tubman, the nineteenth-century abolitionist and poet Frances Harper, Sojourner Truth, Angela Davis, and Winnie Mandela. The images of Black women activists, both U.S. Black American and African, from different time periods, are shown accompanied by only the clicking sound of a slide projector as the images change. As the song's music and the chorus "Oooh ladies first, ladies first" begin, the video switches between two different scenes of Queen Latifah. In the first scene, with two female dancers dressed in African print blazers and combat boots flanking her, Queen Latifah is wearing a black pants suit with a gold and black African print sash diagonally across her body. The sash and her sleeves, with gold stripes around the wrist, give the look a military and Afrocentric feel. In the second scene Queen Latifah is alone and is wearing a head wrap and a white military-style suit while authoritatively studying a large chess-board map of Africa, on which the camera angles focus on South Africa.

Sisters, Philadelphia, Penn., 1996. Courtesy of Jamel Shabazz.

In these scenes and images, which represent only the first twenty seconds of the video, Queen Latifah displays Black consciousness—a mix of Black Nationalist and Pan-African sensibilities as well as an Afrocentric hip hop aesthetic.[17] The core tenets of Black Nationalism and Pan-Africanism are self-determination and self-reliance for African-descended peoples (Dawson 2003; Harris-Lacewell 2006). These tenets are demonstrated in Queen Latifah's video in the selection of the women portrayed, who link African-descended people across the African diaspora; in the focus on South Africa, which specifically linked U.S. Black Americans with the antiapartheid struggle; and in the military style of dress, which evokes the power of Black self-determination.

Black Nationalism and Pan-Africanism are also defined by the aspiration toward and adoption of alternatives to the social, political, economic, and cultural epistemologies of mainstream White American society. In U.S. Black American communities, Islam has consistently been seen as a viable alternative to the White and Christian U.S. mainstream, and as a result the pairing of Black consciousness and Islam is

a consistent feature of the U.S. Black American experience.[18] From all official accounts, Queen Latifah, née Dana Owens, is not herself Muslim,[19] yet her choice of Latifah, a Muslim-identified name, as her stage name is not inconsequential. As an artist who self-identifies as politically conscious, Queen Latifah's name choice reflects a commonly held view within urban U.S. Black communities that Islam is in alignment with Afrocentric and pro-Black sensibilities.[20]

In addition to the aesthetics of style and naming, this alignment is demonstrated in the sampling of male Black Muslim leaders such as Malcolm X, as described by Popmaster Fabel. For example, an excerpt of a recorded speech by Minister Louis Farrakhan introduces the 1989 track "Young, Gifted and Black" by the Brooklyn Five Percenter emcee and hip hop legend Big Daddy Kane. Likewise, the album *Death Certificate* by Ice Cube features excerpts of speeches by Khalid Muhammad. Black Sunni Muslim men also appear in hip hop music: the legendary hip hop group A Tribe Called Quest end the song "Phoney Rappers" with a clip from a speech by Brooklyn Imam Siraj Wahhaj. In the selections featured, Farrakhan and Muhammad preach that Black people have been divinely appointed as the leaders of humanity and Wahhaj warns against a failing moral center in U.S. society. Through their words of Black pride and social critique, these Black Muslim men serve as aural representations of the Black consciousness that links Islam and hip hop.

This alignment between Black consciousness, Black Islam, and hip hop is also articulated in lyrics. The group Public Enemy (PE) is well known for its "overt references to NOI doctrine, icons and rhetoric" (Floyd-Thomas 2003, 51). On the group's 1988 album *It Takes a Nation of Millions to Hold Us Back*, PE front man Chuck D identified himself as "the follower of Farrakhan, don't tell me that you understand until you hear the man" in the song "Don't Believe the Hype"; in another song, "Bring Noise," he declares, "Farrakhan's a prophet and I think you ought to listen to what he has to say to you" (Public Enemy 1988).[21] Likewise, in Lauryn Hill's warning song, "Doo Wop," she advises, "Yo, my men and women, don't forget about the *deen*, the *sirat al-mustaqim*," and she reprimands her people for "talking out ya neck like you a Christian, a Muslim sleeping with the *jinn*."

In her admonitions, Hill, who is not a Muslim, refers directly to Sunni Muslim beliefs. She cites a verse from the opening chapter of the

Big Daddy Kane, Chicago, 1986. Courtesy of Jamel
Shabazz.

Qur'an, "Al-Fatiha," when she reminds her listeners to stay true to the
"true way of life" (*deen*) and to adhere to "the straight path" (*sirat al-
mustaqim*) and chides them for spiritual hypocrisy—claiming to be
holy but spending their time with devilish beings (*jinn*). Similarly, on
his track "I Ain't Mad at Cha" Tupac Shakur raps about his homie who
"hit the pen and now no sinning is the game plan." His friend, who
converted to Islam in prison, is now a "Muslim with no time for dope
games" who "wants to go to the mosque; no time for females." In addition to describing his friend's personal transformation, Tupac speaks to
the way in which being Muslim in the U.S. Black community is often
identified with not only personal righteousness but also a commitment

to the uplift of Black people as a whole, as evidenced by his verse "When I say I'm living large all you see is the struggle."

The pursuit of righteousness is a recurring theme in hip hop verses composed by emcees from the Five Percenters, a genre Felicia Miyakawa (2005) calls "God Hop." For example, the Brand Nubian song "Allah and Justice" is an adaptation of the Five Percenter anthem "The Enlightener," which is sung at Five Percenter community events. Lyrics such as *"God came to teach us of the righteous way / How to build and be born* on this glorious day" refer back to Five Percenter beliefs, and the song's verses detail the science of Supreme Mathematics, the Five Percenter numerological system, making the song itself a lesson for Five Percenters. The proliferation of such hip hop songs in turn introduces new audiences to Five Percenter beliefs (Knight 2008).[22]

Five Percenter religious practice is structured around "breaking down" numbers and words in order to reveal their deeper meanings on a path to knowledge of self.[23] The kind of linguistic deconstruction and mastery of words required by these teachings has set the standard for rhetorical eloquence and word play in hip hop lyricism, making the list of emcees who are also Five Percenters an impressive one. It includes legends such as Rakim, groups such as the Poor Righteous Teachers, and innovators such as the Wu Tang Clan. Accordingly, Five Percenter ideas have also informed hip hop vernacular. Common phrases in hip hop music and culture, such as "What up God," "dropping science," and "word is bond" come directly from Five Percenter lessons.[24]

While the hip hop golden era is notable for "shifting the center of the rap world . . . decidedly in a Black Nationalist direction" (Chang 2005, 229), the value of golden era hip hop for Black consciousness goes back to the very origins of hip hop music and culture, which are in turn linked to hip hop's early relationship to Black Islam. Afrika Bambaataa, one of the godfathers of hip hop, credits the NOI messages of Black pride and self-respect for changing his own thinking and leading him to reorganize his 1970s street organization Black Spades to form the Zulu Nation:

They [NOI] held the teachings of "You're not a 'nigga.' You're not colored. Wake up Black man and Black woman and love yourself. Respect your own. Turn back to Africa." That started sticking with a lot of the brothers and sisters. . . . And that always stuck in my mind and heart. I said I have to do some type of change to get the mindset of the masses that was following me to lead them to another way. (Chang 2005, 100)

Members of the Zulu Nation are united by hip hop music and the pursuit of a common set of values, which include knowledge, wisdom, understanding, freedom, justice, peace, unity, love, respect, work, fun, science, truth, facts, faith, and the oneness of God.[25] Many of these values are universal, yet they also reflect the influence of Black Islam on hip hop.

The Last Poets, an ensemble consisting of poets and a percussionist, is often cited as the progenitor of hip hop, specifically the art of emceeing. Jelani Cobb refers to the group "as proto-rappers, playing many of the verbal techniques that would later become central to MCs (emcees)" (Cobb 2007, 42). In 2005, in a nod to that history Common featured The Last Poets in his critically acclaimed ode to the 'hood, "The Corner." Coming out of the Black Arts Movement, the aesthetic arm of the Black Power tradition, the work of The Last Poets reflects a Black consciousness perspective, an Afrocentric aesthetic, and the influence of Black Islam.

The Last Poets was formed in 1968 at a commemorative event to celebrate the life of Malcolm X. Reflecting on the group's formation, Abiodun Oyewole identified Malcolm X as the group's "pathway to revolutionary understanding":

Malcolm went through a series of rites of passage—from Malcolm Little to Detroit Red to Satan to Malcolm X to El-Hajj Malik El-Shabazz. All this because this man never stopped trying to develop and recognize the best of himself. Malcolm was saying we need to be more. And we heard that. And he said it better than anybody ever said it. He made things clear to us. So all we wanted to do was to be disciples of Malcolm, in a sense using poetry to illuminate the same values that he had planted in our heads. (Oyewole 2003)

The model of rebirth that Malcolm symbolized and encouraged in The Last Poets is repeated in contemporary hip hop narratives. As Cobb (2007) argues, Malcolm's autobiographical form is replicated throughout hip hop storytelling: fatherlessness and poverty lead to a life of crime, and a stint in the penitentiary leads to penitence and rebirth.[26] It is important to note that while Malcolm X is iconic, his narrative is not singular. Rather, he epitomizes the possibility for Black resistance and redemption that Black Islam represents in U.S. Black communities. Accordingly, even the non-Muslim members of The Last Poets identified with Islam at some point because "it [Islam] touches a lot of brothers who come out of the streets" (Oyewole and Hassan 1996, 31).

Black Islam touched a lot of brothers and sisters because, as Tasleem noted, Black Islam was everywhere. The art and culture described by Tasleem as well as The Last Poets and Afrika Bambaataa, and demonstrated by Queen Latifah show that during the twentieth century Black Islam was a social phenomenon known for advancing the principles of Black consciousness, resistance, and redemption and an interdependent notion of community that was broadly experienced in U.S. Black communities. Through music and poetry, the model of Black Muslim leaders such as Malcolm X, and the practice of Black Islam in everyday U.S. Black life, a body of shared knowledge on Black Islam emerged in urban communities through which Black Islam became Black vernacular culture.

From Afrika Islam's radio show and the lyrics of Common, Lauryn Hill, Public Enemy, and Ice Cube to nods at Malcolm X and Muhammad Ali as icons of Black cool and to Queens-bred and non-Muslim rapper Nicki Minaj's quip "I don't fuck with pigs like As Salaamu Alaikum" (Minaj 2009), hip hop's engagement with Black Islam varies in its intensity. But however meaningful or irreverent, hip hop's early and continuing engagement with Black Islam reflects the enduring impact of Black Islam on hip hop music and culture. This impact manifests itself in many ways but is defined by Black Islam's most significant contribution to hip hop: knowledge of self.

Knowledge of Self as Hip Hop Epistemology

> At exactly which point do you start to realize
> that life without knowledge is death in disguise?
> That's why knowledge of self is like life after death
> Apply it to your life, let destiny manifest (Def and Kweli 1998)

These lyrics are taken from Talib Kweli's song "K.O.S. (Determina-tion)" on the album *Mos Def & Talib Kweli Are Black Star*. Kweli is not a Muslim, in contrast to his friend and musical partner on this album, Mos Def, currently known as Yasiin Bey, who is a Sunni Muslim. The track title is taken from its call and response chorus: "With that, what? [call:] 'Knowledge of Self Determination.' [response]." Kweli's lyrics "life without knowledge is death in disguise" do not describe a physi-cal death but the death of the spirit or mind. This harkens back to the NOI and the Five Percenter belief, as well as Sunni and Shi'i thought, that an individual without self-knowledge is less of a human being and more akin to a beast of burden. Kweli then instructs his listener that with knowledge of self you can be reborn and your destiny will become manifest because you, as a god, the original man, or simply a servant empowered by the decree of the Divine can reach or experi-ence power. The song was released thirty-three years after NOI leader Elijah Muhammad published his seminal text *Message to the Blackman in America* (1965), in which he provides an exegetical exposition on knowledge of self. While neither Talib Kweli nor Mos Def are adher-ents of the NOI, this song indexes the centrality of knowledge of self to hip hop epistemology.

Knowledge of self, as articulated by the Nation of Islam, has been particularly influential in hip hop. Some add it to emceeing, b-boying/b-girling, dj-ing, and graffiti as hip hop's fifth element. References to knowledge of self in NOI theology can be found in the "Lost-Found Muslim Lessons," the NOI catechism taught by W. D. Fard Muham-mad, the founder of the Nation of Islam, to Elijah Muhammad as his apostle. The title "Lost-Found" refers to the condition in which W. D. Fard found the "so-called Negro."[27] According to early NOI belief, U.S. Black Americans are descendants of the original inhabitants of Planet Earth and the ancestors of all humanity, forming the tribe of Shabazz (Muhammad 1965, 31). As "the Maker, Owner, and Cream of the Planet Earth," U.S. Black Americans, descendants of enslaved Africans in the Western hemisphere, who lived in subjugation were seen, in an exis-tential sense, as *lost* or wandering without guidance in the "wilderness of North America." When *found* by Master Fard they would discover knowledge of self and reclaim their rightful position among humankind. Two of these lessons teach that self-knowledge is to be "civilized" and endowed with knowledge of the self and also the social world—the science of everything:

Why did Mossa (Moses) have a hard time to civilize the Devil—2000 BC?

Answer: Because he was a savage. Savage means a person that has lost the knowledge of himself and who is living a beast life. . . . Civilize means to teach the knowledge and wisdom of the human family of the planet Earth. (Lost-Found Muslim Lesson no. 1, Question 2)

What is the Duty of a civilized person?

Answer: To teach the uncivilized people, who are savage—civilization (righteousness, the knowledge of himself, the science of everything in life—love, peace and happiness). (Lost-Found Muslim Lesson no. 2, Question 18)

According to NOI beliefs, when knowledge is coupled with righteousness it leads to peace, happiness, and the dominion that is the natural right of the "original man." Elijah Muhammad offers an exegesis on knowledge of self in his *Message to the Blackman in America*. I quote this exposition at length below in order to highlight three themes—time, learning, and action—which define knowledge of self as taken up in hip hop.

It is knowledge of self that the so-called Negroes lack which keeps them from enjoying freedom, justice, and equality. This belongs to them divinely as much as it does to other nations of the earth. It is Allah's (God's) will and purpose that we shall know ourselves. Therefore He came Himself to teach us the knowledge of self. (Muhammad 1965, 31)

We must become aware of the knowledge of self and the time in which we are living. You must know these things whether you agree that Elijah Muhammad is on time or out of time. If what I say is out of season, it goes for nothing. If I am on time or in season, then all I say will bear fruit. . . . It is time for us to learn who we really are, and it is time for us to understand ourselves. . . . Trace over the earth. Check back 5,000, 10,000, or 20,000

years ago. Look at history. Who were those people? They were our people.
(Muhammad 1965, 34–35)

I am for the acquiring of knowledge or the accumulating of knowledge—as we now call it; education. First, my people must be taught the
knowledge of self. Then and only then will they be able to understand
others and that which surrounds them. Anyone who does not have a
knowledge of self is considered a victim of either amnesia or uncon-
sciousness and is not very competent. . . . Gaining the knowledge of self
makes us unite into a great unity. Knowledge of self makes you take on
the great virtue of learning. . . . We need an education, but an education
which removes us from the shackles of slavery and servitude. . . . The acquiring of knowledge for our children and ourselves must not be limited
to the three R's—reading, 'riting and 'rithmetic. It should instead include
the history of the black nation, the knowledge of civilization of man and
the universe and all the sciences. (Muhammad 1965, 39–41)

The so-called Negroes must be taught and given Islam. Why Islam? Islam,
because it teaches first the knowledge of self. It gives us the knowledge of
our own. Then and only then are we able to understand that which surrounds us. "Know thy self" is the doctrine Socrates espoused, and this
is the base of the educational system in America. The religion of Islam
makes the so-called Negroes think in terms of self and their own kind.
Thus, this kind of thinking produces an industrious people who are self-
independent. (Muhammad 1965, 57–58)

The first of the three central themes is time. Knowledge of time, dia-
chronic and synchronic, is critical to knowledge of self. Muhammad
directs his readers to "trace over the earth. Check back 5,000, 10,000,
or 20,000 years ago. Look at history," and knowledge of self relies on
knowing the past—where the self originates. This knowledge of the past
is particularly valuable because it facilitates correct knowledge of the
present—the self in time—enabling individuals to interpret their condition in the here and now. In the particular case of U.S. Black Americans,
argues Muhammad, this kind of knowledge is essential to undo the centuries of "mis-education" (Woodson 2013) that has led many Blacks to
believe they are inferior to Whites. The narrative that was dominant in

the United States at the time Muhammad wrote *Message to the Blackman* and that persists today contained a history of the world that depicted White people as subjects and Black people as objects. As the adage goes, "knowledge is power," and Muhammad thus argues that once empowered with knowledge of time, the Black individual is able to reinterpret his or her subordinate position and see it not as an inevitable result of Black inferiority but, as in NOI theology, as a specific juncture through which Black people are meant to regain their rightful position among humankind.

The second theme, which follows from the first and is critical to knowledge of self, is learning. Muhammad is for "the acquiring of knowledge." Indeed, the knowledge of time is acquired through deliberate study. It was a pedagogical imperative within the NOI that adherents be required to study and memorize the Lost-Found Muslim Lessons, which included a rendering of scientific facts such as the circumference and age of Planet Earth. Being well versed in a range of facts was critical to knowledge of self, in and across time, and also drew on alternative knowledges that converged and diverged with mainstream narratives of science and history. Importantly, the learning was deliberate in that it was geared toward freedom from mental slavery. This deliberate learning leads to the third theme of change and action. The journey toward knowledge of self is designed to change the way individuals think; specifically, its goal is that Black people "think in terms of self and their own kind," which will make them industrious and self-independent. For Muhammad, this kind of thinking is meant to reorient Black people away from an integrationist impulse and toward the shaping of a community that is autonomous from White society and envisions Black people as subjects and creators of their own destiny. In this way, knowledge of self works toward the cultivation of an awareness of self and the social world and encourages direct action to change the condition of the "so-called Negro" lost in the wilderness of North America.

These same three themes—time, learning, and action—run through appropriations of knowledge of self in hip hop. The hip hop articulations may adhere to the dispensationalism and Black exceptionalism fundamental to the NOI rendering of self-knowledge; however, more often, as in Kweli's track, knowledge of self is interpreted more broadly. In hip hop, the pursuit of knowledge of self emphasizes being well informed about the past, particularly the alternative histories that privilege the "hidden transcripts" (Scott 1990) of marginalized peoples, as well as being keenly attuned to contemporary racialized, classed, and gendered oppression and the continuities of contemporary subjugation with past repression. Knowledge of self becomes an ethical epistemology vis-à-vis other human beings, animals, the natural world, and notions of the Divine that engenders a commitment to social change through personal transformation and direct action.

Going back to OmarMukhtar's trajectory from the youth center to Black Panther literature to IMAN, OmarMukhtar situated himself in time. For him, Blackness and the Black American struggle for liberation became the means through which he understood his own position as a member of a racial minority. OmarMukhtar's understanding and deployment of Blackness articulates what Sharma identifies as a "global race consciousness" that extends "the meaning of Blackness beyond biology" (Sharma 2010, 230). Blackness operates as "a matter of critical understanding," which prompts awareness of "how various racisms impact interminority relations and maintain the ideological supremacy of Whites" (Sharma 2010, 2). OmarMukhtar also learned through hip hop. Through his meditation on Five Percenter philosophy ("It's like the RZA said"), he discovered what he considered the "core essence" of Islam: being compassionate, truthful, honest, sincere, just. This knowledge was critical, as it redirected him away from the privatized and insular sense of Muslimness dominant in his childhood community and toward a potentially more expansive and more action-oriented sense of Muslim identity.

Knowledge of self is the first bend in the loop of Muslim Cool, and like OmarMukhtar, my teachers moved toward knowledge of self in order to be Muslims. Many U.S. Muslims might object to this claim—that a concept derived from the NOI and interpolated through hip hop could undergird Muslim piety—because of the aforementioned ways in which Black Islam is seen as "outside" orthodox Islamic traditions. Yet for my teachers, the pursuit of knowledge of self reiterated the "centrality in Islamic thought and society of reason and knowledge," arising from the Qur'an's valorization of the human faculty of reasoning, endowed to humankind by God, and from prophetic traditions that elevate knowledge and learning (Rosen 2002, xi).

Among the numerous directives in the Qur'an and the traditions of Prophet Muhammad are instructions that humans should reflect, consider, and contemplate the natural world as a means of reaching spiritual awareness. This is, as quoted above, precisely how Elijah Muhammad explicates knowledge of self. Not coincidentally, the celebrated twelfth-century Sunni scholar Abu Hamid al-Ghazali also championed the idea in his text *The Alchemy of Happiness*. In the first chapter, "On Knowledge of the Self," al-Ghazali counsels Muslims to seek knowledge of self in order to know God: "What art thou in thyself, and from whence hast thou come? Whither art thou going, and for what purpose hast thou come to tarry here awhile?"[28] Like Elijah Muhammad, al-Ghazali also locates knowledge of self in time, learning, and action.

My teachers are diverse. They are Sunni and Shi'a, Arab, South Asian, Black, and Latin@; they are converts and they were raised Muslim since birth. Across this diversity they travel the loop of Muslim Cool and in doing so recover knowledge of self as, once again, a central episteme in U.S. American Muslim identity. In this way, Muslim Cool is also a commentary on orthodoxy, or on what "counts" as Islamic. My teachers were clear about what traditionally stands as Islamic orthodoxy: the oneness of an omnipotent and omnipresent God and the finality of prophethood in the life and body of Muhammad ibn Abdullah, born in the seventh century C.E. They did not claim to include, for example, the Five Percenters under the umbrella of this traditional notion of orthodoxy, but they did seek connections to Black Islam and identified the various traditions of Black Islam as legitimate resources through which they could interpret their own Muslimness.

When Elijah Muhammad taught his followers knowledge of self, he did so in response to racialized exclusion that marked Blackness as a site of social illegitimacy in the U.S. mainstream. He argued that awareness of "civilization-righteousness, the knowledge of himself, the science of everything in life" would return Black people to their legitimate social status. Likewise, Muslim Cool responds to the idea of Blackness as a site of social illegitimacy in the U.S. mainstream and as a site of religious illegitimacy among Arab and South Asian U.S. American Muslims. Through hip hop epistemology, that is, knowledge of self, Muslim Cool reclaims Black Islam and Blackness as a means of critique that informs action.

Rabia

In comparison to OmarMukhtar, Rabia was less likely to cite the RZA with such precision, but she had also traveled the trajectory of knowledge of self to Muslim Cool. Rabia was an eighteen-year-old Pakistani American who was both an IMAN volunteer and one of my key teachers in the field. Sitting around the kitchen island in her family's home in Bridgeview, I asked her, "Does hip hop help you be Muslim?" Without missing a beat she responded, "Yeah," as if the answer was obvious. She continued, "Imagine if I was listening to Nicole Richie?" I countered, "But she is not a singer." Rabia then offered, "OK then, Paris Hilton," who also did not sing. Laughing at herself, Rabia exclaimed, "Well then, Hannah Montana! Imagine if I was listening to that Nickelodeon crap!" Rabia's juxtaposition of hip hop with Nicole Richie, Paris Hilton, and Hannah Montana was telling. Rabia posited hip hop as an alternative to mainstream popular culture—represented by three White women, Richie, Hilton, and Montana—which Rabia saw as without value and potentially injurious (after all, "crap" is colloquial for feces).[29] While I searched for accuracy in her comparison, it seemed to be irrelevant to Rabia that Richie and Hilton were not musical artists, because they, along with Montana, were not hip hop.

One afternoon, while driving from IMAN to an event on the South Side, Rabia, seated next to me in the car, blurted out, somewhat confession-like, "Let me tell you something: the people I used to hang out with smoked weed—and hip hop was on all the time. I didn't really know a different kind of hip hop until this last year when I began going to IMAN." She went on to explain that through Man-O-Wax and others at IMAN she discovered "conscious" hip hop and other forms of alterity related to it, such as vegetarianism. It is worth noting that the soundtrack to Rabia's admission, like the soundtrack to her former friends' marijuana smoking, was hip hop. In fact, her reflection was provoked by what was playing on my car's CD player, "The Score," the first (and thus far the last) album of the hip hop group The Fugees.

Rabia was excited to hear the album, which she had just discovered, and she raved about the first track "How Many Mics," which makes reference to Khalid Muhammad. Since Sunni orthodoxy prohibits recreational drug use, it was clear that Rabia was concerned that her association with weed smoking would negatively affect my opinion of her. I was not moved by her admission of weed-smoking friends,[30] but I was floored by the fact that she had only recently heard "The Score." The Fugees are often seen as icons of "conscious" hip hop, so I expected that as an IMAN volunteer Rabia would be as familiar with them as OmarMukhtar and I, who could recite the album backward and forward. What I failed to account for at the time was not only the fact that she had only recently been introduced to IMAN and by extension to "conscious" hip hop but also her age: when "The Score" was released, Rabia was only eight years old.

I met Rabia at IMAN, where she had been active since she started college. Rabia's family had initially lived in the city but had moved to Bridgeview when she was a young child. Rabia was in college at the time of my fieldwork and had yet to decide between a career in law and one in medicine. She was a commuter student who negotiated her comings and goings with her parents. Rabia's volunteering at IMAN was at times an additional source of tension with her parents, as it represented another reason in addition to school for her to be away from home. Yet Rabia successfully asserted her autonomy—granted less by her parents' wishes than through the sheer force of her own youthful willfulness. Rabia was also something of an urban fashionista: her scarf usually matched the swoosh in her Nikes, and at the time of my fieldwork she was considering dance classes that would add b-girl to her growing list of qualifications. One afternoon we discussed her relationship to her university's Muslim Students Association (MSA), and Rabia explained why she was not very involved with the group:

RABIA: It's . . . I don't know, I guess I never gave it [MSA] a chance, to explore it.
SU'AD: What do you think [made you not do that]?
RABIA: I guess I judge those people in the MSA. You saw how it was! The guys don't even *salam*[31] on you, and then the girls, they just, like, there are some cool girls but some them are just, like, weird to me, so I just don't try to mingle with them.
SU'AD: The other girls, what makes them weird to you?
RABIA: I don't know; to me, they are just like typical desi girls, and that's just not like me at all. So I, like, don't even . . .

Rabia felt out of place at her MSA because she was not "a typical desi [i.e., South Asian] girl." Who is a typical desi girl? For Rabia, such girls were young South Asian American women who "only hang out with other desis, they only speak in Urdu, they only watch desi movies." Furthermore, according to Rabia, beyond the leisure activities of "smoking hookah, going out to dinner and to Cedar Point [amusement park]," they do not do anything that is "valuable." In Rabia's estimation, because the typical desi girl's universe of concerns is limited to "family, desi friends, getting married, and going to medical school," she fits within, rather than challenges, the South Asian U.S. American Muslim community's status quo. It is important to note that Rabia's "typical desi girl" is a bit of a straw desi girl; even within Rabia's description, the "typical desi girl" does not always abide by the status quo. Notably, "smoking hookah" as a leisure activity is not likely to be endorsed by all immigrant South Asian parents.

Rabia's "typical desi girl" corresponds to what Sharma terms "hegemonic desiness" (Sharma 2010). Hegemonic desiness denotes a way of being South Asian in the United States "among South Asian immigrants contending with their new status as [racial] minorities" that pivots on exceptional financial and educational success and ethnic insularity (Sharma 2010, 85). Like Rabia, Sharma also identifies college student cultural organizations as sites of hegemonic desiness. For Sharma's desi emcee interlocutors, being authentically Indian within Indian student organizations meant coming from or aspiring toward middle-class consumptive practices such as suburban living, dressing in Abercrombie and Fitch clothes, and adhering to heterosexual norms (Sharma 2012). "Being Indian" also rested on cultural authenticity, which then made one culturally authoritative, a designation bestowed on certain students because they displayed "cultural knowledge and because they socialized strictly with Indians" (Sharma 2010, 60). Part of this authenticity was also tied to the "religious hegemony of Indian Hindus" (Sharma 2010, 52). Likewise, Maira (2008) describes second-generation Indian Americans who navigated predominately White college environments by engaging in "ethnicizing moves." These are symbolic markers such as dress and jewelry as well as "literally performing their ethnic identity with 'bhangra moves' . . . to assert . . . ethnic identity" (Maira 2008, 56). Both Maira and Sharma show that hegemonic desiness, although somewhat more palatable to the multicultural tastes of White U.S. normativity, is a performance of a particular type of desiness rather than Whiteness.

Importantly, Rabia encountered hegemonic desiness not in a South Asian American student group, where she might have felt marginal as a non-Hindu, but in the Muslim Students Association. This is somewhat ironic, considering how well Rabia fit her MSA's demographic: young, South Asian U.S. American, and Muslim. Because Rabia felt out of place at the MSA, most of my subsequent encounters with the organization, at their events and in the MSA prayer room, took place without her. These encounters were made possible in part by the relationship I developed with a young Puerto Rican convert, Leticia. She had converted to Islam in high school through her South Asian U.S. American Muslim female classmates, and while I was conducting fieldwork Leticia served on the MSA's executive board. Yet her leadership position in the group only confirmed Rabia's view of the MSA.

I met up with Leticia at a small but popular café in her neighborhood, far from the hallowed halls of her university but close to her roots, in Humboldt Park. I was starting a cleanse the next day so had to avoid all the lovely pastries, cupcakes, slices of cake, caribe grilled cheese, and fresh bread and butter at the café—although I did determine that hot chocolate fell somehow within my precleanse program (it was really, really good). We sat in a corner, and Leticia described her experience with the MSA. She explained that she was "working with them [the MSA students] to try not to be so secluded," particularly "the immigrant students [second-generation South Asian U.S. Americans] who think every Black Muslim is a convert. . . . They are also very medical- and science-focused." Part of her efforts involved getting the MSA to cosponsor an event with a Latin@ fraternity about Latin@ Muslims and collaborating with antiracist groups on campus to fight Islamophobia.

"Working with them" was hard work. Leticia found that her South Asian U.S. American Muslim college classmates were either unwilling or unable to see the need to be active in the broader college community, let alone the city of Chicago. Part of this resistance arose from attitudes of anti-Blackness that played themselves out through microaggressions, such as assuming a Black Muslim must be a convert and thus less schooled in the religion. Although Leticia is Latina and not phenotypically Black, anti-Black attitudes had direct implications for Leticia's authority as an MSA board member and for her feelings of belonging as a convert to Islam. She recounted being subjected to racialized class-based prejudices, such as a Muslim classmate's question and comment: "Leticia, are those your Jordans? They are nice. You are so ghetto!" At this MSA, hegemonic desiness operated as a performance of Muslimness in which class mattered. This made Leticia feel out of place for being "so ghetto" or failing to be appropriately middle class.

Leticia also echoed Rabia's description of male-female interactions at the MSA. She explained that after being seen chatting in front of a campus building with "two guys I knew and one from MSA," she was reprimanded by a fellow student, who told her that this was inappropriate behavior. Leticia concluded that "maybe because I was on the MSA exec board I might have a little more leeway [to talk to members of the opposite gender because of the demands of the position], but to be outside doing that" was considered unseemly. While I was conducting fieldwork, the MSA's prayer space was remodeled to include a high wall between the male and female prayer areas, and there was implicit social pressure to sit and socialize separately at MSA events. Thus the prevailing notions of piety seemed to hinge to some extent on gender segregation; as Leticia put it, at MSA "everything is separate."

Not too long after Rabia's confession on the car ride, I visited her again at her family's large suburban home, which not only housed her immediate family members but also was a frequent way station for relatives newly immigrated to the United States. Seated at the kitchen table, I watched while Rabia enthusiastically informed her mother about a food cooperative that sold organic *zabiha* meat (meat slaughtered according to Islamic jurisprudence). Rabia's mother was a very devout Muslim and accordingly purchased only zabiha meat for her family. Therefore, while she was quite pleased with Rabia's insistence on zabiha, at that moment her sole concern was that the meat was killed properly.

Through her participation in IMAN's programming Rabia had been introduced to a number of ideologies around food, such as vegetarianism and the concept of *tayyib*. The term "tayyib" appears in a Qur'anic verse that enjoins Muslims to eat food that is *halal* (permissible) and tayyib (good and wholesome).[32] Muslim advocates of organic farming argue that tayyib is consequently a necessary condition of a proper Muslim diet and that in order for that condition to be met, animals must be raised humanely (Abdul-Matin 2010). Dietary prescriptions such as these can be found in a number of prophetic traditions that encourage moderation in eating and drinking as well as limits to the consumption of meat, along with the Qur'anic prohibitions on pork and alcohol. Yet Rabia's enthusiasm for organic halal meat had not been ignited by the dietary discourses of the Hanafi orthodoxy of her home community but rather through hip hop's interpolation of Black Islam.[33]

There are a number of hip hop songs that speak to the necessity of eating healthfully and prescribe certain rules for eating. The chorus of A Tribe Called Quest's track "Ham n' Eggs" declares, "I don't eat no ham n' eggs, cuz they're high in cholesterol," and each member of the crew, when asked "Do you eat em?" responds with "No, not at all" (ATCQ 1990).[34] In the song "Be Healthy," dead prez's Stic.Man rhymes, "I don't eat no meat, no dairy, no sweets, only ripe vegetables, fresh fruit and whole wheat" (dead prez 2000). Likewise, KRS-One released an early hip hop manifesto against beef. This song, entitled "Beef," narrates the perils of factory farming, including the "fear and stress" of the cows, which transfer to the humans who "thaw it [frozen beef] out with the blood and season it / then you sit down and begin eatin' it" (BDP 1990). Importantly, many of these songs' directives can be traced back to Black Islam.[35] This is done implicitly by ATCQ when the group members collectively eschew ham, evoking the "no pork on my fork" mantra of U.S. Black American Muslims, and when Stic.Man eats only whole wheat bread, referencing the NOI prohibition against white bread. It is also done explicitly when KRS-One directs his listeners to "Read the book *How to Eat to Live* by Elijah Muhammad, it's a brown paperback" (BDP 1990).

In her work on U.S. Black American Muslims, Carolyn Rouse (2004) examines diet as a means of "ingesting ideology." She discusses Elijah Muhammad's prohibition of what he called "slave food"—foods such as collard greens and sweet potatoes that are commonly used in Black Southern cuisine. Muhammad labeled these foods "slave food" because he argued that they "are unfit for human consumption" as they were discarded by the slave-holding class and were given to Blacks only to emphasize the latter's allegedly subhuman status. Accordingly, for Muhammad eating these foods reproduced the logics of Black enslavement and blocked the path to knowledge of self. Muhammad, who located his teachings within the broader Islamic tradition, also encouraged moderation in eating and drinking and limited the consumption of meat. He viewed such prescriptions as necessary for spiritual purification in order for Blacks to reclaim their God-given roles on earth. After Muhammad's death and the transition of many of his followers to Sunni orthodoxy, many of his proscriptions were abandoned and "soul food" was reincorporated into the Black Muslim diet (Rouse 2004). But Muhammad's fundamental message that "you are what you eat" endures. Black Muslims, following the traditions of Black Islam, can be found, for example, lauding the benefits of honey as a prophetic medicine that can help overcome the disproportionate health problems affecting Black Americans and praising the prohibitions on alcohol and drugs as fundamental to curbing the substance abuse that wreaks havoc on Black communities (Rouse 2004). Food choices and taboos thus remain a key technique of liberation in Black Islam.

I never heard Rabia invoke the term "slave food," but I knew her introduction to organic zabiha meat to be informed by this history. She learned much of the history under the tutelage of Man-O-Wax, who was himself a vegetarian and encouraged healthy eating among youth.[36] Her journey through knowledge of self can be charted in her consumption not only of food but of hip hop—The Fugees as well as local hip hop artists such as D-Nick the Microphone Misfit, who ran workshops with IMAN's youth participants and whose song "Abnormality" features these lines:

> from the lies, the scandal, the food pyramid
> the suckas that invented that need to do a bid
> you want freedom from disease and abnormality
> 'cause you don't want this stuff affecting your reality.

Accordingly, Rabia's *learning* through knowledge of self included the ability to identify inequality as systemic. Moreover, Rabia was tuned in to what healthy eating means in *time*. She was concerned about both factory farm animals and food deserts, and she took her first step toward *action* with her mother. Rabia was consistently passionate about learning and about being a part of social change. During the time I knew her, she drafted a number of social justice projects, including a campaign to address the lack of hygienic conditions in Cook County youth jails and an urban farming effort on the South Side. Not all of her projects were actualized, but they all demonstrated the way in which knowledge of self as hip hop epistemology enabled social understanding and action linked to Black Islam. By thinking and being a U.S. American Muslim through Blackness, Rabia made the final turn to Muslim Cool.

Fatema

> It [the 'hoodjab] means [being] connected to a certain type of people or culture; people who are down with the hip hop scene, that whole Afro-centricity thing too, people who are very Afrocentric but not actually African. I think it's cool because it connects you to not only a culture but also a way of thinking, and it can connect you to hip hop, because hip hop is a form of expression that opens you up—you are open-minded, you are fighting for people who don't have a voice, and the very fact that you are wearing it but you are not from an African culture shows you can connect to African culture as well, and it has potential to make you a part of a larger movement.

In this comment, Fatema, one of my key teachers in the field, was responding to a question I had posed regarding a particular headscarf style, the 'hoodjab (described in detail in chapter 3), that is often worn in U.S. Black American Muslim communities and also by young U.S. American Muslim women, Black and non-Black, engaged in hip hop culture. I was visiting Fatema at the apartment that she shared with her brother, located near the university where she was a junior. I had met Fatema at IMAN, where she was working on community mapping projects and coordinating youth programming. Fatema described being drawn to IMAN because she was seeking out meaning in her life and "wanted to do more than going to weddings every weekend." She was Pakistani U.S. American and, like Rabia, felt that most of her South Asian U.S. American Muslim peers were preoccupied by concerns that were "shallow when the world is much deeper." She saw herself as different from her peers and was motivated to do something, but she did not think that something could happen in the "'burbs" where she grew up. Therefore, Fatema made a conscious choice to move outside the suburbs

to be active in addressing "deeper" concerns. This move included trans-
ferring to a university in the city of Chicago.

In the course of explaining why the 'hoodjab headscarf style was
"cool," Fatema reiterated Man-O-Wax's hip hop trajectory, described
earlier. She identified hip hop as "a form of expression that opens you
up" and that connects to "that whole Afrocentricity thing" and "a larger
movement." Her use of the term "African" was not flippant nor a gloss
but rather Diasporic and an indication of the Afrodiasporic roots of hip
hop. She further explained that connecting to Blackness through hip
hop, even when "you are not from an African culture . . . has potential to
make you a part of a larger movement." Thus as for OmarMukhtar and
for Rabia, for Fatema hip hop was epistemology, knowledge of self that
comes through learning in time and leads to action "fighting for people
who don't have a voice" through her participation in social justice efforts
aimed at alleviating Black suffering.

Fatema, Rabia, and OmarMukhtar are three young U.S. Muslims who
are stereotypically distant from Blackness—they are not only non-Black,
but also the children of immigrants who grew up middle class and in the
suburbs and are subsequently expected to acclimate, if not assimilate, to
Whiteness. Yet it is precisely because of this distance that their stories
most vividly illustrate how Muslim Cool works to cultivate U.S. Muslim
identities through Blackness. At the same time, because of this distance,
it would be easy to locate their self-making within a discourse of cultural
appropriation, which I interrogate when I turn to Fatema's headscarf
in chapter 3. But here I follow Sharma (2010) to suggest an alternative
interpretation for this non-Black Muslim self-making through Blackness: as an extension of earlier traditions of Afro-Asian and Arab-Black
American solidarity.

OmarMukhtar drew on the Black radical tradition to reorganize his
conceptions of himself as an Arab U.S. American Muslim in ways that
challenged his community's sanction of Blackness. Likewise, the Black
radical tradition looked to struggles in locales such as Algeria to re-
conceptualize the Black struggle in the United States as part of a global
anticolonial struggle. As Sohail Daulatzai narrates, anticolonial movements as depicted and disseminated in films like the *Battle of Algiers*
provided "an alternative grammar of resistance and a unique language
of revolt" for Black Power activists (Daulatzai 2012, 80). And in 2014,

after Israel's assault on Gaza and the protests that arose across the United States in the aftermath of numerous consecutive shootings of unarmed Black men and women, some U.S. Black American leaders again globalized Black struggles in the United States by looking to Palestine. One hip hop example of this is a track by Beatnick and K-Salaam (an Iranian U.S. American Muslim) with Talib Kweli and M1 (of dead prez) called "Checkpoints: From Ghetto to Gaza." This song represents an extension of an early tradition of solidarity with the Palestinian struggle (Lubin 2009).

Likewise, there is a tradition of Afro-Asian solidarity. U.S. Asian American activists such as Yuri Kochiyama and Grace Lee Boggs were critical actors in the Black Power movements of the twentieth century (Ho and Mullen 2008; Lee 2013). The "little red book," *Quotations from Chairman Mao Tse Tsung*, and Communist China inspired the revolutionary activism of the Black Panther Party and other 1960s Black radical activists (Kelley and Esch 1999). The technique and discipline of martial artists such as Bruce Lee influenced the development of hip hop dance (Schloss 2009), and the martial arts are a staple in U.S. Black Muslim life. Furthermore, martial arts as a philosophy of self-discipline and self-defense is a common theme in hip hop music and imagery (Banjoko 2004), most famously exemplified by the Wu Tang Clan.

In terms of specific Black and South Asian solidarities in the United States, Mufti Sadiq, the first Ahmadi missionary to the United States, proselytized to Black communities by connecting the South Asian struggle against British colonialism with the struggle against U.S. racism (Curtis 2009). In her work on hip hop desis in the twenty-first century, Sharma (2010) argues that engaging Blackness through hip hop is not a move to appropriate Blackness but a move that rejects notions of race and ethnicity that essentialize Asian Americans as a model minority and Black Americans as their antithesis. Thus, hip hop becomes a way to disrupt narratives that divide and conquer Asian U.S. Americans and Black U.S. Americans in order to prop up white supremacy.

Through Muslim Cool, Fatema, Rabia, and OmarMukhtar extended these legacies of solidarity through hip hop's and therefore Black Islam's emphasis on understanding *and* action. All three have now graduated from college and to a certain extent from IMAN, but they continue to embody Muslim Cool in their personal and professional lives, pursuing "the understanding of how to get justice, freedom, and equality" as well as "love, peace, and happiness." Their interactions with real-life Black people in activist projects that directly confront the violence of racism helped to prevent the flattening of Blackness in their own consciousness. The relationships to hip hop and Black people that they developed through their activism meant engaging knowledge of self *as Muslims* traveling the loop of Muslim Cool.

Toward the end of OmarMukhtar's reflection, he cited the Five Percent: "It's like the RZA said—[this statement is] a Five Percent thing I like to carry around—'You need knowledge, wisdom, understanding, justice, freedom, equality, love, peace, and happiness.'" Like a sample that is looped to create a musical track, Yahya repeated these words— words in which the RZA is citing the Supreme Mathematics of the Five Percent—throughout his commentary. This citation is deeply significant because it traces the loop of Muslim Cool. Through hip hop, which is critically informed by Black Islam, U.S. Muslims turn to Black Islam as a way of thinking and a way of being Muslim.

My teachers demonstrate a relationship to the Islamic tradition and Muslim piety that has been made through the founding theologies and experiences of Black Islam. Notions of the Islamic tradition and Muslim piety have been "hot topics," particularly in the aftermath of 9/11. The discourse of orientalism (Said 1979) and related concepts such as the "clash of civilizations" (Huntington 1993) construct the murky objects "the West" and the "Muslim world" (are they places? spaces? cultures? discourses?) as entities divided by fundamental differences of religion, politics, and a whole host of sensibilities. Critically, these differences presuppose and naturalize the superiority of the West. The attacks of 9/11 and their political, cultural, and discursive aftermath have led to an increased interest in this "difference."

Anthropologists have generally responded to this interest by attempting to undo the elisions between Islam and violence by sharing a more complex vision of Muslim life. In particular, work on piety (Mahmood 2005; Hirschkind 2009), building on the work of Talal Asad (1986, 1993, 2003), has sought to trouble the naturalization of (White)[37] Western supremacy through ethnographic inquiries into Islamist movements that articulate ways of being that are often explicitly oppositional to secular liberal humanism. Whereas Euro-American scholarship tends to presume the universality of the secular liberalist notions of the nature of the self as autonomous and always seeking autonomy and of a "natural" teleology of history and human progress, these studies have critically highlighted the multiplicity of self-making. However, this work has been critiqued as treating piety or religiosity as the only or primary thing of interest to Muslims, for focusing on "paradigmatic models" as the epitome of piety with no room for ambiguity and ambivalence (Schielke 2009), and for taking pious practice out of its broader context and the conversations pious Muslims are having with other, related discourses (Deeb 2009).

Muslim Cool stands both within and outside the terms of this debate. My teachers would never refer to themselves or their aspirations as trying to be pious. The piety intervention focuses on embodiment, specifically on how piety manifests through efforts to perfect one's performance of religious ritual. My teachers engaged in ritual practice to different degrees, but ritual was not what their piety hinged on. In fact for many, exemplified by OmarMukhtar, the quest for piety described in the anthropological literature distracts from the real point of being Muslim, which for them is advancing social justice. Further, paradigmatic models of piety can align with orientalist/secular imaginaries that would presume a necessary opposition between Islam and hip hop. Such opposition is necessary when pitting the Muslims against the West. But these are not the terms of debate for my teachers. While as Muslims they are also implicated in these debates, the frame of their engagement with hip hop was not "civilizational" but racial. Linking their Muslimness to Blackness, which is often absent in the popular and academic discussions of piety, their sense of Muslim identity was not forged in opposition to "the West" but in opposition to white supremacy.

Emerging at the meeting of hip hop and Black Islam, like a hip hop sample Muslim Cool is composed through the loop of knowledge of self. Young Muslims are doing epistemological work—learning and pursuing knowledge of self through hip hop, which loops back to Blackness and Islam. For non-Black Americans of color like OmarMukhtar, Rabia, and Fatema, this move diverges from romantic notions of Americanization in which White middle-class normativity is a much sought after ideal (Sharma 2010). Young Muslims moving toward Blackness and using hip hop to form their Muslim identities are reorganizing their conceptions of the self and the world and in the process challenging hegemonic forms of knowledge (Hill 2009) in U.S. American Muslim communities in which many view hip hop and Black Muslim practices through the lenses of anti-Blackness. This is a powerful intervention by young Muslims across race and class whose relationships to Blackness, Black people, and hip hop are mediated through faith and activism.

2

Policing Music and the Facts of Blackness

In the fall of 2007 DJ Man-O-Wax resurrected "Turntable Dhikr," a live DJ set he had first started working on six years earlier. As the name implies, Man-O-Wax used the turntable to perform *dhikr*, a custom of remembrance practiced by Muslims around the world. The turntable, a record-playing device, is the hip hop DJ's instrument: through the skilled use of the turntable, DJs create new music by cutting, scratching, and mixing prerecorded sound. The practice of dhikr typically includes chanting the names of God and prayers upon the Prophet Muhammad and his family, as well as prayers for the self and for one's community. The instrument of dhikr is, customarily, the voice. During an interview about Turntable Dhikr at the IMAN office, Man-O-Wax described his motivations as follows:

> I thought, man, it would be cool if I took all these different Muslim references in hip hop, and chop them up into samples, and then I brought in different dhikr styles from different countries, a little African, Middle Eastern and the [Indian] Subcontinent on purpose, and that was it. It was me trying to do the same thing that Sufis who make dhikr with music do, [but] as a DJ.

Outside of his work with IMAN, Man-O-Wax is a member of the Zulu Nation and a founding member of the hip hop crew the Fifth Element Warriors (FEW). At the time of my fieldwork FEW was a multiethnic (U.S. Black, White, and South Asian American) and multifaith (Muslim, Rastafarian, and nondenominational) all-male crew.

I watched Man-O-Wax perform Turntable Dhikr along with members of his crew on a number of different occasions. I first viewed Turntable Dhikr at IMAN's Community Café, which was also the first public performance of the live DJ set. At Community Café, the predominately Muslim and multiethnic audience response to Turntable Dhikr was enthusiastic. Subsequent performances I witnessed at an MSA dinner and at the yearly convention of the Islamic Society of North America (ISNA) were markedly different. These invitations to perform Turntable Dhikr came from young Arab and South Asian U.S. American Muslims whom Man-O-Wax described as using music to push social boundaries in their communities. Accordingly, at the performances I observed (and at others I did not) in the Arab American and South Asian U.S. American Muslim communities of Chicagoland, Turntable Dhikr was at the center of controversy.

The audiences at the events I attended consisted mostly of young Muslims of Middle Eastern and South Asian descent, and overall they neither enthusiastically cheered nor jeered Turntable Dhikr. There was however, at each performance, an assertive contingent of audience members who made their strong objections known. These were not older folks, as one might expect, but young people who would pull event organizers to the side and passionately urge them to shut down Turntable Dhikr during the performance or denounce the set at its conclusion. During our conversation I offered Man-O-Wax my then-nascent theories as to why the set was so controversial:

> SU'AD: I think a couple of things are happening [at the performances of Turntable Dhikr]. One, there is maybe a general ambivalence toward music.
>
> MAN-O-WAX: Right.
>
> SU'AD: Then, there is the sense that what is religious is very different from everything else.
>
> MAN-O-WAX: Yep.
>
> SU'AD: Then, there's this sense of this inability to think of the body as an instrument. Then, it's the fact that it's a turntable and it's hip hop and it is related to black people, so all—
>
> MAN-O-WAX: All this together just made it like *haram* [forbidden] upon *haram* upon *haram*! [Laughs]

Man-O-Wax and I laughed at his quip "haram upon haram upon haram" because we shared an understanding of the fraught musical context of U.S. American Islam and the ways in which music is policed in U.S. American Muslim communities. U.S. American Muslims, like

Muslims around the world, are embroiled in a debate on the permissibility of music. Those who argue for the impermissibility of music cite a *hadith* (narration of Prophet Muhammad's words and deeds) in which the Prophet Muhammad is reported to have forbidden music.[1] This tradition along with ancillary texts is used to justify the prohibition of all forms of music except percussion instruments. Other Islamic scholars contest the veracity of this tradition and argue for music's permissibility.[2]

Lay Muslims who argue for the permissibility of music also offer as proof for their position the rich musical traditions, whether expressly spiritual or folkloric, that can be found in just about every Muslim community across the globe. My observations of the private lives of U.S. American Muslims indicate that they enjoy music without necessarily adhering to any conditions or limitations on it. In the United States, Muslims who do not accept the blanket prohibition of music typically turn their focus to questions of instrumentation, audience, and content: Which instruments are Muslims allowed to play? Can women sing and/ or dance in front of mixed-gender audiences? Does the music in question follow the Qur'anic injunction to "enjoin the right and forbid the wrong"? These questions and the policing they produce are particularly acute when it comes to the use of music in public Muslim spaces.

In U.S. American Muslim public discourse the policing of music is typically regarded as theological and thus "unraced." However, in my work on Muslim Cool I found that when determining what is and is not "Islamic," not all music is treated equally, and what is at stake in policing music is a racialized notion of the Islamic tradition. This chapter looks at specific public and private music performances by Muslims and for Muslims to examine how music is policed at the intersection of Blackness and the Islamic tradition. It focuses on instances in which music is accepted as religiously licit yet policed in a manner that articulates two different, though related, contemporary "facts of Blackness": its disavowal and its instrumentalization. At first blush, these two concepts may seem contradictory: one is a rejection of and distancing from Blackness, while the other is its opposite, not a distancing from but an engagement with Blackness. Yet both, I argue, reproduce the devaluation of Black life. This devaluation, I maintain, is not particular to U.S. Muslims, but U.S. Muslim engagements with music reflect the dominant discourse on Blackness in the United States today.

Debates about music illustrate the tensions around race and power in U.S. American Islam. These tensions, described in the Introduction, are based on contestations over authenticity that are tied to conflations of nationality, culture, and religious authority. In U.S. American Muslim discourse, Blackness often can make no natal claims to an "Islamic East." As a result, one "fact of Blackness" is its disavowal. Unadulterated, Black music is seen as "un-Islamic" and therefore must be strictly policed in order to align with proper Muslim practice. This has specific consequences for Muslim Cool, namely a U.S. American Muslim musical landscape that challenges Muslim Cool's performative claims to the Islamic tradition, which are made through Black music. Muslim Cool is also confronted by the other fact of Blackness—its instrumentalization. Black bodies are hypervisible in U.S. Muslim musical spaces, and the typically *male* Black performing body of U.S. American Islam is not disavowed but used as a tool. The Black Muslim performing body is a tool that is appropriated for non-Black ends and through this instrumentalization Black Muslim men (and women) are flattened into essential Black subjects.

The Facts of Blackness: Disavowal and Instrumentation

Frantz Fanon, the Martiniquean psychiatrist and decolonial philosopher, theorized the "fact of Blackness" in a seminal essay. He argued that in the encounter with Whiteness the Black person finds that he or she is no longer a subject with personhood and agency but an "object in the midst of other objects" (Fanon 1967, 109). As an object, "the Negro is an animal, the Negro is bad, the Negro is mean, the Negro is ugly" (Fanon 1967, 113). Over time this objectification of Black people becomes naturalized, normalized, and a "'collective representation' and a *fact* in its own right" (Goffman 1959, 17; italics added). These facts, as Fanon argues, are woven by "the White man . . . out of a thousand details, anecdotes, stories" (Fanon 1967, 111).

Critically, these "facts," like all stereotypes, are not simply self-presentations taken out of context, but myths of power/knowledge (Foucault 1990) that become institutionalized. These "facts" flatten out Black humanity so that the body's epidermis and its movements become "merely a representational iconic body . . . that can be read in a transparent chain of signification; the black body reduced to stereotype and metaphor" (Noble 2005, 133). This iconic body is not merely a constellation of physical features; rather, "styles [and] cultural practices" are "metonymically linked to racialised bodies" and "can become objectified and alienated from the selves that are lived through them and the bodies that animate them" (Noble 2005, 134).

Objectified and alienated from the individual and collective Black experience, Blackness functions as an abstraction of mythic proportions that repeats specific racial histories to uphold the racial status quo. In the United States, associations between race and bodily practices configure a grid of associations in which Whiteness is the norm and representative of that which is valuable, historically rooted, and fully human. Blackness is, in comparison, characterized by lack—lack of value, history, and humanity. Blackness is necessarily deficient, and this deficiency engenders a complex valuation of Blackness in terms of morality: Blackness is that "against which the norms of White society are defined, and by extension, through which they may be defied" (Samuels 2004, 147–48).

On the one hand, Blackness epitomizes the lack of morality, which carries a negative value when juxtaposed against idealized Whiteness. Blackness is the site of leisure instead of hard work, criminal activity rather than lawfulness, erotic excess in lieu of sexual restraint, and an ecstatic Christianity that talks loud and foolishly to God. On the other hand, Blackness is "a symbol of social conscience," particularly for a class of liberal Whites like Norman Mailer's (1961) "White Negro" (and Brooklyn's hipsters), for whom the White norm is attainable but is experienced as a barrier to self-actualization (Monson 1995, 398). These Whites overcome the barrier to the "true" self by appropriating Blackness's alleged lack of moral restraint. Consequently, there are two paradoxical facts of Blackness: Blackness that is disavowed, as Fanon identified it, and Blackness that is instrumentalized.

Hip hop stands as an iconic example of these two facts of Blackness as they have played out in the late twentieth and early twenty-first centuries. In what Tricia Rose has called the "hip hop wars," hip hop is often singled out for attack as the perpetrator of the high crimes of misogyny, violence, and conspicuous consumption. But such attacks, rather than identifying the ways in which these themes, which do circulate in hip hop music, are reflective of broader U.S. American histories and trends, portray hip hop as the singular problem of Blackness. For example, in the spring of 2015 there was a media dustup after the release of a video recording of members of the Oklahoma University chapter of the Sigma Alpha Epsilon fraternity chanting anti-Black racial slurs. Many, including the president of Oklahoma University, saw the behavior of the students as endemic of a longer and unresolved U.S. history of anti-Blackness. In contrast, the hosts of the (left-leaning?) MSNBC show *Morning Joe* blamed it on hip hop, claiming that the SAE members likely learned to use the n-word from hip hop—specifically singling out the music of Waka Flocka—which is consumed by large numbers of White youth.

Hip hop is also instrumentalized. A favorite target of critics of conspicuous consumption, hip hop is, ironically, also used as a marketing tool—to generate consumer desire. Furthermore, hip hop is used as a form of cultural capital (and, as I explore in more detail in chapter 5, cultural imperialism). This was done famously during the first presidential campaign of Barack Obama. A self-proclaimed hip hop head, Obama responded to his democratic rival's political attacks by brushing his shoulder in a clear reference to popular Jay-Z song "Dirt Off Your Shoulders." Hip hop in this instance was the cultural capital of "Black cool"—unruffled, dominating, and marshaled for political power.

The paradox of these facts of Blackness—disavowal and instrumentalization—is rooted in the rise of what Jodi Melamed identifies as the official antiracism of neoliberal multiculturalism. Official antiracism, as the name implies, makes antiracism a proclaimed virtue and goal of the state. Accordingly, it marks a "racial break" with older, pre–World War II state discourses regarding race that were explicitly White supremacist. As Melamed argues, although formally antiracist, the state enacts racialized codes of stigma and privilege that "institutionally validate some forms of difference" while invalidating others (Melamed 2011, 11). In this contradiction, "formally antiracist liberal capitalist modernity revises, partners with and exceeds the capacities of white supremacy without replacing it or ending it" (Melamed 2011, 6–7).

In the official antiracism of neoliberal multiculturalism, Blackness is privileged when, for example, a Black president not only is cool but— due to his elite education, heterosexual masculinity and fatherhood, and work as a community organizer and government servant—represents the story of Black racial uplift through successful post–civil rights integration. In contrast, Blackness is stigmatized as "bad Blackness" when it is related to other kinds of bodies and behaviors, such a single mothers on welfare, and these forms of racialized privilege and stigma naturalize structural inequalities (Melamed 2011). The figure of the Black president, then, is marshaled as "good Blackness": a U.S. Black American performativity that is *appropriately different* and aligns with the state's vision of itself as officially antiracist.

What is critically important about the duality of good Blackness and bad Blackness is that the facts of Blackness it engenders—disavowal and instrumentalization—work jointly to devalue Black life in the contemporary United States.[3] The discourse of postracialism arose immediately following the election of the United States' first Black (and hip hop head) president. Postracialism was a natural outgrowth of the antiracism of neoliberal multiculturalism, now affirmed by the Obama presidency. Advocates asked how the United States could have a Black president and still be plagued by anti-Black racism, concluding that it could not and that Obama's election constituted proof positive that Americans are beyond racism.

This argument is easily countered by even a cursory examination of the continued disproportional disadvantage U.S. Black Americans experience in areas such as incarceration, employment, and education. However, the Blackness of the Black president is operationalized as an instrument, using the rhetoric of the culture of poverty and personal responsibility, to disavow other Blacks such as the incarcerated, the unemployed, and those who have left the failing public education system. The parallel work of disavowal and instrumentalization disables discourse, policies, and practices that could potentially eliminate inequality by normalizing the structural racism that is the actual cause of Black disadvantage. Accordingly, disavowal and instrumentalization sustain racial status quos in the United States, including within U.S. American Muslim communities.

As described in the Introduction, unequal power relations frame interracial interactions within the U.S. American Muslim community; specifically, South Asian and Arab U.S. American Muslims wield an ethnoreligious hegemony over U.S. Black Americans. This hegemony is grounded in cultural capital based on claims of proximity to the Islamic tradition. This cultural capital yields a power to erect and police boundaries of the "Islamic" in ways that either disavow Blackness or instrumentalize it. As a result, the policing of certain kinds of music by these Muslims often reinscribes the facts of Blackness and consequently the devaluation of Black life.

While they participate in the work of anti-Blackness, as non-Whites Arab and South Asian U.S. American Muslims have a complex relationship to Blackness *and* Whiteness. As Sylvia Chan-Malik has discussed, for Arab and South Asian U.S. American Muslims, who are neither White nor Black, it is ethnic particularism rather than assimilationism that enables a limited privilege in relation to Whiteness and Blackness (Chan-Malik 2011, 34). Cultural distinctions such as dress, food, and religion are often retained along with a deep commitment to the "bootstrap" ethos of free market capitalism in alignment with neoliberal multiculturalism (Prashad 2005). This practice of model minority performativity extends the distance between the "immigrant" and a Black cultural distinctiveness in which Black music stands in for Black lack/excess and Blackness is disavowed as un-Islamic. At the same time, Black cultural distinctiveness can be instrumentalized as a useful tool in the reproduction of an ethnically particular Muslim identity. Thus, the maintenance of non-Black cultural distinctiveness can work *within* the racial hierarchies of the United States. Although they do not have the same privileges as White Americans, when they adhere to the facts of Blackness, these non-White and non-Black Muslims reproduce the logic of white supremacy. It is within this context that Muslim Cool, with its validation and celebration of Black expressive culture as an end in itself, offers a counterpoint to the elisions of culture and race that, in the process of policing what is "Islamic," rehearse the facts of Blackness.

Turntable Dhikr

During Labor Day weekend in 2007, Man-O-Wax and FEW were invited to perform Turntable Dhikr at an open mic night at the annual ISNA convention held that year in the northwest suburbs of Chicago. I walked with Wax and the rest of FEW to the ballroom where the open mic was to take place, and there was a lot of anxious energy in the group. We wondered aloud what the crowd would be like—would they "get" Turntable Dhikr? And, perhaps even more importantly, would the crew be able to perform unfettered by ISNA's staff? ISNA had slowly begun to lift some of its past restrictions on music, but this shift was shrouded in ambivalence and as a result musical acts were subject to increased scrutiny.

On our way to the ballroom we ran into a fellow hip hop artist, a U.S. Black American emcee from California named 415. He explained that open mics were part of an effort on the part of ISNA's leadership to compete with what many jokingly call "Club ISNA." "Club ISNA" is a term used to describe the fairly large crowds of unsupervised young Muslims who hang out in conference hotel lobbies till the early hours of the morning during the convention weekend. From my observations, Club ISNA usually got started after the end of the conference's formal programming, which included the official "entertainment nights" that featured prominent Muslim performing artists and were geared toward Muslim teens and young adults. Likewise, the open mic night was also held after the official program to serve as a kind of official "after party" alternative to Club ISNA.

The emcee 415 had attended an earlier open mic the night before and warned us that tonight's open mic might be canceled. The previous evening the open mic had an open sign-up list and a few Muslim punk bands signed up to perform, but before completing their performances had ended up leaving with police escort.[4] However, 415's suspicions had less to do with potential blowback from the night before than with what he believed to be a specific hostility toward hip hop. He exclaimed, "they don't really like hip hop. . . . We are trying to do something good and they don't even know it."

"They," that is, ISNA, was first established as a collective of Muslim Student Associations (MSA) to serve the needs of Muslim migrants at U.S. American universities. Fifty years later, ISNA aspires to facilitate the religious, cultural, and civic development of all U.S. Muslims—immigrant and native-born. This is a noble goal, yet in my observation ISNA mainly attracts middle- to upper-class South Asian and (to a lesser extent) Arab U.S. American Muslims. Given its primary demographic, the musical sensibilities and shifts at ISNA echo those of the broader Arab and South Asian U.S. American Muslim communities, whose interpretations of Islamic orthodoxy have long dictated social conservatism in public spaces. I have attended events organized by ISNA and its related youth organizations (MSA and Muslim Youth of North America, MYNA) since I was a youth. Even when music was allowed in these spaces, the prevalent conservatism meant strict policing of musical performances. This policing included the prohibition of any nonpercussion music, all dance, and all female performances before mixed-gender audiences.[5] Against the backdrop of this historical context, the fact that ISNA *invited* hip hop musicians to perform at its annual conference marked a significant departure from its previous music practices. Indeed, since the early 2000s, musical performance events, including nonpercussion music and female poetry recital, have gone from being an unlikely to a fairly standard—though contested—part of ISNA, MSA, and MYNA conference programming.

The night Man-O-Wax was invited to perform at ISNA, the program commenced with a speech by an Islamic scholar, a South Asian U.S. American male who appeared to be in his mid-thirties. His message for the youthful audience was that in order to have a clear direction in life they must cultivate the "inner self" rather than be obsessed with outward appearance. This cultivation could be attained, he argued, by enjoying the "right kinds of entertainment." He cited a Qur'anic verse in which spouses and children are described as *qurrat al-'ayn*, or the ease of the eye. He then suggested that true Islamic entertainment was spending time with one's family, a somewhat odd admonition at a conference where all events were divided into age sets.

Two other young scholars followed, and their inclusion *before* the performances seemed an intentional move by ISNA organizers to give the youth in attendance some *deen* (religion) along with the *dunya* (worldly life). Yet the presence of religious scholars also legitimated ISNA's inclusion of popular music at the conference. That one scholar implicitly critiqued the very event at which he was invited to speak is indicative of an overarching ambivalence regarding popular culture at ISNA. On the one hand there is deep concern over the persuasive power of mass mediated popular culture that is often at odds with the particular notions of Islamic tradition and custom dominant at ISNA, while on the other there is an urgent desire to harness its power for the perpetuation of those very notions of Islamic tradition and custom.

A counterpoint to ISNA's musical landscape is the community of Imam W. D. Mohammed, which OmarMukhtar referenced in his IMAN initiation story. I also attended the annual conference of this community, now known as The Mosque Cares Annual Muslim Convention, on the same Labor Day weekend in 2007 in a southern suburb of Chicago. The geographic distance between the two conferences (which took at least an hour and a half to cover by car) spatially reflected the distance between these two communities' respective approaches to music. I had participated in this annual convention, like that of ISNA, since my teenage years. At this U.S. American Muslim community's events, there were no prohibitions on musical instrumentation, there *were* occasional dance performances, U.S. Black American musical genres predominated, and women *sang*. A typical song was Suad El-Amin's R&B track "Shahadah." The song begins with lyrics that declare the *shahada*, the Muslim testimony of faith, "We bear witness there is no God but Allah," to the backing of classic rhythm and blues. Further, the song enumerates traditional Sunni *'aqida* (creed), such as belief in God, the prophets, and all revealed texts. This song was released in the 1980s and is now an intergenerational "oldie but goodie"—and one of my personal favorites.

A standard feature of this annual Muslim convention was a public address given by Imam W. D. Mohammed. His audience was predominantly African American, and his lecture that Labor Day weekend in 2007 touched directly on what he called "entertainment culture." Mohammed identified the moral challenges posed by mainstream popular culture, but he did not see the solution to preserving Islamic morality to lie in restricting musical practices. Rather, he was a proponent of using all available styles of music and expressive culture to advance it. In this community that embraced "music with a message," Mohammed's teaching was realized in songs such as "Shahadah."

The shared concern with music's message bridged part of the distance between ISNA and Mosque Cares. In the U.S. Black American Muslim community, the policing of music culture focused on matters of content, not form, yet as in the South Asian and Arab U.S. American communities represented by ISNA, in this community the use of "music with a message" also aimed at the preservation of particular notions of Islamic tradition and custom. In all these communities, the engagement with music was framed by anxieties about the influence of mainstream

American popular culture, particularly on young Muslims. Like the scholar's speech at the open mic night, Imam Mohammed's speech carried a subtext concerning the maintenance and perpetuation of a Muslim identity. As media scholars have recognized, these communities are aware of the ideological potential of popular culture, which works by normalizing certain kinds of social conditions and social norms (Hall 1996; Lipsitz 2001; Adorno 1991). This production and reproduction of normativity can reinforce and but also challenge particular systems of domination and the status quo. This dual characteristic makes music a site of strategic contestation and meaning making among U.S. American Muslims.

As 415 predicted, the open mic seemed to be in limbo when we arrived. We witnessed a series of offstage negotiations between the person who had organized the event and another ISNA staff member, who wanted to end the evening earlier than scheduled even though there were only two artists on the line-up—FEW and a local Chicago emcee called emCF (the CF stood for "Chicago's Finest"). The emcee emCF, also a U.S. Black American Muslim artist, echoed 415's interpretation of ISNA's attitude toward hip hop. He interpreted the delay as a "lack of true respect and interest in the artists and what they had to offer." Furthermore, the crowd, at around two hundred Arab and South Asian U.S. American Muslim youth, was dwarfed by the size of the ballroom. I was told that the crowd was significantly smaller than the previous evening's, which had numbered over a thousand.

Eventually the open mic began, with the above mentioned short scholarly lectures followed by emCF's set, which consisted of only two songs. After emCF, Man-O-Wax and two non-Muslim FEW members, DJ Architect and D-Nick the Microphone Misfit, took the stage. In addition to playing the ultimate hype man to get the somewhat tepid crowd excited, D-Nick opened up Turntable Dhikr with the rap "99 Names of Jah/God/Allah" (according to the Islamic tradition, God has ninety-nine names or attributes):

> 99 ways for people to be guided
> 99 ways for fools to be enlightened
> 99 philosophies with 99 lessons
> 99 servants seeking divine blessing

of the Most Beneficent, Most Merciful, the King
Who guides the chosen people to a state that's serene
with 99 attributes of articulation
99 solutions for any situation
99 questions and 99 answers
99 diminishes with 99 enhancers
99 melodies and 99 rhythms
99 approaches and techniques to hit 'em
There's 99 levels and 99 planes
That's why God is verbalized with 99 names

After D-Nick, the remaining performance used the turntable as a technology of dhikr. DJs Man-O-Wax and Architect cut, scratched, and mixed together samples from hip hop songs that reference Black Islam, such as "Rock Dis Funky Joint" by the Five Percenter group Poor Righteous Teachers and "Traveling Man" by Yasiin Bey. They also sampled Qawwali and Gnawa tracks, representing the South Asian and Moroccan spiritual musical traditions, respectively. Their technique included manipulating samples in order to stretch out and repeat key phrases from their chosen samples such as "As Salaamu Alaikum" (peace be upon you), "Ya Rasulullah" (O Messenger of God), and "We are the future of God's plan." The audience seemed to take a while to warm up but appeared especially excited to hear musical samples drawn from Qawwali, which may have been familiar to those with South Asian Muslim ancestry. Yet there was still something of an overall disconnect between the performers and the audience; as OmarMukhtar, who was also in attendance, remarked, "This was not the right crowd." From my vantage point, this disconnect did not appear to be the result of hostility but of the fact that some in the audience in fact did not "get it": they did not understand *turntablism*—even though this crowd, consisting of young people who had largely grown up in the United States, was undoubtedly familiar with hip hop.[6]

But the more significant disconnect that evening was that between the audience and the loop of Muslim Cool: hip hop was not seen as a conduit to Muslimness but as a divergence from proper Muslim practice. Throughout the performance, a group of five to seven college-aged Arab and South Asian American men congregated near one corner of the stage. These young men appeared determined to bring an early end to Turntable Dhikr, because they believed it was haram. They did not seem to be officially affiliated with ISNA but argued passionately with the evening's host. As the Turntable Dhikr performance went on, these dissenters continued to put pressure on the host, and on their urging the latter inched closer and closer to the stage and closer and closer to shutting down the performance. Turntable Dhikr is about a twelve-minute set, and as it ended FEW's b-boys took the stage to dance. At that point the event organizer went up to the stage and told the crew they would have to end after this final song. Once they had left the stage, a wider debate on Turntable Dhikr ensued.

Contrary to 415's claim that "they don't like hip hop," the dissenters insisted that neither the music nor the dancing was problematic; instead, the cause of their concern was turntablism. One Arab American young man in a white *thobe* (long male dress) complained that Turntable Dhikr was sacrilegious because it was impermissible "to scratch Allah's name." An Arab Canadian Muslim music producer who joined the debate concurred by claiming, "It says that in the Qur'an." I asked the obvious follow-up question: "Where [does it say that]?" He was unable to produce "chapter and verse" but promised to email me later. Of course, I did not expect to receive either an email or explicit textual evidence. These young men were not Islamic scholars; they were just engaging in the fairly common practice of "daleel-slaying" (debate focused on instant citations of textual evidence, or *daleel*) among lay Muslims.[7]

While these young men could not cite authoritative textual daleel for their position, they had arrived at it by marshaling another kind of evidence: through analogy, they extended general guidelines aimed at preserving the sanctity of God's name to the turntable.[8] Examples of such guidelines include proscriptions against distorting Qur'anic verses by way of intentional mispronunciation, the requirement of ritual purity when reciting the Qur'an (in which God's names are frequently mentioned), and prohibitions on taking items, from newspapers to pendants, with God's name inscribed upon them into a ritually unclean space, such as a bathroom.

Man-O-Wax was not unaware of these sensitivities. He was careful and deliberate in his manipulation of samples:

There's some people who just don't like the mixing of music with spiritual things. And there are some people who just don't understand the technology part. When someone is singing and does something extra, even with Qur'an, adds an inflection, it is the same thing [as the turntable]. But even so I purposefully, because I knew I was using my hand, did not do that when it said Allah or certain things like that. I purposefully scratched the "bis" [of "bismillah," a common phrase meaning "in the name of God"] but let the "Allah" play out [without manipulation]. Other than that, I wasn't DJing Qur'anic verses, and again it was people's [prerecorded] voices saying the words [in the samples], and so there were layers to it and thought behind it.

As Man-O-Wax mentioned, a trained Qur'anic reciter who follows the firmly orthodox rules of *tajwid* (Qur'anic recitation) extends and constricts her or his recitation of Allah's name. Likewise, a Sufi practitioner will repeat the name of God over and over much in the way a DJ repeats sounds by pulling and releasing a record. Arguably, then, the turntable is an ideal technology for dhikr. However, the group of dissenters saw the turntable not as a technology for remembrance but as haram—and thus parallel to practices that undercut the reverence for God's authority that is fundamental to Muslim belief.

As Man-O-Wax noted in the quotation at the beginning of this chapter, Turntable Dhikr was seen as "haram upon haram upon haram." Accordingly, the objections to Turntable Dhikr partially reflect a broad ambivalence toward popular culture in many U.S. American Muslim institutions. However, it is insufficient to analyze these objections without attending to the ways in which the facts of Blackness circulate within the interracial dynamics of U.S. American Islam. The objections were also about race, specifically Blackness. The ISNA convention constitutes what Karim (2008) calls an "ethnic Muslim space," namely, a Muslim space in which one ethnic group predominates. Importantly, ethnic dominance is not just a quantitative reality—and as Karim notes, there is typically some, even if very little, diversity in ethnic Muslim spaces (2008, 53). Rather, ethnic Muslim space describes a qualitative experience in which "the power structures of race and class affect" how U.S. American Muslims construct space (2008, 55). As Karim details in her own ethnographic research, "the ISNA conference represents a privileged immigrant space in relation to poor African Americans who cannot afford to attend" (2008, 55). In the context of the unequal power relations that define the "indigenous-immigrant" divide, ethnic Muslim spaces dominated by Arab and South Asian U.S. American Muslims are typically spaces where Blackness is rendered invisible or marginal. ISNA, like other U.S. American Muslim institutions of its ilk, is often critiqued for reproducing these forms of erasure.[9]

The Turntable Dhikr dissenters were also engaging in this form of erasure and operating outside the epistemology of Muslim Cool. For Muslim Cool, Blackness is the loop through which Muslim identity is constructed and links to the "Islamic" are established, whereas in the discourse of the dissenters Blackness represents a break with the "Islamic" that needs to be policed. Policing in everyday life is a technique of control and power. Those who police either have or are seeking to obtain the power to determine borders and boundaries, who belongs and who is the outcast, and what is authoritative and what is authentic. Hence, policing is the power to enforce codes. Code means the representation or renaming of a thing, idea, or concept and its conversion into another form, which can be obscure to some but transparent to others. Code also denotes laws and regulations over bodies and behavior.

Policing and codes have a long history in the associations between race and the body that animate the facts of Blackness. Slave passes and branding marks, freedom papers and a variety of restrictions on mobility and lifestyle both before and after emancipation (including limits on owning property, giving witness testimony, and being "idle")—all these were official Black codes that regulated Black life and gave rise to the facts of Blackness.[10] These official Black codes are extended in current policies such as stop and frisk laws that also make it criminal to be young, Black, and "idle." Yet Black codes are not only official laws. Today the officially antiracist state also polices Blackness through codes of racialized stigma and privilege, which include the coded use of language (Lopez 2015), to determine and delimit the acceptable boundaries of Blackness.

With this historical memory and contemporary context in mind, I hold that objections to Turntable Dhikr are not necessarily or even primarily born of considerations of doctrine. The Turntable Dhikr dissenters did not wield the power of the state, but they were emboldened by the cultural capital of proximity to tradition and the subsequent power to enforce codes in places such as ISNA, even though they were not official representatives of the institution. Their power to effectively mark Turntable Dhikr as "haram" was created through elisions of culture and race that distinguish between the categories "Islamic" and "un-Islamic" in normative ways that specifically make Blackness marginal or exclude it from proper Muslim practice. Man-O-Wax did *not* scratch Allah's name, but that is not really the point. The claim that scratching Allah's name is haram was a disavowal of Blackness *in code*. It is true that in their loud and aggressive objections, the dissenters never explicitly mentioned race and Blackness. But this silence does not constitute evidence of the absence of race as a subtext. Their turns on Blackness were subtle and slight—in the manner of a code—and in this encounter they embodied the "other" of Muslim Cool: the ethnoreligious hegemony that polices and enforces codes to establish the acceptable boundaries of Blackness.

(Black) Music Is Haram

Known as the "Hip Hop Imam" because of his support and advocacy for Muslim hip hop artists, Imam Al Hajj Talib Abdur-Rashid, a U.S. Black American, has been in a leadership position at Harlem's historic Mosque of Islamic Brotherhood since the 1980s. The late U.S. Black American imam Shaykh Allama Al Hajj Ahmad Tawfiq established the Mosque of Islamic Brotherhood (MIB) and the mosque claims descent from the Muslim Mosque Incorporated established by Malcolm X before his assassination. True to its genealogical claims, MIB promotes a U.S. American Muslim identity that marries the Sunni tradition with pan-African sensibilities. Therefore, despite his New York City base, Imam Talib has a national profile and was often in Chicago at the invitation of IMAN. He shared the following story with me during an interview at his mosque:

> A few years ago I was at a fund-raising event in Brooklyn for a local mosque. The event, as most Muslim events are, was top heavy with speakers, but they had some entertainment, I guess to break it up a bit. They had these drummers, a scintillating, extremely talented ensemble of Muslim Senegalese African drummers. I was sitting on stage with a

group of imams who were African American and Arab imams; I don't even think there were any continental African ones on stage at the time. As soon as the drummers came out and started playing, I watched, with great interest, as most of the African American imams got up and excused themselves from the section. They were doing it, as far as I could tell, out of a sense of piety. The Arab imams sat there, along with myself. As I am sitting there with imams who are from Saudi, Egypt, and a couple of other countries, I noted with great interest that they knew what they were listening to. Our people [the drummers] come out, *bada bada baaa* [drumming sound], the Africans born in America get up, [saying,] "Excuse me, *astaghfirullah*" ["I seek refuge with God"; a common reaction to something religiously suspicious], and leave, Arabs who are not from this country are sitting there like "Oooh, did you hear that? Listen to that!"

So then the brothers give this brilliant *bada bada baaa* and they finish *BOOM!* And the place was dead quiet, and I sat there looking at the audience, they don't know what to do, people have told them so many things. They didn't want to clap, because that's *astaghfirullah*; they didn't want to praise Allah, call up a *takbir* [the phrase "Allahu akbar," "God is greatest"], that was *astaghfirullah*; so the audience sat there frozen, like statues, and I said to myself, this is crazy! It gave me an idea of the cultural confusion, the seed of cultural confusion that has been sown amongst our people here in America. And because our people here in America are so sincere, our desire and effort to understand the *deen* and practice it well, and people come over and slide stuff up under us, and because our few indigenous scholars are not addressing these kind of cultural issues, it creates confusion and paralysis as we saw that night. . . . Now that's the general framework. It is based upon those things, this general quandary, a conflict between Arab culture disguised as Islam and the Islamic practice of African people born on the continent or born in America.

The picture Imam Talib painted underscores the conflations of race, religion, and culture that emerge from the intersection of Blackness and Islamic tradition. Echoing Man-O-Wax's comment "There's people who don't like mixing music with spiritual things," Imam Talib identified a similar disavowal of music as a form of piety among the U.S. Black American imams in his story. Imam Talib interpreted this disavowal as the consequence of a "cultural confusion" born of the hegemonic influence of "Arab culture disguised as Islam." This is a hegemony that has been deleterious to U.S. Black American Muslims whose religious sincerity, according to Imam Talib, has made them vulnerable to a form of Islamic charlatanism. Thus, under the undue influence of "Arab culture disguised as Islam," he argues, some African American Muslims have come to alienate themselves from their own cultural traditions—Afrodiasporic and U.S.-based—in their quest to be good believers.

It must be noted that Imam Talib contrasted the group of U.S. Black American imams with a group of imams whom he identified as Arab but who did not disavow the music. Imam Talib's phrase "Arab culture disguised as Islam," then, is not a reference to Arab Muslim culture as a whole but to certain hegemonic interpretations of Islam coming from the Middle East. Imam Talib's configuration echoes Jackson's (2005) concept of "Immigrant Islam," which does not refer to all immigrant Muslims but to an ideological framework. Imam Talib used these "Arab imams" who "knew what they were listening to" as a counterpoint to what he saw as a cultural confusion among U.S. American Muslims more broadly. The rest of the audience did not depart the hall with the U.S. Black American imams, but they were, according to Imam Talib, also confused; they knew neither what they were listening to nor how to respond to it. In Imam Talib's view, hegemonic interpretations of Islam coming from the Middle East have thus made an indelible impact on how all U.S. American Muslims negotiate their musical practices: they have heard so many "astaghfirullahs" that they are unsure what is "Islamic" and what is "un-Islamic."

The cultural confusion and Arab Muslim religious hegemony Imam Talib identified are indexes of a "crisis of authority" facing contemporary Muslim communities (Grewal 2013). Muslims who live as religious minorities or within Muslim-majority countries dominated by non-Muslim Euro-American military, political, economic, and cultural might are asking critical questions of religious identity: What does it mean to be Muslim? How does one do Islam "right" in the here and now? Who can authoritatively answer these crucial questions of contemporary Muslim life? As Zareena Grewal (2013) argues, central to this crisis are debates over "tradition," making the maintenance of "tradition" the most critical heuristic deployed to preserve specific notions of Muslim identity. Tradition emerges as a critical heuristic because the well-established sites of religious authority such as the 'ulama' (religious scholarly class) that Muslims historically relied on to interpret and thus authenticate tradition either have been deemed irrelevant or corrupt or are facing significant challenges from other spaces of authority such as the state and the Euro-American academy (Grewal 2013).

This crisis of authority is particularly acute for U.S. American Muslims subject to increasing forms of state surveillance and violence since 9/11. U.S. American Muslims vie with each other for the power to authenticate the "true" or "real" Islamic tradition in order to confront the "us versus them" discourse of the U.S. American mainstream (a discourse that comes, in different forms, both from those who might call themselves "conservatives" and from "liberals" or secular humanists). The confusion Imam Talib described stems from this uncertainty about "tradition": what counts as part of the Islamic tradition, and subsequently, what counts as a legitimate form of Muslim piety? The Senegalese musicians were drumming, which is a practice that falls well within the category of religiously permissible music according to even the strictest opinions on music. Furthermore, as Senegalese Muslims, the drummers arguably represent Islamic tradition, since Islam has been practiced in Senegal since the eleventh century C.E. Nevertheless, per Imam Talib's description, the U.S. American audience remained uncertain about the performance— they were unable to determine whether it was indeed "Islamic."

It is here that the intersection of Blackness and "tradition" becomes key. Grewal (2013) theorizes the notion of "the Islamic East as archive" to map the discursive and performative impact of the moral geographies constructed by U.S. American Muslims. As an archive, the "Islamic East" is a site to look back to and toward in order to uncover, recover, and re-create resources that authenticate and authorize ideas, concepts, and practices done in the "West." Although a deeply symbolic space, almost an Islamic elsewhere, the Islamic East also embodies specific places such as the Middle East and, for Grewal, Islamic West Africa. Yet the archive is not an innocent location. It is my contention that U.S. American Muslims, Blacks and non-Blacks, rarely think of Africa as an archive for Islamic authenticity and authority, as evidenced by its absence from the intellectual genealogies of U.S. American scholars who are most popular among U.S. American Muslims, such as Imam Zaid Shakir, Yasir Qadhi, and Nouman Ali Khan, who studied in Syria or Saudi Arabia.[11]

This devaluing is particularly true of Africa south of the Sahara but can also be claimed for Morocco and Mauritania, both Arabic-speaking African nations. Although Mauritania is the pedagogical home of the well-known U.S. American scholar Hamza Yusuf, who, as Grewal argues, has consequently legitimated it as an archive of tradition, Africa is still marginalized in comparison to sites such as Tarim (Yemen), Damascus (Syria), and Medina (Saudi Arabia). Cairo is also an important archival site where popular scholars such as Suhaib Webb and Sherman Jackson have been trained, but although physically located in Africa, it has for all intents and purposes been siphoned off the continent. Mauritania too, though an African nation, is seen as more legitimate than say, Senegal or Nigeria as an archival site in U.S. American Muslim public discourse.

Senegal is the home of the African American Islamic Institute, established in the 1980s, where some of the earliest U.S. Black American *huffaz* (Qur'an memorizers) were trained, but this fact is not widely known in the mainstream U.S. American Muslim public square. That such information would be relatively unknown is a by-product of the way in which Africa (save Egypt, Morocco, and Mauritania) has been effectively erased from the Islamic tradition. The erasure is made possible by the chronic disavowal of Black people within Muslim communities. As a legacy of African slavery, the Arabic term *'abd*, which means slave, is still used, though not uncontested, to describe African-descended people. The term "Black" itself "remains an insult in many parts of North Africa and the Middle East . . . and Africa is still often viewed as violent and uncivilized" (Curtis 2014, 24). Likewise, scholars report experiences of race-based discrimination faced by African-descended communities in South Asia (Curtis 2014). Importantly, notions of anti-Blackness in the Middle East and South Asia have been compounded by modern white supremacist ideas of Black inferiority. The erasure of Africa from the archive is a critical deletion that enables the categorization of Black music as un-Islamic.

As a result, the fact of Blackness throughout much of the transnational ummah is that it is negatively valued; consequently, Blackness and the Islamic tradition are seen as necessarily distinct and diverging. Accordingly, the heterogeneity of Black ethnicity, the difference between, say, being Senegalese and Muslim and being U.S. Black American and

Muslim, is inconsequential. What made the audience described by Imam Talib uncertain about drumming and the U.S. Black American imams repudiate it was its Blackness, and what Imam Talib identified as cultural confusion was, I argue, the enforcement of Black codes through acts of self-policing.

In Imam Talib's narrative, self-policing happened in two instances: the audience's uncertainty and the U.S. Black American imams' walking off the stage. These choices and sentiments marked Blackness as distinct from tradition and thus as necessarily (in the case of the imams) or potentially (for the audience) un-Islamic—even though, in the case of drumming, legal permissibility was not in question. Moreover, the self-policing of Blackness by U.S. Black men engages in a "politics of pious respectability." Such self-policing reenacts the politics of respectability pursued by African Americans since the nineteenth century (Higginbotham 1994) as a means to make claims to authenticity and belonging. In this case they are responding to a hegemonic narrative—discussed in more detail in chapter 4—that conflates particular sets of Arab and South Asian Muslim cultural specificities with piety and repudiates Blackness. At the same time, while policing is about power, the self-policing by the audience was not necessarily a collective "power grab." However, it does signal the power of hegemonic definitions of the "Islamic" to bracket Blackness as being outside the tradition.

This point is further illustrated by an event I attended about a month before the Turntable Dhikr performance at ISNA. It was a concert event sponsored by Muslim American Society Youth (MAS Youth). MAS Youth, which has chapters all over the country, is a division of the Muslim American Society that caters to young professionals and high school students. MAS was established in 1993 and, with its distant relation to Islamic revivalist movements in the Arab world, describes itself as a "movement that uses the teachings of Islam to better society" (MAS 2014).[12] Like ISNA, MAS Youth aspires to include U.S. American Muslims across race and ethnicity. But my observations in Chicago and New York City indicate that both the staff and the community they serve are primarily Arab U.S. American Muslims.

The event, called "Voices in Praise: Celebrating Muhammad (pbuh)," took place in a concert theater in the same Chicago suburb in which ISNA held its convention. The concert was part of a larger campaign to "increase awareness about Islam's Prophet Muhammad" in order "to break stereotypical images of Islam and its prophet and to encourage dialogue and discussion" (MAS 2007). As at ISNA's open mic, hip hop was a featured musical genre at this concert. On the bill was Native Deen, a well-established Islamic hip hop group whose members are all U.S. Black American men, and a White British "dawah-pop" artist, who was the opening act.[13] The headliner was Sami Yusuf, an internationally known European Nasheed (religious praise song) artist of Middle Eastern descent. The crowd was mostly preadolescents with their parents, predominantly of Middle Eastern descent, along with a significant South Asian American contingent.

After finding a seat in an empty row I was joined by a group of boisterous Arab U.S. American teens who had come, with one young woman's mother as chaperone, from Milwaukee, Wisconsin. This group, which I dubbed the "Milwaukee Seven," was very friendly, intended to enjoy the show, and seemed determined to get the rest of the crowd to do the same. Most of the crowd remained seated during the Native Deen hip hop performance, but the Milwaukee Seven did not. They did not exactly dance in their seats, but they did clap, shout, and sway; as one of the seven remarked, "Who sits down at a concert?" The event's Muslim security guard answered her rhetorical question by repeatedly asking the Milwaukee Seven to remain seated.

The Milwaukee Seven were among a small minority of audience members who actually stood during the hip hop performance. This muted response stood in remarkable contrast to how the audience responded to the final act, the Nasheed singer. During Sami Yusuf's performance, the entire audience rose to their feet and swayed and clapped to the praise music, much as I have seen audiences react in the Middle East. I did not see the security officers reprimand audience members as they had the Milwaukee Seven; even if they had tried, they would have been no match for the sheer number of excited spectators.

The difference in audience engagement between the respective performances of Native Deen and Sami Yusuf is worth examining. Sami Yusuf headlined the concert, but Native Deen has its own national and international reputation, and it clearly had fans in the audience. Although most audience members remained seated during the Native Deen portion of the concert, some sang along with Native Deen songs, and there was a postconcert throng of young fans who clamored for the artists' autographs. Moreover, the music of Yusuf and that of Native Deen address the same themes of religious piety. Nevertheless, despite familiarity and similarity, the audience were policed and self-policed during the Native Deen performance. Moreover, unlike the audience Imam Talib described, this American Muslim crowd knew what they were listening to and when not to self-police—when it came to Sami Yusuf.

Sami Yusuf's genre, the Nasheed, is popular and has a long history in a number of Muslim-majority nations. Among U.S. American Muslims, Nasheed music is typically regarded as indubitably "Islamic" despite differences of scholarly opinion. This scholarly debate is, however, of little consequence, because Nasheed music's cultural location is "the archive of the Islamic East." Therefore, Nasheed music carries the weight of religious authoritativeness for the lay Muslim. The Nasheed's archival roots in the Islamic East are further bolstered by its primary aesthetics. While Nasheed songs popular among U.S. American Muslims are becoming more pop-oriented, they still tend to reflect Middle Eastern and South Asian aesthetics in terms of the instruments, rhythms, and language and in terms of the artists themselves, who are typically male, of Arab or South Asian heritage, and often American or British citizens or living in the Middle East or Asian subcontinent. None of this is meant to deny the devotional value of Nasheeds but to underscore that what makes Nasheed music compelling is not only its devotional potential but also the authority it embodies thanks to its perceived roots in the archive of the Islamic East. This point is critical, because the obscuring of these extrareligious dynamics and the conflation of cultural specificities with religious permissibility are key to defining Black music as inherently un-Islamic.

Returning to the events in Brooklyn and Chicago, the singing of Sami Yusuf was read as permissible because of his ties—in his music, performance, and body—to the Islamic East. Accordingly, his musical performance was considered "Islamic" by default, and open enjoyment of his performance was likewise religiously valid. The same kind of legitimacy was not afforded to the African drummers, although their drumming was technically less religiously ambiguous than the music of Sami Yusuf or Native Deen. Yet this inconsistency is very consistent once we see it as an enforcement of Black codes. Indeed, what ties the drumming, Native Deen, and Turntable Dhikr together is their Blackness via music. This Blackness is delinked from the Islamic archive and linked to the facts of Blackness in the U.S. context in which U.S. American Muslims operate: by association, Black music too comes to be seen as hypersexual, hyper-violent, and downwardly mobile. This linking fosters a discourse of anti-Black racism that combines with the elision of Africa from the Islamic East as archive to place Black musical traditions beyond the Islamic pale. Importantly, this is an implicit move. When the designation "Islamic" defaults to the Islamic East as archive, then the cultural practices of U.S. American Blackness are necessarily "un-Islamic." As a result, African drumming is dubious, and hip hop, whether Turntable Dhikr or Native Deen, is marked as Black music and consequently is strictly policed by U.S. American Muslims.

Instrumentalization as the Other "Fact of Blackness"

One summer while conducting research I attended a small party held at the home of one of the Palestinian U.S. American friends of Lati-fah, another of my key younger teachers.[14] The family lived right on the invisible border between the city of Chicago and the southwest suburbs. The family's home was also along the trail of the Palestinian exodus from the South Side of Chicago that has taken place over the last few decades. I was there with Latifah and one other U.S. Black American Muslim female teenager. All the other partygoers were young Palestinian U.S. American women. I had come to know these other young women by observing the way in which they, like Latifah, circulated between IMAN and an Arab American nonprofit organization also located on the south-west side of the city.

Despite working within the same organizations and even extending party invitations to one another, their friendships were often tenuous. While this is fairly typical for U.S. American teens and young adults, this was different in that the women seemed to divide themselves along a "good Muslim girl/bad Muslim girl" axis. This axis spun on cultur-ally normative and culturally transgressive presentations of self that indexed their ideas about being Muslim. Therefore, while wearing a headscarf served as an obvious general signifier of a "good Muslim girl," the headscarves of the "good Muslim girls" were part of a series of practices through which they tried to embody "proper" Arab U.S. American femininity. Their sense of propriety was displayed in the specific way in which they wore their scarves—pinned under the chin, common in many Middle Eastern countries—as well as in the way in which they held their bodies and their tongues. They attempted to embody a quiet modesty, in contrast to the "bad Muslim girls" who left their hair and necks uncovered and were louder and more aggressive in their presentation of self. The "bad Muslim girls" also displayed, in their clothing and language, a clear identification with hip hop culture and urban Blackness. This identification was present but much more subdued in the "good Muslim girls." It seemed to me that the hip hop identity of the "bad Muslim girls" was a subversive performance of Blackness in response to certain impositions of Arab U.S. American cultural norms.

Divided along this axis, the two groups clustered at opposite ends of the small basement where we were all gathered, which took away a bit of the festivity that is a "girl party." The girl party, in U.S. American Muslim communities, is a social event held at homes or in rented halls that is designed to be a space where Muslim women can let their hair out (or down), literally and figuratively, in an all-female environment. One of the main activities at about every girl party I have attended is dancing. This party was no exception, and dancing, specifically belly dancing, commenced as soon as the host played some contemporary Arab pop music. Latifah and I both danced with skill, surprising those around us as well as each other since we had never danced together before. Yet despite how much I enjoy dancing of any kind, I began to feel extremely uncomfortable, as the young Palestinian U.S. American women and the host's Palestinian immigrant mother left the dance floor in order to watch the "spectacle" of the two dancing (Black) girls. My discomfort increased as I began to consider our dancing in the context of the Black entertaining body as well as the history of Black slavery in the Middle East. As I eased off the dance floor, I made this point, in a joking way, to Latifah, who seemed to understand and joined me.

What did it mean to dance as Muslims in Black and female bodies, in the contexts, local and global, present and historic, of that Chicagoland basement girl party? Were Latifah and I using our bodies to be accepted while playing into tropes that returned us to our "place"? Alternatively, when our bodies dominated the dance floor, did this push back against the broader U.S. and U.S. American Muslim context in which our Blackness was implicitly disavowed? These questions are driven by a critical awareness of the history of Blackness, particularly that of enslaved Black bodies in the United States and the Middle East. These histories, though separated by space and time, are parallel in the ways in which Blackness and gender intersect to shape the Black female enslaved reality in the United States. The historic narratives conjured up by that moment in the basement are the subtext through which Black female bodies continue to be objectified in contemporary mediums such as film, TV, and music videos—spaces in which U.S. Americans, like these young Palestinian American women, have become accustomed to enjoying the spectacle of the Black female body. The historical narratives on which I drew to interpret that moment may not have been shared by the rest of the young women, and if asked, they might have argued that it was "just dancing." But my reading is not an evaluation of any individual biases these young women may or may not have had; rather, it is a critical engagement with race as a structural condition of sociality in the United States.

As a condition of Muslim sociality, the meeting and meaning of the facts of Blackness within U.S. Muslim life engender a complex racial-religious landscape. Each person at that basement party was Muslim and therefore, according to Muslim beliefs, equal, yet the women in that basement, myself included, were also operating in the context of a local and national Muslim community in which claims to Muslim authenticity were tied to race and class. Thus our interactions took place against the backdrop of the anti-Black discourse of Arab U.S. American ethnoreligious hegemonies, which is further complicated by past and present iconic representations of the Black female body fueled by the anti-Black discourse of white supremacy. Therefore, in that context and in that moment Latifah and I, despite sharing the faith of our Palestinian U.S. American spectators, ceased to be completely ourselves; instead, our racialized bodies intersected with history, and we became embodied signifiers or "facts of Blackness."

The question of how our bodies as Black women, even as Black Muslim women who were friends with the Palestinian U.S. American spectators, were interpreted is critical for Muslim Cool. Muslim Cool operates within the complex racial-religious landscape of U.S. American Islam discursively, through performances such as Turntable Dhikr, a concert, or a girls' dance party. In the act of these performances Muslim Cool comes up against the fact of Blackness as disavowal, when policing is used to bracket Blackness outside the Islamic tradition. However, Muslim Cool is also implicated in the other fact of Blackness—its instrumentalization through the Black performing body.

Within this complex racial-religious landscape, the Black performing body of American Islam is more often male than female. It is in the performances of Black men as preachers and artists that Blackness is broadly sanctioned in the public spaces of U.S. Muslim communities. I have observed this phenomenon both within predominantly African American spaces and within spaces in which African Americans are a minority or absent.[15] In the latter spaces, including the countless small and large educational, entertainment, and social events I have attended over the years, the following pattern repeats itself: Black male Muslim bodies on stages in front of non-Black Muslim audiences.

For example, there is a nationally prominent U.S. Black American imam who is known for his aptitude for fund-raising. It is not uncommon to see him at events across the country, invited to rally support for a cause such as building a local institution in a predominantly Arab or South Asian U.S. American Muslim community or raising donations for a humanitarian crisis in the Middle East and South Asia. While he is loved and lauded by Arab and South Asian U.S. American Muslims for his abilities, his local inner-city masjid continues to struggle financially. Furthermore, since 9/11 some U.S. Black Muslim men have occasionally been put forward to mainstream U.S. media as representatives who will come off as "American." Finally, in addition to being marshaled for such causes, male U.S. Black Muslim artists, most often hip hop emcees and poets, have also been deployed to attract young South Asian and Arab U.S. American Muslims, as in the ISNA open mic night, to religious spaces the latter might otherwise avoid.

At first blush, the imam and the emcee may appear to play disparate roles, yet they have much in common. In U.S. Black American culture, preaching is in fact an art, relying on the same mastery of lyric, rhetoric, sound, and improvisation demanded of the emcee. Additionally, both preachers and emcees often face the expectation of community leadership—that they will use the bully pulpit to speak truth to power.

In U.S. Muslim life, when these two characteristics, namely, style and resistance, are abstracted and essentialized as "facts," Blackness is instrumentalized. Reduced to a fact of Blackness, Black Muslim men become a representational iconic body, or what Nicole Fleetwood terms "black iconicity," "in which singular images or signs" of Blackness "come to represent a whole host of historical occurrences and processes" (Fleetwood 2011, 2). As icons, U.S. Black Muslim men are totemic, with a symbolic power that can be appropriated in South Asian and Arab American Muslim communities.

> Went to Islamic school with Arab and Desi kids
> Clowning me on my race showin' me what wicked is
> Fast forward 15 years later, now I'm on top
> They think Black Boy's the ish 'cause they sprung on hip hop
> I don't take it personally
> Them hiding their dreams in me
> Purpose of creating me
> Was not for jive parody
> Nor life taking
> Chart breaking
> But truth saying and love making
> Making God's love manifest
> In my mind's pen
> And my heart's paper.

These verses are taken from a scene entitled "Black Boy aka Raheem" from my performance ethnography *Sampled*. In this scene I aimed to capture the racialized landscape of Chicago Islam and reconstruct, at least partially, the narrative of African American Islam in Chicago since 1975, which to date has received little attention in the academy. This particular selection follows the narratives I was told in the field by young Chicago Muslims such as emCF. In emCF's retelling of his experiences in an Islamic school in which he was one of a few African American students, as hip hop music and culture had grown to dominate U.S. youth culture, a shift had taken place in the valuations of Blackness amongst his peers—from repudiation to instrumentalization. Likewise, in Black Boy/Raheem's narrative, his position in the eyes of his former classmates shifted: as Black Boy (as opposed to Raheem, which is his given name), he came to be idolized. This idolatry is a direct product of hip hop's global commodification, in which the young Black male stands as the ultimate representation of hip hop authenticity and Black cool (Kelley 1997; Kitwana 2006; Rose 2008). Thus, whereas once he was excluded because he was Black, now he is iconic and a totemic embodiment of Black cool.

In this context, Fanon's theorization of the "fact of blackness" generated in historical narratives and contemporary tales is particularly useful. The instrumentalization of Blackness in many parts of the U.S. Muslim community is evident in the perception of the Negro as not ugly or mean but as *baddd*. He has enough swag and anger to make rousing speeches and songs, yet his leadership is rarely relevant offstage. While non-Black imams and artists are also asked to perform, and thus conjure a different symbolic power, stages are not the only places where these non-Black male bodies are elevated. In contrast, the stage is the sole location in which most Black male bodies wield any semblance of authority in non-Black Muslim U.S. communities.

This shift in the valuation of Blackness noted by my interlocutors and its related "facts" lead to the instrumentalization of U.S. Black American cultural aesthetics in U.S. Muslim communities. This instrumentalization can be seen in moves toward a more expansive approach to hip hop at sites such as the ISNA conference. Accordingly, policing and the enforcement of Black codes have accompanied the inclusion of hip hop. Muslim hip hop artists, the overwhelming majority of whom are U.S. Black Americans, who perform at ISNA and similar venues typically complain of the ways in which their music is policed in these locations: songs are prescreened for appropriate content, and artists are asked to rhyme over percussion-only music tracks. Their bodies are also policed, as the poet Amir Sulaiman explains in the documentary *Deen Tight*:

> Every year it's like a bit of a fight [Director: A fight between?] between the musicians, artists, and the organizers as far as what's permissible, what can they do: "No, you can't use this instrument," "No, you can't use this recorded song." Even to the point, saying, you know how rappers, they have a certain hand gesture? They say you can't use these hand gestures. Not, like, grabbing the crotch or anything but just the way like an emcee

moves. I mean, you know, a certain manner, a way. [Director: Don't act black?] Basically! Like that in itself is almost, like, impermissible. What makes you Black and American is haram." (Davis 2010)

Descriptions and discussions of gender and performance among U.S. Muslims typically center on gendered restrictions facing women. Indeed, young female Muslim emcees have to fight for the mic (Khabeer 2007). Yet as Sulaiman explains, even male bodies are policed, as certain gesticulations may be prohibited. Sulaiman describes a policing that is racialized—the enforcement of Black codes. Enforcement is key to the instrumentalization of Blackness in that it defines what Blackness is for and what is it not for. Thus, while emCF, Amir Sulaiman, and Black Boy/Raheem are not "invisible men," as totemic icons that non-Black Muslims, young or otherwise, may "hide their dreams in" they are not perceived as three-dimensional human beings. Likewise, their Blackness continues to undermine their claims to Muslim authenticity and authority, because implicit in the instrumentalization of Blackness is the enduring notion that "what makes you Black and American is haram."

Legitimacy as a Muslim is a deeply felt need for recognition within the U.S. Black American Muslim community in Chicago and beyond (McCloud 1995; Jackson 2005; Karim 2008; Chan-Malik 2011). This need for recognition is a by-product of the marginalization many Black Muslims face within the larger U.S. Muslim community. Yet whereas marginalization can be akin to invisibility, in which the subject is not recognized and thus of little social consequence, the visual field is more entangled. Invisibility and hypervisibility (being seen but misrecognized) are nodes of subjectification that shape the experience of racialization for Blacks (as well as for other people of color and Whites), since distance from the "unmarkedness" of Whiteness depends on Blackness's visual properties (Hartman 1997; Moten 2003; Yancy 2008; Fleetwood 2011). The dynamics of Black hypervisibility are maintained within the multiracial and multiethnic subject positions of U.S. Muslims. As Latifah and I found at the basement party, as emCF and Black Boy experienced in their careers, and as Amir Sulaiman witnessed at his show, in the move away from repudiation toward instrumentalization, Black Muslim bodies are hypervisible in Muslim musical spaces, flattened into essential Black subjects reproducing well-worn "facts of Blackness."

Policing according to code repudiates Blackness in its fullness, leaving as the only sanctioned Blackness that which is circumscribed into an instrument. Consequently, although the facts of Blackness, namely, disavowal and instrumentalization, can take different forms, both do the same work: devaluing Black life. When Blackness and its history, experience, and cultural production are stigmatized as un-Islamic, and this stigma becomes naturalized and normalized as fact, the implicit statement is that Blackness is of no value. Likewise, when Blackness and its history, experience, and cultural production are instrumentalized, configured as a tool to be used when necessary and tossed away when no longer needed, that too makes the implicit statement that Blackness has no value in and of itself—its only value lies in its contribution to non-Black development. Critically, while the examples I have examined centered on U.S. South Asian and Arab ethnic Muslim spaces, policing Blackness is not only the purview of Arab and South Asian U.S. American Muslims. Indeed, some U.S. Black Muslims engage the "Islamic" by repudiating Blackness.

For Muslim Cool, these facts of Blackness have specific consequences. They position Muslim Cool in a battle against narrowly racialized notions of what is and is not Islamic, notions that are racialized because what is at stake is not the religious permissibility of a type of music or a performance but rather its *Blackness*. The "battle rhymes" of Muslim Cool reject disavowal to reproduce the Islamic tradition *through* Blackness, in the case of FEW through Dhikr on a turntable. Muslim Cool articulates a connection to tradition through an unpoliced and uncoded Blackness, which makes it a counterdiscourse to the ethnoreligious norms of hegemonic Arab and South Asian U.S. American Muslim institutions and communities. Muslim Cool enables greater performative possibilities through Blackness, and as such it is in tension with instrumentalization. Whereas instrumentalization is fundamentally the use of Blackness for non-Black ends, for Muslim Cool Blackness is a means of being Muslim, whether on stage or, as explored in the next chapter, in everyday life.

3

Blackness as a Blueprint for the Muslim Self

SCENE: SARA

(A sample from "Doo Wop (That Thing)" by hip hop artist Lauryn Hill plays as three models come onto the stage and do coordinated shoulder-shimmies reminiscent of a 1960s female R&B group. As the sample ends, the models freeze into poses and Sara enters.)

NARRATOR

This here is Sara.

SARA

(Waves and smiles brightly at audience and excitedly walks between the models, examining them)

NARRATOR

She's decided that she is going to start wearing a scarf. Tomorrow she will join the ranks of the *hijabis*. Today, she has to pick what kind of hijabi she'll be. You see, as personal as her choice might seem, it is also a very public one. Her choice will be her first voice in the world. She could go for Traditional . . .

TRADITIONAL

(Comes to life, yawns, and looks bored at the audience)

SARA

(Stops, examines, and interacts with Traditional)

NARRATOR

Traditional . . . is, well, what people think of when they think of wearing a hijab. Ok, maybe not all people but most people. Oh well, maybe not even most people but some people, in some parts of the world, in some parts of their brains would say, "This is Tradition!" but maybe some others might just say it's "modern Middle East conservative," and still others might call it "extremist" gear. Hmm . . . Traditional is pretty loaded, and since her family is already trippin' that she's about to *hi-jab*, Sara's gonna pass.

HIJABI-LITE

(Comes to life and begins to model her outfit)

SARA

(Moves over to Hijabi-lite and follows the model's movements)

NARRATOR

Then there is always the old standard: *Hijabi-lite*! From Friday prayer to Islamic conventions, this virtual uniform is donned by hijabis from California to the New York Island, marking them Muslim *and* just *short* of suspicious. Hijabi-lite features a mid-length tunic or dress, purchased from H&M, that is paired with pants. While having graduated from wearing a white cotton lace scarf with *everything*, Hijabi-lite is not a risk-taking ensemble; it's moderate, middle class, mostly mainstream, *and halal-certified*!

HIJABI-LITE

(Smiles and gives a thumbs up)

SARA

(Turns her thumbs down and moves over to 'Hoodjabi)

NARRATOR

The newest addition to the hijab choices is edgier and grimier than the rest and comes with street cred—that *no longer needs to be earned*!

'HOODJABI

(Throws her hands in the air into a B-girl stance and does break dancing moves during the narration)

SARA

(Struggles to follow 'Hoodjabi's dance moves)

NARRATOR

Great choice if she wants all the coolness of Blackness and 'hoodness without all the struggle. Now, she'll have to bear with the "partial hijab" comments, and everybody's fear that she's becoming like [whispers] "those shiftless negros." But the hip hop style is cooooooool! Colorful scarf-to-the-back and "'hood" gear. And she so desperately wants to be cool. . . . Don't we all? And just 'cause she comes from the suburbs don't mean she's out of touch.

SARA

(Throws a Black Power fist in the air)

NARRATOR

She learned that slavery was really bad and some of those Africans were Muslim . . . and she's going to do something about all this injustice! So it doesn't matter if she's never been south of Roosevelt; at the end of the day aren't we all being screwed over anyway? At least that's what she's heard somewhere.

SARA AND 'HOODJABI

(Smile at each other and stand with backs to each other in a B-girl stance)

NARRATOR

Yeah, 'Hoodjabi could work.

(Lauryn Hill sample plays again as Sara intertwines arms with 'Hoodjabi and they go off stage. At the same time Traditional and Hijabi-lite look on in shock and dismay, shrug shoulders, and intertwine arms as they go off stage.)

END SCENE

I composed and performed this scene as part of my performance ethnography *Sampled: Beats of Muslim Life* during my last few months in the field. The scene is inspired by the vignette "The Hairpiece" in the

Sara Deliberates (Artistic Rendition). Courtesy of Eve Rivera.

play *The Colored Museum* (Wolfe 1987) in which two wigs owned by
a U.S. Black American woman, who is primping in front of a mirror,
argue over which style the woman will choose. The main character in my
vignette is a young Muslim woman named Sara who has recently decided
to wear a headscarf. During this scene Sara examines three headscarf
models in order to determine what style she will wear. The first model,
"Traditional," wears a long black *abaya* (dress) and a headscarf with
a subtle print that is worn by wrapping the rectangular scarf's edges
around the hairline and under the chin so that only the model's face
is exposed. The second model, "Hijabi-lite," wears loose-fitting pants,
a knee-length, pastel-colored tunic, and a color-coordinated scarf that
also covers her hair and neck. The final model wears a headscarf that
is tied at the nape of the neck and wrapped like a chignon, along with
jeans, sneakers, large earrings, a Palestinian *kufiya*, and a Che Guevara
T-shirt. I had initially named this style "Hip hop hijabi" but, as I will
explain later, subsequently renamed it "'Hoodjabi." As Sara deliberates,
the voice of the narrator, whom I play, punctuates the pros and cons
of each choice to illustrate that Sara's decision is not merely a personal
preference but a sartorial choice that is also a sign. Accordingly, which

Models Pose (Artistic Rendition). Courtesy of Eve Rivera.

kind of hijabi Sara chooses to become has implications for how she will be "read" in her Muslim community.[1]

Stylistically, the 'hoodjab—a headscarf tied at the nape of the neck with the scarf's ends wrapped in a bun—is reflective of a head wrapping style that comes from the broader Afrodiasporic tradition. It is precisely through these Diasporic origins that my teacher Latifah came to be attracted to the style. Like her U.S. Arab American friends, Latifah, who is U.S. Black American, typically wears her scarf like the "Hijabi-lite" model in the Sara scene above. Yet Latifah also found the 'hoodjab style cool. She told me, "It seems cooler to me," and said that she "feels Blacker" when she wears the 'hoodjab. In fact, Latifah had been playing with the idea of wearing the 'hoodjab more regularly, much to the chagrin of her close Palestinian U.S. American Muslim friends. These friends evaluated the 'hoodjab based on the stylistic practices of the Chicago Palestinian community and and therefore felt that it did not meet the requirements of "proper" hijab, as exemplified by the Hijabi-lite model in the scene above. She explained, "They were baggin' on me, I am actually thinking of wearing it like that, back and tied up, and they were like, 'NO! Don't do that! You are going to go to hell!'"

Sara Tries Out 'Hoodjabi (Artistic Rendition). Courtesy of Eve Rivera.

Whether made out of purple cotton or black silk, when tied and twisted in a particular way a headscarf becomes a cultural artifact. In the instances described above, the headscarf became a 'hoodjab, an artifact of U.S. Muslim culture formed at the intersection of race, gender, hip hop, and Islam in the United States. This self-making through style is motivated to counter the racial and ethnic hegemonies of the contemporary United States, namely, what critical race scholar Hortense Spillers identifies as "the ruling episteme" that provides the racial logic "of naming and valuation" in the United States (Spillers 2003, 208). According to Spillers, this episteme works through a "class of symbolic paradigms that (1) inscribe 'ethnicity' as a scene of negation and (2) confirm the human body as a metonymic figure for an entire repertoire of human and social arrangements" (Spillers 2003, 208). In this way ethnicity, which she defines as Black and White, operates as explanatory shorthand that needs no explanation—it is always and already known what name and value to give to Blackness and Whiteness. In this construction, the body is key as it becomes the symbolic and physical location upon which the episteme of U.S. racial hierarchies reinscribes itself.

The ruling episteme that names and values plays out in the sites of Black popular culture. This is particularly true for hip hop, in which "what is Black" is often equivalent to "what is 'hood." Likewise, in social policy, 'hood bodies are metonymic figures—shorthand that explains away the discrepancies between Black and White outcomes in the United States. Yet in the contested space of Black popular culture the hegemony of U.S. racial hierarchies is confronted by related namings and valuations that are wrought from within Black communities (Hall 1998). Within this alternative ruling episteme is what Stuart Hall describes as the "repertoires of black popular culture": style, music, and the body (Hall 1998, 27). According to these alternative valuations, style is not the "sugar coating" but itself the subject, music is an alternative and critique of western logocentrism, and the body as a "canvas of representation" is a site of agency.

Muslim Cool is a racial-religious self-making that has a complicated relationship to this racial syntax. Thus I follow the "'hood" in "'hoodjab" to examine what is both problematic and productive about Muslim Cool as racial-religious performativity by U.S. Black and non-Black Muslim women. Importantly, my focus on this particular Muslim female headscarf style is not meant as an investment in the popular fetish over what Muslim women wear. Rather, I have selected the 'hoodjab because it is emblematic of the convergence of religion, race, femininity, and hip hop in the United States. Accordingly, this chapter examines the complex relationship between Blackness and an aesthetics of self-making in which Blackness becomes a blueprint for the Muslim self.

Black Cool in the 'Hood[jabi]

The first time I performed *Sampled*, I recruited a few people I had met in the field. One of these was a young college student named Noreen. Noreen was an IMAN volunteer whom I knew relatively well, although she was not one of my main teachers. When I asked Noreen to play the role of the "Hip Hop hijabi" she suggested that I call the style "'Hoodjabi" instead. She went on to explain that while she had been interning at an elite university the previous summer her White female supervisor had joked with her, "I should call you 'hoodjabi, because you are so 'hood." Yet despite being described as "so 'hood," Noreen is not from the 'hood at all. Like many of the Pakistani American Muslims in Chicago, she hails from the suburbs.

I asked Noreen why she thought her supervisor, whom she considered a friend, had called her a 'hoodjabi. Noreen pointed to her own behavior: "I was the only Muslim woman in a very academic center and the university [environment] was bland," and therefore she behaved, or performed, in a manner that seemed to contrast with the stodginess of her surroundings. More specifically, Noreen thought her supervisor's comments were elicited by the kind of "lingo" she used: "I used to say *fo' sho'*, *bzounce*, and *peace out* a lot." These words and terms—fo' sho' ("for sure"), bzounce or bounce ("to leave"), and peace out ("goodbye")—come from the reservoirs of African American Vernacular English and Hip Hop Nation Language (Alim 2006b). Ironically, however, Noreen credited her introduction to these terms to a White female college friend whom she described as "a typical White girl from the suburbs, but very sweet . . . Julie. Julie always said *fo' sho'* and then I started using it. . . . I guess my supervisor was surprised," Noreen explained, "to hear me use words most [people] associate with the 'hood."

Likewise, I got the impression that Noreen was surprised to find her supervisor calling her 'hood, as if wondering what an older White woman would know about the 'hood, anyway. In spite of the appearance of cognitive dissonance, neither the fact that Noreen's older White supervisor would have ideas about the 'hood nor the fact that the very things that made Noreen so 'hood had been transmitted through a "sweet" and suburban young White woman are surprising. Rather, they reflect a discourse on the 'hood—performativity and appropriation—that plays a critical role in defining contemporary Blackness.

To understand the 'hood's emergence as a concept and a descriptor it is important to briefly trace its antecedents: the slum, the inner city, and the ghetto. Like the 'hood, these terms often serve as euphemisms that disguise the way in which "race, space, and class have been historically and systematically ordered in the collective consciousness" (Forman 2002, 43). In the seminal text *Gold Coast and Slum*, Harvey Warren Zorbaugh identified the slum as a "distinctive area of disintegration and disorganization" in which White ethnics and communities of color were sites of social pathos resulting from "environmental" or structural conditions (Zorbaugh [1929] 1976, 129). In contrast to the slum, with its relative racial heterogeneity, the inner city surfaced as a descriptor when White flight, suburban growth, and targeted disinvestment in cities came to redefine the U.S. landscape. Although its meaning has become obscured, the term "implicitly refers to racially inflected conditions of danger, violence, and depravity" that always operate in contrast with "ideals of calm, safety, and security attributed to nonurban or suburban spaces" (Forman 2002, 43). Whereas the slum has fallen out of favor in the media and policy discourse in the United States, the inner city is code for urban "disintegration and disorganization" that is specifically Black.

Likewise, "ghetto," despite having roots in Western European religious discrimination, carries a racial inflection in which pathos is rooted in culture rather than in structural inequalities. In the United States, this race-ing of space has evolved in such a way that "ghetto" and Blackness are now two sides of the same coin. Comparing the ghetto to impoverished ethnic enclaves or to Zorbaugh's slums, Loic Wacquant contends that "ghetto and ethnic neighborhoods have divergent structures and opposite functions—one is the springboard for *assimilation* via cultural learning and social-cum-spatial mobility, the other a material and symbolic isolation ward geared toward *dissimilation*. The former is best figured by a bridge, the latter by a wall" (Wacquant 2004, 7). Fellow sociologist Mary Pattillo argues for the necessity of attending to class diversity and defines the ghetto as "the entirety of the spatially segregated and contiguous black community" (Pattillo-McCoy 2000, 105). Her conceptualization is attuned to the ways in which the ghetto was a home space and a location of struggle in Black popular music in the 1960s and 1970s (Forman 2002). Yet as a descriptor the ghetto has been picked up in policy and media narratives to become, akin to the inner city, a reductive conflation of Black people, poverty, and space (Forman 2002).

Murray Forman identifies one of the first iterations of "the 'hood" in the single "Boyz-N-The Hood" released in 1986 by the late Los Angeles emcee and producer Eazy-E (Forman 2002).[2] Unlike the slum and the ghetto, the 'hood emerged from within the U.S. Black community itself. Further, the 'hood is more than a colloquial rendition of "neighborhood."[3] It is a discursive intervention that redefines the urban spaces of U.S. Black life in terms of cultural production, innovation, and pride, and as such the cultural move away from the ghetto toward the 'hood is a reclamation of a more dynamic notion of raced and classed urban spaces.[4]

For example, Scarface, a celebrated emcee (formerly of the Houston-based rap group Geto Boys) who is also Muslim, offers the following definition of the 'hood on the official remix of the 2005 song "The Corner":[5]

> There's Crips on the corner
> Bloods on the corner
> GDs and Vice Lords
> so it's thugs on the corner
> There's children havin' fun, so it's love on the corner
> O.G. with triple beams hold they drugs on the corner
> There's cops on the corner
> dope fiends that walk around in they socks is on the corner
> but I love 'em so I'm a honor
> There's life on the corner
> death on the corner
> We fightin' till our very last breath on the corner.

The corner here is both a metaphor for the 'hood itself and a particularly meaningful site in the 'hood, a motif that is common in musical, literary, and social scientific renderings of life in urban U.S. Black communities. In his verse, Scarface's juxtaposition of children and "thugs" positions them as *equally* inhabiting the corner, thereby invoking the simultaneity of life and death in the 'hood. Later on the same track, Yasiin Bey rhymes:

> Granmama hit me with three words
> "Son, keep prayin'"
> This shorty hit me with three more
> "Son, keep blazin'"
> They both deep statements
> from two unique places
> real forever real
> I just love to hear the streets say it:
> Corner.

Bey also identifies equal value in both sides of "the corner," perhaps pushing the motif a bit further, from life/death to life/life. *Granmama* represents a perspective, "Keep prayin'," that is grounded in an orientation toward God. This perspective can be seen as life generating because it follows a moral prescription that rejects nihilism, which some argue is the defining characteristic of young urban U.S. Black life (West 1994). Although that logic positions *Shorty* (a young person) as the embodiment of nihilism, for Bey the shorty's advice, "Son, keep blazin'," is just as valuable. Grounded not in the transcendent but in the here and now, the shorty's counsel offers another perspective, which has the quality of the hustle—brilliance, ingenuity, and tenacity—and also gives life to "the corner," a central location in "the 'hood," a section of the city, segregated by race and class.[6]

Stuart Hall (1998) analyzes Black popular culture as a "contradictory space" and "a site of strategic contestation" in which Black expressive cultures are simultaneously embodiments of Blackness that emerge, not unproblematically, from within Black communities themselves and reproductions of Blackness that are appropriated and/or commodified outside Black communities. While in this instance he uses space primarily in the abstract sense, it is the sense of space *as an identifiable place*, constructed through "hierarchical power relations" (Gupta and Ferguson 1992, 8), that plays a central role in the production, consumption, and circulation of Black popular cultures. Accordingly, John Jeffries adds "the city" to Hall's list of the repertoires of Black popular culture. Jeffries argues that "in black popular culture, the city is hip. It's the locale of cool. . . . The city is where black popular styles are born. . . . Black music, although it often has roots in traditions that are distinctly rural, is always radically transformed and remixed by urban city dwellers" (Jeffries 1998, 189). Thus, the 'hood, hip hop's remix of Black urban home spaces, is the locale of Black cool. At this site of contestation, complex Black meanings stand beside representations that rely on familiar myths that "make" Black people cool: deviance and primitivism.

Take another "so 'hood" moment as an example. In 2007 DJ Khaled, a Palestinian U.S. American Muslim from Miami, produced a song entitled "I'm So 'Hood" that featured popular U.S. Black hip hop artists Rick Ross, Plies, Trick Daddy, and T-Pain. T-Pain, who was also raised Muslim, sings the hook:

I'm so 'hood
Yeah, I wear my pants below my waist
and I never dance when I'm in this place
because you and your man is planning to hate.
I'm so 'hood
And I got these golds up in my mouth
and if you get closer to my house
then you know what I'm talking 'bout.
I'm out the 'hood.
And if you feel me put your hands up
My 'hood niggas can you stand up
If you not from here you can walk it out
And you're not 'hood if you don't know what I'm talking 'bout.

In the music video for this song, these lyrics are accompanied by images of "the 'hood" that include scenes of Black children throwing up "turf" signs and a police chase. These images mirror the lyrics' simultaneous emphasis on deterioration and pleasure. Ruin paired with the conspicuous consumption proliferates in many imaginings of Black U.S. American communities in mainstream popular culture—imaginings taken up by individuals who may not be Black, as is the case with DJ Khaled, nor from the 'hood, as is the case for DJ Khaled and T-Pain. Their appropriation of the 'hood is deeply invested in the Janus-faced caricature of Black urban communities as places of ruin and pleasure. These artists also use place to claim their hip hop "authenticity" as well as their marketability as representatives of Black expressive culture. The song reflects a broader "über-'hood" discourse in U.S. American popular culture that reinforces a sense of the 'hood's underclassness by representing it as "a space of play and pleasure amid violence and deterioration" (Kelley 1997, 44). This über-'hood discourse has produced a set of iconic representations, specifically the video vixen and the bejeweled emcee, that have come to stand in for the totality of the Black American experience, reifying deviance and primitivism as "facts of blackness" (Fanon 1967).

It is by way of this über-'hood discourse that I want to come back to Noreen's story of the 'hoodjab. According to Noreen's analysis, her academic supervisor marked her as a 'hoodjabi at least in part because of the language she used, language that made Noreen "so 'hood." Yet not all the terms Noreen used have origins in the 'hood. *Fo' sho'*, for example, has origins in the rural South (despite migrations northward and toward cities). But the kind of precision that would recognize diversity within the Black experience is typically unavailable when applying, as Noreen's supervisor did, the über-'hood discourse. Hence, the supervisor moved effortlessly from "fo' sho'" to "so 'hood." Moreover, she did more than call Noreen "so 'hood": she also anointed Noreen a 'hoodjabi—that is, she wrapped Noreen's 'hoodness into her religious headscarf. This move to connect the 'hood and the hijab is significant, because stylistically the scarf style Noreen wore is drawn from the Afrodiasporic practice of head wrapping among women.

Historians have recorded the use of head wraps among Black American women since the institutionalization of racial slavery in the United States. For enslaved African women, headscarves "afforded some protection from the sun, kept the hair clean, helped preserve patterns of braiding and wrapping, [and] concealed telltale scars or African country marks" (White and White 1998, 58). Such utilitarian uses of head wraps would continue in the aesthetic practice of Black women in postabolition America, particularly among those who worked as domestics. Furthermore, during the eighteenth and nineteenth centuries headscarves were put to ritual use in Christian, Muslim, and Vodun ceremonies. Elaborate wrapping styles were also used by Black women as sartorial opposition and resistance to White U.S. American norms of propriety (Griebel 1995). This symbolic use is a precursor to the "Black is Beautiful" era of the 1960s and 1970s, when Black women embraced head wraps as a display of Afrocentric pride.

In the mid-eighties hip hop artists such as the Jungle Brothers of the Native Tongue collective offered a less militarized Black nationalism and popularized an Afrocentric hip hop aesthetic in the form of African cloth medallions, kente prints, and head wraps. Native Tongue member and hip hop legend Queen Latifah firmly established head wraps in the hip hop aesthetic. Cheryl Keyes describes Queen Latifah as a "Queen Mother" emcee:

> The "Queen Mother" category comprises female rappers who view themselves as African-centered icons, an image often suggested in their dress. Women in this category adorn their bodies with royal or kente cloth

strips, African headdresses, goddess braid styles, and ankh-stylized jewelry. Their rhymes embrace Black female empowerment and spirituality,
making clear their self-identification as African, woman, warrior, priest-
ess, and queen. (Keyes 2012, 401)

Keyes's explicit reference to spirituality in her outline of the Queen
Mother emcee once again underscores the influence of Black Islam on
hip hop. The practice of head wrapping in hip hop aligns with Black
Muslim practices that advocate head coverings as a form of female modesty, "empowerment and spirituality," and self-identification as "African."

Drawing on her ethnographic fieldwork among U.S. Black American Muslim women converts, Carolyn Rouse (2004) observes that
headscarves among African American Muslim women are part of the
negotiation of an intersectional identity—Black, female, and U.S. American. Rouse argues that when U.S. Black American Muslim women cover
their hair and bodies as Muslims, they "author a new female aesthetic"
that is the simultaneous expression of religious devotion and a spiritual
politics that rejects the feminine standards of white supremacy (Rouse
2004, 63). As authors of this critical aesthetic, Black Muslim women
reclaim the Afrodiasporic headdress as Islamic, in contradistinction
to the hegemonic legitimacy often afforded solely to Arab and South
Asian styles of head covering, such as those worn by the Traditional and
Hijabi-lite models in the Sara scene at the beginning of this chapter.

The style Noreen called "the 'hoodjab" descends from this U.S. Black
Muslim head wrapping tradition but it does not encapsulate it. Many
U.S. Black Muslim women tie what they call their *khimars* without any
particular reference to hip hop.[7] There are many U.S. Black American
Muslim communities in which this type of headscarf, wrapped in a bun,
along with a number of styles akin to the West African Gele, is the predominant way of wearing a khimar, irrespective of age, class, or musical taste. In stark contrast to the proclamation of my teacher Latifah's
U.S. Arab American friends, U.S. Black Muslim women who wear their
scarves tied up in a bun not only do *not* believe it will lead them to hell
but also advocate for the style as a legitimate form of obedience to divine
ordinance and a means of making life on earth a little bit more heaven-
like—by eschewing the self-hate that comes from accepting the confines
of white supremacy. Of course, U.S. Black Muslim women are not mono-

U.S. Black American Muslim Headscarf Styles 1.
Courtesy of Author.

lithic, and there are others who would echo the "bagging" of Latifah's U.S. Arab American friends and maintain that the style does not fulfill the requirements of hijab and some who do not wear headscarves at all.

From the way Noreen told the story, it seemed that her supervisor had invented the term 'hoodjab in a somewhat offhand manner. However, her quip was shorthand for a series of deeply embedded associations between race, space, and class. These associations mark how the fundamental contradictions of Black popular culture shape Muslim Cool: the 'hoodjab is at once a reflection and a reduction of a dynamic lived experience. Yet as Hall notes, "however deformed, incorporated, and inauthentic are the forms in which black people and black communities and traditions appear and are represented in popular culture, we continue to see, in the figures and the repertoires on which popular culture draws, the experiences that stand behind them" (Hall 1998, 27).

U.S. Black American Muslim Headscarf Styles 2. Courtesy of Author.

Thus, while on the one hand the term 'hoodjabi is a negation of the complexities of Black urban life, hip hop, and Islam, on the other hand Muslim Cool as a lived practice of Muslim identity can be excavated from these associations.

At the time of my research Latifah had recently become friends with Naeemah, also a U.S. Black American Muslim woman in her late teens. Both were emerging artists and activists-in-training at IMAN. After knowing them for a while through IMAN, I asked them to meet me for a formally recorded interview. We met up at the café nearest to IMAN, which was a midway point between where I lived, close to IMAN, and where they lived, Latifah at the city limits and Naeemah in a southern suburb. Latifah did not have her license yet (and not because she was not old enough; this remained a running joke until she finally got her license years later), so she got a ride with Naeemah and Naeemah's mother, who, in a reasonable move to vet me as I was still a stranger at that time, also came to the meeting. Over the best café treats the chain café-restaurant could provide, I asked Latifah and Naeemah: Is hip hop important to you? Latifah explained:

> I think it is really important to me, man. 'Cause, I don't know, 'cause back then when I didn't really use to listen to it, and then when I found out . . . like I really started to get into it. I don't know, it just made life different, more . . . *pop* to me! [Laughs] I don't know, I don't know how that sounds—
> SU'AD: Like, more exciting?
> LATIFAH: Yeah, like more exciting, more . . . I don't know how to explain it, man, but it's important to me, man . . .
> SU'AD: Wait, let me think . . . more exciting . . . do you think it made you more interested in different things?
> LATIFAH: Yeah! I don't know, it kind of made me feel like more Black, when I was younger I looked kind of Mexican. [Laughs] It [hip hop] made me get more in touch with my Black self. . . . [With hip hop] I started to get more in touch with myself and started to figure out who I am. I am at the age when I am like, "Who am I really?" "What I am I really about?"

Earlier in our conversation, Latifah said her older brother had introduced her to hip hop when she was around eight years old. However, "back then" she had not listened to hip hop because she had been "strict." Accordingly, when her brother would turn on a local Chicago video music show, "The Box," she would tell him to "turn that haram stuff off." But as she explained to me, when she matured and reached "that age" at which she began to interrogate her own identity more deeply, hip hop was no longer that "haram stuff" but rather came to play a fairly critical role in helping her "connect with [her] black roots."

The connections to Blackness that Latifah made through hip hop were directly related not only to her social maturation but also to the sociality of the environment in which she grew up. As described earlier, Latifah's primary social group was predominately Arab U.S. American Muslim. As a result, Latifah often found herself "the only Black person in the room." The ethnic makeup of her circle of friends was due to a series of factors. First, she lived on the western edge of the South Side of Chicago, which put her closer to Palestinian Muslim communities in the southwest suburbs than to most U.S. Black American Muslims, who tend to live much further east. Additionally, her mother's conversion had been different from that of most of the older adult U.S. Black American Muslims I encountered in the field, who had initially been members of the Nation of Islam and had adopted a Sunni identity after the death of Elijah Muhammad. In contrast, Latifah's mother converted to Islam in the early 1980s under the tutelage of a cousin who was already a Sunni Muslim. When she first became Muslim, Latifah's mother was connected to a network of U.S. Black American Muslim women, but over time, she explained, the "other sisters either moved away or left Islam." This left her to find religious fellowship and, most importantly, the religious education she passionately desired outside the U.S. Black American Muslim community in Chicago.

Like most converts, Latifah's mother was attracted to Islam's message of universal kinship among Muslims. Yet she acknowledged the experience of anti-Black racism that many U.S. Black American Muslims describe in their interactions with the Palestinian community in the area. For her, however, the spiritual knowledge she gained and was able to expose her young children to seemed to outweigh any slights she might have encountered. When Latifah was young, her mother regularly attended religious classes at the large Palestinian masjid in the southwest Chicago suburb of Bridgeview. Latifah recalled that her mother was well known among the Palestinian U.S. American sisters at the masjid. Her mother agreed: "I think they [Palestinian Muslims] got used to me."

Similarly, Latifah valued her friendships with her own Palestinian U.S. American cohort. She was thankful that "most of my friends are Muslim; [they] help me get better with my deen [religion]." Likewise, Latifah never explicitly described any direct racially discriminatory acts by her Palestinian U.S. American friends. This contrasts fairly starkly with stories told to me by other U.S. Black American Muslims in the field. While Latifah did not see herself as an object of overt racism, she did identify microaggressions of anti-Black racial prejudice and exclusion that framed her relationships with her friends and their families.

LATIFAH: The youth I know . . . the community they are a part of, brought up in, is a community that is not really accepting of all cultures. We are all good [as friends], but there is something behind their eyes, something is not right. [Laughs]

SU'AD: . . . [They] secretly hate you?

LATIFAH: No, not that. They just don't know about other cultures, are not involved in other cultures, as I am; I am involved in a lot of different cultures. Big thing with them is their parents: a lot of Arab people said to me they prefer black people, marrying-wise, to marry, but their parents wouldn't allow it, so they are not going to learn much till they leave home.

Since Latifah found value in her close friendships with her Palestinian U.S. American peers, her comments created a bit of distance between her friends, who helped her stay on the Islamic straight and narrow, and "Arab people," who felt pressure to enact anti-Black racism. Yet presumably these prejudices were also part of the backdrop of Latifah's friendships since, for example, Latifah and her girlfriends were all at the marrying age but the eligible single men in the households of her close female friends were ineligible for Latifah because she was non-Palestinian and Black. Latifah did openly describe some of the frustrations she experienced in all-Arab American environments:

I am, like, the only Black person who works there [a local Arab American nonprofit] since she [pointing at Naeemah] left, and I hated her because of that! I hated her because of that because I was the only Black person there and they were driving me crazy! Because I was, like, getting out of touch with who I am! I was sort of like "Oh, yeah" to their culture and their ways and started to get out of touch with myself.

These moments of exclusion as well as other moments of inclusion created a complex racial landscape. Specifically, Latifah articulated a desire to be in social spaces that, unlike the Arab American nonprofit where she worked, featured U.S. Black American cultural norms and practices. It is within this context that Latifah experienced what I read as a "longing" for Blackness that she addressed through the racial aesthetic performance of Muslim Cool.

Performance, Race, and Identity

Drawing on his work on the meanings of race and class within U.S. Black American communities, John Jackson Jr. argues that racial identity and subjectivity "make sense in people's daily lives in terms of performances, practices and perceptions" (Jackson 2003, 161). Thus, race is an everyday performance recognized in phenotype but also via bodily practices, such as language, dress, and gesture, which are acts of "racial performativity . . . that shore up social identity" (Jackson 2003, 187). Embedded in this language of performance, as illustrated in Jackson's turn of phrase "racial performativity to *shore up* identity," is the question of authenticity. If one has to "shore up" one's racial identity, does this mean the identity is necessarily "inauthentic"? This question of authenticity underscores the intersubjectivity of race and ethnicity and the role of bodily performance in the articulation and experience of these identifications. Racial meanings are not objective facts but rather constructed intersubjectively. As such, what counts or does not count as Black, White, Latin@, Arab, and so on is an embodied practice, in terms of phenotype and performance, that draws on shared meanings. Therefore, one's claim to a racial identity can slip from one's grasp and require the reaffirmation of racial belonging. Tied to this question of authenticity, racial performance is an intersubjective making of the self. Erving Goffman has argued for the "presentation of self" constructed in everyday interactions through which "the individual . . . presents himself and his activity to others, the ways in which he guides and controls the impression they form of him, and the kinds of things he may and may not do while sustaining his performance before them" (Goffman 1959, xi).

Individuals and groups of individuals thus take on sets of bodily practices, what Goffman calls a "social front." The social front provides cues meant to communicate a particular perception of the self to its audience, much like an actor communicates a role in a play (Goffman 1959). Goffman also emphasizes that these presentations of self are often routines through which "social relationships" take shape (Goffman 1959, 16). These routine performances have been defined by a number of later scholars (Turner 1987; Bourdieu 1990; Kondo 1997; De Certeau 2002) as "repetitions, imitations, and reiterations" (Kapchan 1996), which comprise a performativity that creates and reinstantiates social norms as well as relationships (Butler 2004). Thus defined, performance seems to retain traces of the stage's inauthenticity, and "performing race" can be interpreted as the enactment of an externalized presentation of self that is not reflective of an internal subjectivity.

Yet the presentation of self is not necessarily an artificial display or a labored oppression of one's individuality in which one is always "on" and can never be one's "true" self. Rather, Goffman contends with the question of authenticity by arguing for a range of self-presentations between cynicism and sincerity. The cynic is "the performer who may not be taken in at all by his own routine" and is therefore distinct from the performer who "can be sincerely convinced that the impression of reality which he stages is the real reality" (Goffman 1959, 17). Likewise, Jackson holds that "masking . . . is not just the fake performance of the self, but also a mechanism for its constitution, through and through (Jackson 2005, 228). Hence, Jackson also invokes the notion of sincerity to complicate thinking around race and its relationship to self-making. Offering sincerity as authenticity's "cognate ideal," Jackson argues for the possibility of experiencing racial identity as not merely the "straight jacket of identity politics" (2005: 22). Racial sincerity foregrounds the intersubjectivity of racial identity to do away with authenticity tests but not with the experience of race that "can feel so obvious, natural, real and even liberating," namely, "walk[ing] around with purportedly racial selves crammed up inside of us and serving as invisible links to other people" (Jackson 2005, 15). Thus, the sincere presentation of self, racial or otherwise, may be an intentional practice that seeks not to delude but to make the inner self and to make that self accessible to others.

For Latifah, the performativities enabled by Muslim Cool built links of racial sincerity that bridged the disconnect that she experienced in her social environment and enabled her to "feel more Black . . . [and] in touch with [her] Black self." Muslim Cool is critical here because Latifah's identity is intersectional—she identified a need to connect to her "deen" *and* to connect to her Black self. In the absence of appropriate social spaces and the experiences and relationships with Black culture that they would engender, practices of racial performance that asserted Black identity became important for Latifah. Critically, her assertions are not caught up in the tropes of authenticity. My argument is not that Latifah saw herself as "inauthentically" Black but rather that she felt disconnected from that sincere Blackness that invisibly linked her (in ways she "didn't know" how to articulate) to other Black people. However, the social spaces and relationships surrounding her proposed a binary opposition between the deen as one distinct subject and Blackness as another. This binary created the longing for Blackness that Latifah articulated. Because Muslim Cool is rooted in the intersection of Islam and Blackness, it fundamentally disrupts this binary and creates new performative possibilities for a young U.S. Black Muslim woman such as Latifah.

Latifah's performance of Blackness can be traced to her engagement with hip hop as a Muslim woman doing art and activism. As a spoken word artist and singer Latifah drew heavily on the repertoires of Black popular culture. She employed style and music rooted in Black expressive culture, from the way she held a note and dropped a verse to the way she moved her body in forms. Further, Latifah was a participant in activist projects, such as a youth mapping project on the South Side, which centered on Blackness and Black people. By Black people I am referring to the residents of IMAN's neighborhood, who were among the primary beneficiaries of the organization's community development work. By Blackness I am referring to the iconic role U.S. Black Americans play as paramount symbols of the struggle for freedom. Critically, as detailed in chapter 5, Blackness as an icon of liberation struggles and the specific roles Black Muslims have played in the struggle for Black liberation are continuously reinforced in hip hop and at IMAN. Therefore, in contrast to her role at the other nonprofit where she worked and even to some extent her relationships with her non-Black friends, Latifah's activism at IMAN enabled her to engage in a performance of Blackness as activism.

Muslim Cool was a conduit for this kind of sincere racial performance in Latifah's considerations of the 'hoodjab. While not all U.S. Black Muslim women call their head wraps 'hoodjabs or wear scarves in this manner, the style is a multiply symbolic icon of Blackness. As we have seen, it symbolizes the broader U.S. Black American embrace of Afrocentricity. It is an iconic representation of the Afrocentric hip hop aesthetic and it signals the role U.S. Black Muslim women have played in bringing this aesthetic into the American Muslim nomenclature of religious dress. In fact, the isomorphism between the scarf style and Black identity is so strong that Naeemah told me that she "feels odd" when she wears her scarf in a different style. This isomorphism, I argue, is magnified in the encounter between the U.S. Black Muslim woman and her non-Black coreligionists. The 'hoodjab can be a particularly powerful symbol in the context of the naming and valuations of U.S. American Islam experienced by Latifah that misname and devalue Blackness. Furthermore, I believe that Latifah's sense of "feeling blacker" when wearing this style is due to the style's predominance in many African American Muslim communities *and* its relationship to Black cool and popular culture. Because of this intersection between Islam and Black cool in America, Latifah is not simply styling her scarf in a particular way; she is using Muslim Cool as the performative blueprint for her sincere Black Muslim self.

Performing Muslim Cool across Race

Since Noreen was neither U.S. Black American nor raised in a Black Muslim community, I was curious as to how she came to wear her khimar styled in a bun. She explained to me that she had first admired the style on others and then learned how to wrap her own scarf from Fatema, who is also Pakistani U.S. American. When I asked Fatema about her own introduction to the style, which she calls the "hip hop style," she explained:

> I don't think that I actually started wearing it that way until I started working on the South Side and starting seeing more people from IMAN, mostly African American and Arab, wear that particular style. And I think I must have seen at least one or two Pakistani people wear it, and then I felt even more so, "Oh, ok, this is something I can do as well." A lot of times the way people wear hijab is very cultural as well, so there was a part of me that didn't want to try and be something that I am not. Pakistanis wear their scarves very differently, tucked in behind the ears. I never wore it that way but I did like the way African Americans were wearing it, which in some ways is connected to the ways it is worn in Africa. I am pretty sure I saw it on Erykah Badu, too, and I was just like, "Oh cool!" There is definitely some sort of link to pop culture. Initially I was just excited by the fact I could wear my hijab and show my earrings and my necklace. I liked how it was versatile, I could wear it that way and

it didn't have to immediately mean, when someone saw me, "Oh, she's a Muslim." And yes, part of it is that it's cool because it's different and it's cool because I can wear earrings.

Fatema's narrative, like that of Latifah, inspired the "Sara" scene that opens this chapter. Throughout my fieldwork, Fatema and I discussed her relationship to hip hop and the 'hood in light of her racial and ethnic identity and socioeconomic background: she was the daughter of Pakistani immigrants to the United States who had settled in an upper-class Chicago suburb. Fatema was conscious of how she looked: a bubbly hyphenated American—her Pakistani heritage was not necessarily evident—in the *freshest kicks* (most up-to-date sneakers), who almost always rocked her head scarf tied in the "hip hop style." Indeed, the apparent disconnect between her racialized hip hop dress and 'hood activism on the one hand, and her own racial and class position on the other, was very acute for her.

Fatema told me that when she first started working at IMAN, "I was really excited but then realized I had to step back and learn." Full of her typical enthusiasm, she had come to the table ready to work, but she had been taught knowledge of self and thus gained an awareness of how her participation in the organization's work was complicated by her racial position and class privilege. Specifically, as a wealthy young person there were opportunities afforded her because of her class privilege; as a middle-class Asian U.S. American she was "relatively valorized" (Kim 1999) in comparison to the Black community with whom she engaged at IMAN; and as a South Asian Muslim she was relatively privileged in the U.S. Muslim community. Hence, she trod lightly regarding wearing this particular headscarf style because she understood that style matters and accordingly that the khimar carries racial and cultural weight. The character Sara in *Sampled* not only has to decide what her personal preference for hijab will be but also, like Latifah and Fatema, has to contend with the ways in which other Muslims will "read" her (and potentially forecast her final abode) based on her scarf style. Furthermore, this reading of a Muslim woman's headscarf is done not only within the Muslim community but by non-Muslims as well.

In her monograph on college-aged Muslim women Shabana Mir (2014) looks in depth at the "double scrutiny" by Muslims and non-

Muslims that her interlocutors experience with respect to their sarto-rial choices as Muslim women. One of the debates among the young women in her study concerns the question whether wearing a headscarf facilitates or restricts their ability to teach their non-Muslim peers about Islam. The "hijabis" (i.e., women who wear head scarves) in Mir's study argue that the simple act of wearing the hijab is a teaching tool and a symbol that speaks even when the wearer may be silent. Yet the "non-hijabis" contend the opposite. The need to teach peers about Islam is driven by the desire to combat dominant stereotypes about Islam and Muslims. The non-hijabis thus argue that in light of the orientalist gaze that prefigures a Muslim woman as either a proponent or a victim of Muslim fanaticism, wearing a khimar reinforces that image and fore-closes any potential learning (Mir 2014).

This debate resonates with Fatema's comment that wearing the "hip hop style" doesn't immediately mark her as a Muslim. Fatema's decision was not about whether or not to wear a hijab; rather, it was about what kind of headscarf style would facilitate interactions across religious dif-ference. At the same time, because culture and style matter, Fatema's assessment of how her Muslimness would be read was also culturally and spatially located. Fatema viewed the hip hop style as not imme-diately identifiably Muslim because it is stylistically distinct from the modern Middle East conservative head scarf style (what I call "Tradi-tional" in the Sara scene) that dominates the imagination of the White American public, and it is thus free of the latter's stigma. While there are, because of Black Islam, also cultural locations in which this style is easily identified as Muslim, for someone like Fatema, who comes from a Pakistani immigrant and suburban background, the style eliminates all associations with orientalist renderings of "the Muslim woman." Thus, for Fatema, this scarf style enabled an approachability that was signifi-cant to her as a budding activist who saw being approachable as key to community work.

Yet it is also precisely because of the 'hoodjab's connection to Black Muslim female practice that the style also gave her access to forms of sartorial pleasure as a Muslim woman. It granted Fatema a wider aes-thetic playground because she "could wear earrings and necklaces" that could be seen. It also gave her access to the possibility of being marked as "cool" because wearing it made her identifiable with icons of a sort of Black activist cool such as Erykah Badu. Instead of constituting an enclosure that prevents access, Blackness in this instance, through the repertoire of style, was a point of accessibility for Fatema on a number of different levels. However, given Fatema's status as a non-Black Muslim woman of color, this accessibility was gained through a technique of cultural appropriation that does not escape the syntax of history and the symbols of race.

In the United States, cultural appropriation is often cast as the adoption of a passing fad, which, in the particular case of Black expressive cultures, conjures up the specter of minstrelsy. White American youth are often seen through this lens when they take on practices borrowed from Black expressive culture. Scholars note that White appropriations of Blackness are part of a lifecycle in which "White American males spend their early years as imaginary Indians and their teens as imaginary Blacks before settling into a White adulthood" (Leslie Felder [1964], quoted in Roediger 1998, 361). Yet even in the face of these historical continuities, scholars point out that White youth also evade simplistic typologies: their bodily practices should be seen as "complex and contradictory parts of a terrible past and of what is bound to be a long struggle to transcend it" (Roediger 1998, 359). Likewise, Maira argues that class and racial location complicate the racial politics of cool. She finds that for wealthy Desi youth hip hop is often a "transitional flirtation with Black popular culture on the road to mainstream capitalist success" (Maira 2008, 58–59). Their ephemeral engagement with hip hop stands in contrast to the stance of young Desis from working-class families, who, she argues, use hip hop to form alliances with Black communities around shared class and racial marginalization (Maira 2008).

Alternatively, some scholars conceive cross-racial borrowing as a manifestation of a sort of racial utopia in which racial boundaries are easily crossed as a means of interracial understanding. Arguing that "destabilizing the racial signifier is not enough," Dorinne Kondo critiques liberal humanist theorizing that presumes that "cross-racial impersonations" inherently transcend racial difference because they violate "racial perimeters" (Kondo 2000: 100). Kondo persuasively argues that in this formulation of racial utopia, race, gender, and sexuality are still seen as "mere attributes of identity" rather than as "historically shaped axes of power and inequality" (Kondo 2000, 82). Hence, the act of performing

Blackness by non-Blacks is not enough; performances must acknowledge and then destabilize the power structures that continue to perpetu-
ate violent exclusion and marginality. Thus, Kondo asserts that racial
crossings truly work toward antiracist ends only when politics and ac-
countability to marginalized communities are foregrounded.

When Muslim Cool is done across race, it is indubitably informed by a
racial politics of cool in which Blackness and cool are synonyms and sites
of youthful exploration and abandonment. This was somewhat at play in
Fatema's identification of the 'hoodjab scarf style as "cool because it's different." "Different" in this instance marked the style's distinctness from
the norms of her own U.S. Pakistani American and immigrant community. But while Fatema's efforts to separate herself from that community
may carry echoes of the supermarket aisle kind of cultural appropriation,
it is key to see them in light of the other connections Fatema sought to
make. Her class identity did not lead to a mere brief fling with Black
popular culture. Rather, in the manner called for by Kondo, Fatema attempted to mediate her relationship to Blackness not just by wearing a
Black Muslim headscarf but through her interactions with real-life Black
people engaged in activist projects that directly confront the violence of
racism. I use the word "attempt" here quite pointedly. I found that Fatema
was always acutely aware of the way her khimar choice could be read by
Muslims and non-Muslims alike as a gross form of appropriation. Thus,
although she became comfortable enough to wear her hijab in various
Afrocentric styles, from buns to Geles, Fatema's mediations were never
complete. Her attempts were marked by racial sincerity. She did not seek
to be sincerely Black or to disavow being a Pakistani U.S. American.
Rather, she described her appropriation of the "hip hop style" as a way
to connect and be connected to Afrocentricity as a "larger social movement" for justice. Thus, she did not seek to transcend race but rather
sincerely sought Blackness as a means to interracial solidarity.

I have constructed here a genealogy of a Muslim woman's headscarf in
the United States that goes back to hip hop, Black slavery in the Americas, the Black female experience, and Black Islam. Through this genealogy, I make a distinct departure from the broader academic discussion
of Muslim women's dress. This literature is often either couched in an
Islamic studies context or highly polemical. Accordingly, scholars tend
to either debate the status of "hijab" as a religious requirement or argue

for a western liberal narrative in which the hijab is an oppressive practice. Further, social scientific academic treatments of the topic in the United States generally frame the practice as a negotiation between "Islamic" values and "American" values, without giving adequate attention to style.

In an article on college-aged American Muslim women of Pakistani and Arab ancestry, sociologists Rhys Williams and Gira Vashi contend that for the women in their study, "wearing hijab is . . . a practical and useful response to living as young women in the nexus between two cultures and as members of a minority faith" (Williams and Vashi 2007, 285). Here, conflict in the lives of U.S. Muslims is set up as necessarily bicultural, imposing a dichotomy that posits "America" and "Islam" as undifferentiated wholes, distinct only in contrast to the other, and that forecloses the possibility of diversity within and overlap across these "wholes." Likewise, adopting this bicultural clash perspective others have argued that making the choice to wear a hijab represents a process of Islamization that projects a "public Islamic identity," which interrupts the expected pattern of assimilation (Haddad 2007). Particularly in the post–9/11 context, this process has also been described as a kind of embodiment of resistance to anti-Muslim racism in a manner similar to the way the hijab was used in anticolonial movements in North Africa and the Middle East (Haddad 2007).

At first blush, the comparison of (non-Black) U.S. Muslim women with Muslim women in Africa and Southwest Asia appears fairly reasonable. Yet when these non-American women are used as the sole vantage point through which to analyze Muslim women in the United States, the comparison ultimately reinforces the America/Islam cultural binary. Instead, we could compare young Arab American and South Asian U.S. American Muslim women to other Muslim women much closer to home, such as U.S. Black Muslim women for whom headscarves "represent the decolonization of the third world body" in the context of white supremacy at work in the United States (Rouse 2004, 62–63).

More complexity is found in the scholarship's framing of the hijab as representing not only resistance to but also acceptance of the state. In this frame, a hijab is worn as a symbol of an American Muslim identity through which young Muslim women enact their acceptance and expectations of the state—namely, the expectation that their rights as American citizens, including freedom of religion, will be honored (Williams and Vashi 2007; Haddad 2007). Yet this kind of recognition by the state is elusive. Unfortunately, as long as scholarship is wedded to a bicultural framework, it will also play a role in blocking such recognition.

When "America" is posited as a transparent category, its surrogacy for white normativity is obscured, which then reproduces not only an unproductive bicultural model but also white privilege itself. Likewise, "Islam," though also treated as transparent, is not an unmarked category but a metonym for racially, ethnically, and temporally specific Muslim practices spatially located outside "America." Thus, despite the best of intentions, in effect the very belonging these young women are seeking is denied to them through the frames of scholarly analysis, thereby reenacting the exclusionary logic of belonging in the United States.

In contrast, I have offered a nuanced analysis of the stylistic particularities of the U.S. American Muslim female headdress that locates this practice squarely within the performance of race.[8] To that end I have not used the term "hijab" as a catchall for a Muslim woman's headscarf but used the terms head wrap, headscarf, and khimar interchangeably with hijab to foreground the diversity of the U.S. Muslim community in my discussion. Accordingly, with this genealogy of the 'hoodjab my aim is to be analytically and methodologically inclusive. Moreover, by examining the interactions and intersections among different groups of Muslims, I complicate not only the meanings of the practice of female modesty, but also the ways in which we understand this religious community and the United States itself.

It's Complicated

Theorizing through the 'hoodjab, I hold that Muslim Cool is a technology of racial-religious performativity that constructs and "shores up" social identity. The 'hoodjab marked my teachers' identities as Muslim women in the United States, underscoring the ways in which expressions of Muslim womanhood are implicated by ideas about Blackness. Blackness is central to the racial-religious performativity of the 'hoodjab and consequently to the process of self-making—the development of a sense of self and of belonging as a raced, gendered, and religious subject in the United States. As a "performance," Muslim Cool reiterates the definition of race as a social construct that is formed and functions within contexts of power and inequality (Omi and Winant 1994; Gregory 1999; Hartigan 2005; Lipsitz 2006). Race is not a primordial essence, and its performance is something that must be learned and relearned.

Importantly, Muslim Cool's privileging of Blackness is entangled in the epistemes of naming and valuation. In many ways, Noreen, Fatema, and Latifah as well as Noreen's boss all identify the 'hoodjab as cool because it signifies hip hop, which in turn signifies Blackness, which is valued as the ultimate repository of cool in the United States. Further, as a material artifact of Black cool that is identified with Muslims, the 'hoodjab style makes the Muslim woman who wears it cool. The 'hoodjab thus loops through hip hop, Blackness, and Islam, and this loop is not without its problems.

When Blackness operates as a metonym for cool, the 'hoodjab can be a "site of negation." For Noreen's boss, the 'hoodjab was an emblem of the über-'hood narrative of Black life as poverty and pleasure, a story in which the complexities of place, class, and race become irrelevant. The 'hoodjab also exemplifies a negation of Black Muslim women. Academic narrations of Muslim women in hijab that overlook style presume that the Muslim women's headscarf is worn only in ways that tie it to the Islamic East. This aesthetic elision is an erasure, albeit unintended, of U.S. Black Muslim women and their authorial imprint on the sartorial landscape of Islam in the United States.[9] This erasure, then, is a reinscription of the ethnoreligious hegemony that Muslim Cool contests through embodied practices such as the 'hoodjab.

Indeed, representations and appropriations of Blackness are polysemous: Blackness holds a multiplicity of meanings. Blackness as cool is also a shorthand for righteous resistance to white supremacy as well as non-White hegemonies. The polysemous character of Blackness as cool holds potential for young Muslims doing Muslim Cool. For Latifah and Fatema the 'hoodjab was a technology of Muslim Cool that served as a conduit of self-making through racial sincerity. In this way, Muslim Cool highlights the links between race, gender, and religious subjectivity in the United States. Religious identity is not transcendent but rather is produced intersubjectively through complex racial pathways. Muslim Cool and its techniques of Blackness also reiterate race's sincerity; it is unsettled and unsettling. Race is a tie that binds, in all the possible senses of the term.

4

Cool Muslim Dandies

Signifyin' Race, Religion, Masculinity, and Nation

Eight different Black American men adorned the covers of the August 2008 issue of *Ebony* magazine. These eight different men on eight different covers represented an effort by the magazine to pay homage to one very powerful characteristic they had in common: Black cool. These men had been declared among "the 25 coolest brothers of all time" (Cobb 2008). Featured in a twenty-page photo spread, the members of this distinguished cohort included Jimi Hendrix, President Barack Obama, and Jay-Z. Alongside each photo was a brief explanation of what made each man *cool*, be it his walk, his virtuosity, his poise, and so on. The photo spread began with a short introduction, "The Genius of Cool: The 25 Coolest Brothers of All Time," written by historian William Jelani Cobb. Cobb explains:

> It doesn't take much to understand that "cool" is a form of Negro Zen, honed under the worst of circumstances this land could offer. If America built its society on efforts to keep black folk perpetually off balance, cool was the ultimate retaliation—a way of not only remaining balanced, but making it look effortless. Look at the key elements of cool—self-possession, elegance, and the ability to be fluent in body language—and it becomes obvious that cool was our antidote to the heat of hateration. (Cobb 2008, 68–69)

In this introduction, Cobb attempts to parse out the origins and elements of a "you know it when you see it" type of social phenomenon. Cool is easily identified but remains theoretically elusive. Cobb identifies the earliest iterations of cool from the Yoruba of West Africa—an ethnic group whose members were among the enslaved in the Americas. Yet in spite of these distant Yoruba roots, Cobb sees cool, as we now know it, as inextricable from the specific Black experience in the United States. Cobb argues that cool is a spirit-mind-body state of equilibrium and insight that has enabled U.S. Black Americans to withstand the assaults of white supremacy. Furthermore, Cobb posits that cool is a practice that has been perfected and passed on through the language of the body. Thus, cool is something performative and embodied that we are able to "see," and therefore recognize, over time and space. In this definition, cool is fundamentally U.S. Black American (thereby making my earlier use of the modifier "Black," as in "Black cool," redundant). But while Cobb appears to locate what makes cool cool in the U.S. Black American experience, his emphasis on cool as an embodied practice reiterates Stuart Hall's (1998) claim that style and the body are the repertoires of Black expressive culture. These repertoires, which are not the sole purview of U.S. Black American expressive cultures, highlight the fact that the Blackness of cool is fundamentally *Diasporic*.

Published eight months after the election of the first Black U.S. president, the photo spread is a celebration. It is a visual redemption of U.S. Black men from the "crisis of Black masculinity." The belief that Black male life is especially precarious is common within U.S. Black American communities. This belief became even more widespread in the wake of the numerous highly publicized deaths of Black men and women at the hands of the police and of vigilante citizens beginning with the murder of Trayvon Martin in 2012. Yet this precariousness also means social death. For example, social justice activists have shown that Black, particularly male, outcomes can be predicted in grade school. What they initially called the "school-to-prison pipeline" traces the high rates of Black male incarceration to systemic disparities in education, housing, wealth, health, and state violence. Recently, I have heard activists rename this process the "womb-to-prison pipeline." This renaming expresses the reality faced by many Black men, namely, that subjected to the necropolitics of the state (Mbembe 2003, 40), Black men in the United States may be counted among the "living dead."

Three years into the second term of the first Black president, Compton-based emcee Kendrick Lamar released his third album, *To Pimp a Butterfly*, to critical acclaim. The song "i" on that album is set up as a live performance that is interrupted by what sounds like a fight between audience members. Lamar breaks up the fight by passionately asking:

How many niggas we done lost, bro?
This, this year alone
Exactly. So we ain't got time to waste time my nigga
Niggas gotta make time bro
The judge make time, you know that, the judge make time right?
The judge make time so it ain't shit
It shouldn't be shit for us to come out here and appreciate the little
 bit of life we got left, dawg

This interruption rehearses a familiar scene in the discourse on the crisis of Black masculinity: young Black men fighting/hurting/killing young Black men. Lamar implores his audience to stop fighting by citing the physical deaths of those "we done lost" and the social death of state violence, "the judge make time." The familiarity of this interruption and of Lamar's intervention reflects what remains contested about the commonsense uncertainty of Black male life in the United States: what is its root cause? Are Black men nihilists entangled in pathological behaviors, or are Black men severely constrained by systems of inequality that fundamentally identify Black male life as disposable?

The performance of cool has been a central concept in the analysis of this crisis and the debate over its origins. In *Cool Pose* (1992), authors Richard Majors and Janet Mancini Billson identify Cobb's "Negro Zen" as an attitude of detachment and disinterest in the White mainstream that functions as a psychological defense mechanism against the marginalization and exclusion young Black men experience in America (Majors and Billson 1992). Black cool as a Black male response to systemic racism is a reiteration of an older sociological concept, "soul" (Rainwater 1970). "Soul," as an academic subject, was born out of the "ghetto ethnographies" of the 1960s, which "challenged the more conservative culture-of-poverty arguments and insisted that black culture was a set of coping mechanisms that grew out of the struggle for material and psychic survival" (Kelley 1997, 19). In the eponymous anthology (1970), sociologist Lee Rainwater described soul as a "style of Negro adaptation . . . [to] economic and political marginality" (Rainwater 1970, 8). In the same volume, Ulf Hannerz theorizes "soul" as a rhetorical device that reflects ambivalence about the causes of this social, political, and economic marginality (Hannerz 1970). According to Hannerz, the modest expansion of opportunities during the civil rights era created uncertainty among U.S. Black men in the 'hood as to whether structural inequalities or personal failures perpetuated their social immobility (Hannerz 1970).

This group of theorists argues that despite this agenda of adaptation as self-preservation, both soul and the cool pose are forms of self-sabotage that inculcate a value system that leads to lower achievement, incarceration, broken families, and homicide. In her book *We Real Cool*, bell hooks brings a Black feminist perspective to this conversation. She holds that Black men are in crisis because they cannot "hope for more than a life locked down, caged [and] confined," but also because they are encouraged to embrace cool in the form of a patriarchal masculinity (hooks 2004, xxi). For hooks, patriarchal masculinity is the real threat to Black male life because it ties Black men to a model of manhood that is entangled in the very system of white supremacist imperialist capitalist patriarchy that dominates them. She encourages Black men to "turn away from patriarchal notions of coolness . . . in the direction of a legacy of black male cool that remains life-enhancing, a legacy of grace" (hooks 2003, 158).

Among the "coolest brothers of all time" featured in *Ebony* were two U.S. Black *Muslim* men: Muhammad Ali and Malcolm X. Their inclusion was not inconsequential: it conjures up the relationship between Blackness and alterity that undergirds Muslim Cool. In U.S. popular culture, cool is a stance of opposition to and confrontation with dominant social norms, and in a nation defined by racial inequality, Blackness is the perpetual id to the White ego. This has made Black folks, as Cobb suggests, the maestros of cool in the United States. Critically, Black cool should be understood as a two-pronged approach. Black cool is an embodied form of resistance to a host of dehumanizing social norms *and* it offers a redemption of Blackness through the creation of separate sets of social standards. Malcolm and Ali epitomized this duality. When Malcolm X famously asked, "Who taught you to hate yourself?" he was urging Black people to reject the logic of white supremacy for a logic of Black self-love. Ali did the same, claiming beauty, greatness, and grace for himself and by extension for all Black men and women. Furthermore, as Muslims, both during and after their time in the Nation of Islam (NOI), they embraced Islam to craft alternative spiritual practices, worldviews, standards, norms, and ways of living—all driven by two key priorities: Black self-determination and Black redemption.

In my fieldwork, I found this performative tradition of Black cool as resistance and redemption in the sartorial choices of a cohort of men I refer to as "Muslim dandies." My use of the term "dandy" is an engagement with recent scholarship that examines Black dandyism as a performance of Black masculinity that begins in early European-African encounters and has been documented in the United States from the early nineteenth century onward (White and White 1998; Miller 2009; Lewis 2015). In her insightful study of Black dandyism in the United States, Monica Miller argues that as a Black performative style, Black dandyism *signifies on Whiteness.*

In his foundational text, *Signifying Monkey* (1989), Henry Louis Gates Jr. identifies "signifyin'" as a rhetorical technique of the African diaspora that appropriates hegemonic White signs in ways that revise the *meaning* of these signs. Acts of signifyin',' which are more than speech acts, stand in an "intertextual relation" to hegemonic Whiteness, but signifyin' is not a blind mimicry that aspires to the mainstream (Gates 1989, 51). Rather, signifyin' is an aesthetic reinterpretation that challenges the status quo (Miller 2009; Gates 1989; White and White 1998). Thus to *signify on Whiteness* is to disarm Whiteness through the use of its own signs. There is currently a renaissance of the signifyin' dandy aesthetic, what curator Shantrelle Lewis calls "Global Black Dandyism" (Lewis 2015). From Brooklyn to the Congo, cohorts of Black men are choosing remixed Edwardian- and Victorian-era style over the archetypical hip hop gear of jeans and white tees. Through a very self-conscious use of colors, prints, fabrics, hemlines, cufflinks, pocket squares, shoes, bags, hairstyles, head wear, and other materials, Black dandies signify on, rather than submit to, the tastes of white supremacy.

The dandy style is also emerging among U.S. Muslim men, and as dandies strive to be men of distinction, Muslim dandies are not a dime a dozen. Rather, they are a small but influential cohort. They are men who are rising in prominence in local, national, and even international Muslim communities, and as a result of their growing stature—people are talking about them—they are the subjects of a U.S. Muslim sartorial discourse around race, authority, and Muslim identity. They are also subjects whose choices inform the stylistic selections of other U.S. Muslim men—whether these men emulate or disdain the Muslim dandy. Thus, the Muslim dandies are tastemakers. All but one of the Muslim dandies I interviewed in my fieldwork were U.S. Black American, and while they were not all from Chicago, they all hailed from major centers of Black life in the United States. Growing up in the city, each had developed a relationship to Blackness by way of hip hop, which had also been their portal to conversion to Islam. They had also had advanced religious training, either in the United States or abroad, and reported finding that the stylistic norms they had valued before Islam—urban, Black, and U.S. American—were untenable if they wanted to be seen as authentically and authoritatively Muslim. Stylistically, most could be considered dandies par excellence; however, not all embraced the term, despite being identified as "dandyish" by others.

This chapter explores this emergent practice of Muslim dandyism and identifies it as an act of Muslim Cool. I argue that in ways analogous to Muslim women's use of headdress, Muslim men, and particularly U.S. Black Muslim men, are using dress as a means to signify on white supremacy *and* on Arab and South Asian U.S. American Muslim hegemonies. I examine how the fashion choices made by Muslim dandies are embedded in class tensions in U.S. Black American communities that are gendered and sexualized. I also show that through their sartorial practices they counter a politics of pious respectability in which claims to authenticity and authority as a Muslim are constructed by privileging certain forms of male dress over others. I end the examination by meditating on what the Muslim dandy teaches us about the position of the Black Muslim man in the war on terror.

The *Ebony* photo spread focused solely on cool as embodied in male bodies, echoing an intellectual tradition that locates Black cool in Black male performativity. A number of scholars have been critical of this tradition within the social sciences because it uses the young Black urban male experience as a proxy for the entirety of the Black experience (Kelley 1997; Morgan 1999). This reification of the young urban Black male not only does not accurately reflect the diversity of Black life but also overdetermines the reality of being young, Black, and male. While attentive to the fact that the Black male is not a stand-in for all Black people, I am also trying to move away from a parallel trend that renders the Muslim woman's experience the only gendered subjectivity that matters in the study of Muslim life.

I am thus extending the investigation of style, begun in chapter 3, to productively use this set of exclusions—Black, male, and urban—to explore Muslim Cool as sartorial choices that engage race, religion, gender, *and* nation. Nation is a particularly important category in this chapter because the Muslim dandy's style seems to explicitly hone in on a particular claim to Americanness. These men are neither U.S. Arab nor U.S. South Asian American; they lack a lineage from the "Islamic East" and consequently some of the privileges of male authority in U.S. Muslim communities. However, they use their Americanness, articulated through their appropriation of certain dress styles, to reclaim the privilege to be authoritative as Black, urban, working-class men—they use dress as a form of resistance and racial redemption. What follows, then, is an extended exploratory meditation on a complex relationship between Blackness and the aesthetics of identity, culminating in the argument that Blackness is a critical site of self-making for U.S. American Muslims.

Class, Gender, and Sexuality

In the stylistic landscape of Chicago, U.S. Black Muslim men sometimes wore the South Asian tunic-and-pants suit, *shalwar kameez*, with "a vest and henna in their beard," as Abd al-Karim put it, or, alternatively, the floor-length *thobe* typically worn by men in the Middle East. Yet it was more common to find U.S. Black Muslim men in an assortment of what Madison Avenue execs euphemistically call "urban" styles. These are styles that come out of urban Black communities (the 'hood) and youth-driven hip hop culture. This attire ranges from the basic—jeans, T-shirts, and hoodies—to more stylized versions. Against this sartorial backdrop, Abd al-Karim—in a tweed double-breasted blazer, slim-cut jeans, and velvet slippers, with a plum-colored bow tie for a pop of color—had a distinct dandy style. His attire was always high quality, but the price of his dandified look was not counted only in dollars and cents.

Abd al-Karim, in his early thirties, is a Chicago native and a *talib al-'ilm* (student of knowledge). This means that he traveled often between the United States and parts of Africa and the Middle East, studying Islamic sciences. During an interview in a mutual friend's backyard, Abd al-Karim shared a string of hilarious stories about how his dandy aesthetic had been interpreted during his early days as a Muslim. He explained that when he first became a Muslim, he was the go-to guy among "the brothers" for leading *salat* (prayer). Within his cohort of newly converted U.S. Black American men he had memorized the most Qur'an at the time—about one *juz'*, or a thirtieth part of the entire text—and he was able to recite fairly well, which made him the most qualified prayer leader to his peers. However, all this changed when he began to "experiment with style." He was passed over for someone who had less knowledge but who dressed the part: "The same brother looked at me and was like, 'No, you [indicating someone else] lead the prayer.' And this was someone who couldn't even make it through *Fatiha*[1] without [an error]."

Here, "dressing the part," meant wearing a Middle Eastern thobe or a shalwar kameez. Although the hip hop aesthetic seemed to be the predominant style of dress among U.S. Black American Muslim men in Chicago, once the man in question had been identified as a religious leader, he dressed differently. Men who were religious authorities tended to wear clothing that in U.S. Black communities was identified more closely with locations such as Karachi and Cairo than with Chicago. I observed this style of dress particularly among U.S. Black American Sunni Muslim men who were not affiliated with the community of Imam W. D. Mohammed or with the Nation of Islam. However, Abd al-Karim believed that the objections to his leadership of the prayer were not only based on his failure to wear a thobe: "Maybe if my look was more identifiably urban, maybe he wouldn't have reacted to me in the same way, but since I was walking around in an ascot . . ." Abd al-Karim argued that his loss of credibility as a religious authority was driven by tensions of class and masculinity among U.S. Black American men:

> ABD AL-KARIM: On the one hand, there is general suspicion of, in this community, anything that indicates middle class values. . . . There is also this suspicion of fashion because they think it has an underlying agenda to emasculate. . . . I think that there are certain styles that the *brothers* regard as particularly feminine. Even without going into detail about those looks, I think *'inayah*, [which is] a certain kind of attentiveness to dress, is seen as—
> SU'AD: Why you acting like—
> ABD AL-KARIM:—a *bint* [i.e., female; we both laugh].

Muslim Dandy Style. Courtesy of Evan Brown.

Technically, Abd al-Karim's socioeconomic class position matched that of the poor and working-class Black Sunni Muslims who formed his immediate community. Yet because the dandy aesthetic draws on elite fashion styles and etiquette, he was read as middle class, which made him an object of suspicion. Underlying this class suspicion, as Abd al-Karim noted, was gender. Dressing the middle-class part was not only a form of elitism but also seen as undercutting working-class Black masculine power. Abd al-Karim's interpretation of his community outlines the broader dynamics of class within U.S. Black American communities.

Class in U.S. Black American communities has long been a topic of academic scholarship. As scholars note (Kelley 1997; Pattillo 2008), early work on class in U. S. Black communities tended either to focus solely on the Black poor or to depict a great divide between the classes that is rarely bridged. In contrast, later scholarship offers a much more nuanced perspective by tracing significant class diversity and its profound effects on notions of Blackness and authenticity, visions of Black progress, and forms of U.S. Black American self-making (Jackson 2003; Pattillo 2007; Gregory 1999). Class diversity is lived in Black communities every day through contact among people of different classes. Such contact is enabled by ties of kinship and friendship, as well as obligations and affective relationships (Jackson 2003). Importantly, class status is not determined by bank account balances, which are typically unknowable to others, but by particular symbols, choices, and bodily performances of status (Jackson 2003; Pattillo 2007). These signs and practices are keys to the operation of "class difference [as] a mode of distinction and judgment" and the class-based intraracial tensions that it produces (Jackson 2003, 63). Many poor and working-class Blacks believe that their middle-class counterparts see themselves as distinct—as better than less wealthy Blacks—and thus stand on high and judge poorer Blacks as being responsible for their own poverty—they are poor because they lack a work ethic (Jackson 2003). Hence, lack of middle-class status can be a source of self-doubt for low-income U.S. Black Americans (Am I poor because I did not work hard enough?), but it can also be a sign of racial treason (The "system" is rigged, so middle-class Black success is the result of "selling out" their people).

Contrary to culture-of-poverty arguments that place all the blame for Black disadvantage squarely on Black culture and behavior, middle-class Blacks, for their part, are well aware of how institutionalized racism perpetuates Black poverty (Pattillo 2007). Yet as Mary Pattillo has illustrated in her extensive work on the Black middle class, middle-class U.S. American Blacks can also carry paternalistic sensibilities that frame their contributions to poorer Black communities as stemming from their deeper pockets as well as their more respectable behavior—a kind of "culture of poverty lite" (Pattillo 2007). This politics of respectability among the Black middle class is always in tension with a competing notion of Black authenticity—keeping it real. Keeping it real reconfigures the middle-class "airs" of respectability as White cultural impositions and signals Black complicity with White domination. Hence, Abd al-Karim's change of dress aroused suspicion.

As noted above, Abd al-Karim linked these class suspicions to gender and sexuality. As I have described elsewhere (Khabeer 2009), "bint" is an Arabic word for daughter/girl that translates in Black Arabic (African American Muslim vernacular Arabic) as "bitch" or, in polite company, "female." Thus, the quip "Why you acting like a bint?" reflects a hostility toward the dandy aesthetic because that aesthetic is interpreted as feminine, as a departure from dominant forms of masculinity, such as those exemplified by jeans and T-shirts. Abd al-Karim interpreted this aversion as a fear of emasculation that was particularly meaningful to "the brothers." In his statement, "the brothers" is an immediate reference to his poor and working-class U.S. Black American Muslim male compatriots, but it is also a broader commentary on the ways in which Black men, as well as Black women, negotiate their performances of gender and sexuality under the ever-present surveillance of the White normative gaze—a gaze that renders Black gender and sexuality necessarily pathological.

Echoing our earlier discussion of racial performativity, gender is not a given but rather is a performance. Furthermore, like the performance of race, the performance of gender is not necessarily artificial or automatic. As Judith Butler has argued, the gendered self is made through improvisations, but its intelligibility to others is constrained by the regulatory power of the male/female binary (Butler 2004). The repeated iteration of gender norms, according to Butler, is what gives regulations their power but also their potential to fail (Butler 1989, 2004). In the potential for failure, for Butler, lies agency, which ultimately culminates in resistance to the regulations of gender norms (Mahmood 2005). Butler's insights continue to represent a significant departure from older ideas according to which gender identity is a natural outgrowth of biological sex and anatomy. Yet because race is not central to her conceptualizations, they fail to address fully the gendered performance of the Muslim dandies I encountered. For this, I look to Hortense Spillers, who has argued that when enacted upon racialized, specifically Black, bodies, the regulatory power of gender entails different orders of gender performance and consequently different means of agency and resistance.

Spillers argues that the male/female binary is indeed a social construct but one that was inaccessible under captivity, as the slave system essentially categorized Blacks as nonpersons or what she calls "flesh" (Spillers 2003). This is not to say that enslaved Black people lost their sense of subjecthood or did not recognize each other as persons, but rather to emphasize the violent logics of racial slavery. This is also not to deny the historical record of Black women's subjection to sexual violence. Rather, it underscores that Black women were also subjected to "male" forms of violence, thus eliding the male/female distinction in the lives of the enslaved: "In other words, in the historic outline of dominance, the respective subject-positions of 'female' and 'male' adhere to no symbolic integrity" (Spillers 2003, 204). Black people were always already failing to perform gender norms, yet Black failure to perform gender correctly did not culminate in agency to resist but rather was reworked as a technique of racial subjugation. Accordingly, it is the "potential for gender *differentiation*," once denied, that operates as a particularly meaningful means of agency and resistance within some U.S. Black American communities.[2]

Abd Al-Karim's sartorial story offers an example of how narratives of Black pathology are built upon symbolic deployments of gender and sexuality. The White gaze regards Black men and women as having either too little or too much sexuality—what Alexander Weheliye identifies as "lack" and "surplus"—and that they do gender in reverse as well. Archetypes of Black men and women in the United States, such as "Uncle Tom," "the buck," "Mammy," and "Jezebel" put these qualities into sharp relief.[3] The "Uncle Tom," a dutiful and loyal Black man who is often pictured alone as the caretaker of a blond-haired girl child, is essentially a eunuch who lacks all sexual desire. His opposite is "the buck," whose surplus of sexuality and violence is a looming threat to the preservation of that very same virginal female Whiteness now signified by the nation. Likewise, "Mammy" is a Black woman who has no desire beyond dutifully caring for her master's children. She contrasts with the oversexed "Jezebel," who wants sex all the time, with anyone, and anywhere and is also a sexual predator (Harris-Perry 2013).

Added to these slavery-era symbolic forms are post-"liberation" ideal types in which Black gender performance is a reversal of the male/female binary. As Spillers notes, "Sapphire" enacts her "Old Man" in drag, just as her "Old Man" becomes "Sapphire" in outrageous caricature (Spillers 2003, 204). Sapphire is an archetype of the Black woman as irrationally and uniquely aggressive and angry (Harris-Perry 2013).[4] According to White normative heterosexual gender roles the male is assertive, a positive characteristic that enables him to be a responsible caretaker of an idealized domesticated female. Yet in Sapphire and her Old Man these roles are reversed, and in that reversal what was once positive becomes pathos.

Importantly, the sartorial critique directed at Abd al-Karim is a response to this representational context in which narratives of Black pathology have persistently obscured structural inequality. Central to the narrative around Sapphire is her alleged role as the matriarch of the Black family in crisis. According to this narrative, immortalized in the now-infamous Moynihan Report,[5] the Old Man is absent because Sapphire emasculates Black men—although this somehow fails to prevent her from accumulating multiple "baby daddies." Sapphire is primarily responsible for this role reversal, which is the root of a series of negative life indicators from out-of-wedlock births to juvenile delinquency. In this view, Black families are dysfunctional because of "the tangle of pathology" that is at the root of Black disadvantage in the United States (Moynihan 1965). This logic is deeply problematic, as it defines "family functionality" on the basis of a married and middle-class White heteronormative nuclear family model. Nevertheless, it continues to be very effective in linking gender, class, and sexuality as a means to write Black people off as nonnormative in order to reproduce the racial status quo in the United States. Abd al-Karim's critics show an awareness of these deeply lodged perceptions of Black pathology and of their inseparable connections with certain items of clothing and stylistic choices. They identify links between style and Black pathology that have particular resonance within the discourse around the crisis of Black masculinity.

I spoke with a young U.S. Black Muslim man who went by the name of LeThereBeAir at the IMAN office to get his perspective on the Muslim dandy. He is a U.S. Black American and in his mid-twenties, and I had first met him when I started fieldwork in Chicago, where he was born and raised. His parents were converts to Islam, and he credits his interest in fashion to his father. When we met he had on a pair of semi-fitted camouflage cargo jeans, a T-shirt, and a jean jacket with the fashion industry's rendition of a Native American print on the sleeves. He was also wearing a "fitted" (a baseball cap), and the contrast of prints and colors he was wearing had a very stylish and cool-looking effect. He described himself as part of a "sneaker subculture" and showed me a cell phone picture of a closet full of sneakers, which he collects to both wear and resell. Accordingly, he was wearing sneakers, and he explained that he chose the particular pair he had on because they were historic—they bore a first-edition color. He told me that when getting dressed he often starts with his shoes and works the rest of his outfit around them. His "sneaker game" was intense; during our interview I furiously took notes, overwhelmed by his command of the styles and trends associated with contemporary hip hop fashion. He described his own style as "streetwear," in contrast to the dandy style, which he admired and called "dapper." He did not consider himself a dandy, and nor do I, because he rarely wore suits or other more formal clothes and accessories. This did not mean he was any less discerning or fashion forward, but his discernment often went unrecognized. He dedicated a lot of time and energy to his style, but "to the rest of the world it's just a T-shirt"; LeThereBeAir's identity was reduced to a fact of Blackness, the young Black man as a thug.

> Late last year I was going to a training, with Google, at the Tribune building downtown. I had this baseball cap on actually, the only one I actually wear. So I'm going into the building and the lady [at the desk] asks, "Where are you going?" and I tell her, "I'm going to Google," and then she, this White lady, asks, "Are you here to deliver food?" I wanted to give it to her but I was like "No!" And she kind of brushed it off and asked for my ID [to get into the building]. I don't like that kind of stuff because I choose to wear a baseball cap or a T-shirt, somebody looking at me like that. I don't know, the racial stuff hurts more; it's like they think you are less than them.

Like the "buck" that precedes it, the image of the "thug" is of a young Black male as hypermasculine, with a surplus of sexuality and violence. The thug also lacks a work ethic, self-control, a value for education, and a value for life itself. The thug is recognized by his clothes—baseball caps, T-shirts, jeans, sneakers, gold jewelry, uncut natural hair, and tattoos. The thug crystallizes the perspective that the crisis of Black masculinity stems from the surplus and the lack of young Black men. When LeThereBeAir complains of being looked at "like that," he is concerned about being seen as a thug and the consequences of being seen that way. LeThereBeAir tells a story of a microaggression—being asked if he was the delivery boy—that is embedded in an economy of sartorial symbols that young U.S. Black American men must navigate to command respect, to be seen, and, as the 2012 murder of Travyon Martin in a hoodie proved, to stay alive.[6] In the past, as today, links between style and Black pathology have fueled punitive legislation and facilitated death. Yet the history of U.S. Black American fashion seems to show that as much as Black people were aware of the dangers of dress, they also chose to challenge that danger through dress.

U.S. Black American Fashion from Slavery to Hip Hop

In their monograph *Stylin'*, Shane White and Graham White argue that dress, and specifically the compulsion to make African bodies fit in "European garb," was a technique of domination during slavery in the United States (White and White 1998, 7). "Clothing was embedded in a system of rewards and punishments designed to make . . . the whole institution of slavery run smoothly" and create hierarchies among the enslaved (White and White 1998, 14). Style continued to be a site in which Whites would reward or censure free Blacks according to whether their dress was deemed appropriate to their inferior station (White and White 1998; Miller 2009). For example, the clothes, parades, and pageantry of free Northern Blacks were openly ridiculed by White northerners. Likewise, free Southern Blacks who failed to "dress the part" as social inferiors were imprisoned and subject to violent attacks, even death.

Clothing was used to dominate, but Blacks also used it in ways that gave material expression to their sense of personhood. In what is really the hallmark of the U.S. Black American fashion tradition, enslaved and free Blacks would take on, embellish, and remake European styles in line with the priorities of color and print of African aesthetics. Postemancipation, dress became central to the politics of respectability among Blacks themselves. Styles considered ostentatious or gaudy by the emerging middle classes and the Black elite were eschewed for more "understated fashion," which underscores the historical nature of the class conflict described by Abd al-Karim (White and White 1998, 168). The sartorial choices of these middle- and upper-class Blacks were undergirded by the desire to subvert notions of Black inferiority, thereby making even the Black elite's preference for the muted tones of respectability a form of signifyin'.

The historical use of clothing as a technique of domination and division by Whites and as a form of signifyin' and expressing competing ideas of authenticity among Blacks reflects the contestation around hip hop dress today, as indicated by Abd al-Karim's story. As a form of dress, hip hop styles are built on certain fundamental clothing items, which have included, at least since the early 1990s, sagging (although not always baggy) jeans, T-shirts, sports jerseys, gold jewelry, sneakers, and fitted baseball caps. Critically, these fundamentals come directly out of the stylistic imaginations of urban Black youth, yet in the tradition of Black fashion these styles creatively appropriate dominant White mainstream aesthetics.

As a teenager in Brooklyn in the 1990s, I recall witnessing the origin of these styles in the remaking of high-end items such as Tommy Hilfiger jeans, Timberland boots, and Ralph Lauren polos into 'hood gear. This produced a look of oversized (and sometimes colorful) jeans and polo shirts paired with Timberland boots whose laces were loosely tied and which were worn in all seasons and for just about all occasions. The reach into the mainstream knew few bounds. For example, Robin D. G. Kelley (1996) noted that young Blacks in California were wearing hockey jerseys, not out of fidelity to a typically all-White sport but because young Blacks made the jerseys *fresh*.

This remixing of mainstream fashion lines is at the root of hip hop fashion's emergence as a trend in the marketplace and as a subsequent source of revenue for established lines such as Hilfiger and for new Black-owned fashion companies such as Karl Kani, FUBU, and Phat Farm (Fleetwood 2011; Neal 2013). In her analysis of hip hop fashion, Nicole Fleetwood holds that this profitability is embedded in the marketing and consumption of Black male iconicity. Tied to the "fixity of the black male body," she argues, "hip-hop clothing style is virulently and heterosexually masculine" (Fleetwood 2011, 160).

Class, like gender and sexuality, is also an important dimension of these styles. Hip hop fashion styles are tied to ideas about the 'hood, making them decidedly working class. Moreover, jeans and T-shirts, the staples of hip hop fashion, underwrite styles that tend to err toward casual dress according to mainstream fashion norms. Nevertheless, the suit has also been a key ensemble in the hip hop wardrobe, but without raising the same class ire that Abd al-Karim describes.

Old school hip hop artists such as Dana Dane, Slick Rick, and Big Daddy Kane were known for their fashion sense. From album covers to performances, they often wore and talked about wearing dapper suits, which were read as signs neither of middle-class elitism nor of emasculation. Kane, who was typically flanked by beautiful women on his album covers, was also shown wearing a suit. On the album covers for *Smooth Operator* and *Prince of Darkness*, Kane's suits are evidence of his virile heterosexuality. Likewise, in the lyrics of the hip hop classic "La Di Da Di," Slick Rick narrates his style and vanity in descriptive detail as part of his specifically masculine braggadocio:

> I woke up around ten o'clock in the morning
> I gave myself a stretch up, a morning yawning
> Went to the bathroom to wash up
> Had some soap on my face and my hand on a cup
> I said, "um, mirror mirror on the wall
> Who is the top choice of them all?"
> There was a rumble dumble, five minutes it lasted
> The mirror said, "You are, you conceited bastard!"
> Well that's true that why we never have no beef
> So I then washed off the soap and brushed my gold teeth
> Used Oil of Olay cause my skin gets pale
> And then I got the files for my finger nails
> True to the night and on my behalf
> I put the bubbles in the tub so I could have a bubble bath
> Clean, dry was my body and hair
> I threw on my brand new Gucci underwear
> For all the girls I might take home
> I got the Johnson's baby powder and the Polo cologne
> Fresh dressed like a million bucks
> Threw on the Bally shoes and the fly green socks
> Stepped out house stopped short, oh no
> I went back in, I forgot my Kangol
> then I dilly dally ran into an alley
> Bumped into my old girl Sally from the valley (Doug E. Fresh and
> MC Ricky D 1985)

Slick Rick's narration is littered with luxury items: Polo cologne, Gucci underwear, Bally shoes, and a Kangol hat. His self-care is meticulous and aimed at attracting women, the first of whom, Sally, he encounters in an alley, which locates him as squarely heterosexual and in the 'hood. Here, Slick Rick is akin to what Manthia Diawara (1998), riffing on Walter Benjamin (2006), labels "homeboy flaneurs." Homeboy flaneurs are young men "who dressed up to be seen, and see themselves being admired by others" (Diawara 1998, 242). Diawara's flaneurs were young Black and Latino males who would saunter up and down the streets of New York City's Greenwich Village in the early 1990s. Although Diawara and Slick Rick focus on male experiences, I too remember getting "fresh dressed like a million bucks" to take the train from my 'hood in Crown Heights up to West Fourth Street to walk up and down Eighth Ave, to see and be seen.

The twenty-first century saw an extension of the hip hop suit tradition in the rise of the hip hop mogul. Embodied in figures such as Sean Combs, Russell Simmons, and Jay-Z, the hip hop mogul is "typically male, entrepreneurial, prestigious in both cultural influence and personal wealth, . . . typically young, typically African American and typically tethered either literally or symbolically to America's disenfranchised inner cities" (Smith 2003, 69). The hip hop mogul is an icon of the U.S. American bootstrap narrative. Working-class status is central to the autobiographies of all hip hop moguls. Further, for the male hip hop mogul, suiting is also a sign of virile sexuality under the broader banner of masculine power—something that Ilyas, one the dandies I interviewed, called "getting your grown man on."

Old school and contemporary hip hop suiting is also linked to modes of consumption that are central to the "ghetto fabulous aesthetic" (Mukherjee 2006). To be "ghetto fabulous" describes the consumption of luxury items—"bling"—by poor and working-class Blacks. These consumption habits are much maligned in the discourse of respectability as bad behavior and fiscal irresponsibility; yet, as Roopali Mukherjee discusses, the "audacious poses of bling serve [as] emphatic affirmations of working class black urban life" (Mukherjee 2006, 600). Likewise, Diawara places consumption at the "center of the struggle for the black good life" that "puts . . . stereotypes of blackness in the marketplace and obtains the highest prices for them" (Diawara 1998, 273).[7]

High-end clothes and accessories are meant to be inaccessible from certain race and class locations, and through this inaccessibility they reproduce race and class hierarchies. Thus, for Blacks to purchase high-

COOL MUSLIM DANDIES | 157

end clothes and accessories or knockoff versions of them is to signify on Whiteness and to enact a form of Black redemption. The full material enjoyment of this Black redemption is limited: the hip hop moguls' success is primarily individual (though it may reach the closest kin, hip hop artists are always "putting on his mans and dem"). Yet it is performatively accessible for the collective: even if you do not have Jay-Z's "paper," you can still dress the part. Accordingly, rather than being seen as elite and effeminate, these suited hip hop Black men symbolize heterosexual masculine power and working-class aspirations.

As members of the hip hop generation, the U.S. American Muslim dandies I spoke with likewise described their deployment of the suit as a sign of heterosexual masculine maturity. Ilyas from California, one of the dandies par excellence, described his aesthetic as being "on your grown man." The idea of the "grown man," I found, was key in many dandies' narrations. For Jihad (Chicago) and Faheem (Oakland), the grown man was embodied by "the men in my family." This included grandfathers, fathers, and uncles whose sharp dressing had inspired their own choices. For Faheem and others, familial inspiration also came from the scholar and public intellectual Dr. Sherman Jackson. Jackson is known for wearing well-tailored and well-put-together suits. Jackson's dress is notable because as a U.S. Black American Muslim man and a religious scholar in a suit, he is seen to be making a sartorial intervention in the family of the *ummah*. So inspired, Faheem got a dress shirt tailored in the French cuff style Jackson is known for among Muslim dandies—a style Ilyas referred to as a "Dr. J throwback."

The grown man included other members of the "ummah family"— the "suited and booted" man of the NOI's male training league, the Fruit of Islam.[8] In addition, as men of color from urban communities, the Muslim dandies also took masculine style inspiration from what we might consider the other side of the moral spectrum: pimps, players, and street hustlers known for their style. Hence, despite accusations of "acting like a bint," for these Muslim men of color the dandy style fell squarely within a tradition of Black masculine sartorial expression: the desire to look good, to see and be seen as central to being Black, male, and cool.

Yet as the resistance described by Abd al-Karim illustrates, this expression of Black masculine sartorial tradition does not always translate well in Muslim spaces. In my conversations with non-dandy U.S. Black American men, the Muslim dandy was regarded with ambivalence or deep concern. Bilal, a forty-something Chicago cab driver, had reservations about the style. Bilal's go-to outfit was generally a *kufi* (cap) and a *kameez* (long shirt) worn with jeans and sneakers. He did not object to the dandy style per se, particularly because he highly respected Abd al-Karim, "but for me, I like to wear things so these [White] people out here know I am a Muslim." In contrast, Hamza, a thirty-something computer technician from D.C., gave the Muslim dandies the proverbial "side eye." I was intrigued by this because, to my untrained eye, Hamza was a good dresser and, like the Muslim dandies, placed value on style. Yet Hamza felt the dandy style should be avoided because it was "too effeminate" and could possibly be "interpreted as homosexual"; thus it was not, for Hamza, properly manly. Hamza's concern about the appearance of homosexuality was rooted in his belief that same-sex desire was a moral wrong but also in his worry that a nonnormative masculinity would reduce Islam's esteem within urban U.S. Black American communities that valued gender differentiation.

The concern over the Muslim dandy's potential departure from normative Black masculinity struck me as paradoxical for two reasons. First, as already explained, there is a long tradition of looking good among U.S. Black American men. And second, based on my observations, Muslim dandies tended to be deeply invested in the idea of the Islamic tradition—namely, the corpus and consensus of Sunni and Shi'a orthodoxy. This is a tradition made up of gendered ritual and social laws, which made adherence to gender distinctions a valuable act of piety for Muslim dandies. The apparent paradox is partly reconciled when these objections are considered in view of the racialized politics of pious respectability.

The Politics of Pious Respectability

Like Abd al-Karim, Ilyas had a reputation that preceded him. My first encounter with Ilyas was thus with his legend. People talked about him because despite his relatively young age he was a successful businessman involved in ventures from fashion to technology. He was also, at the time, a very eligible bachelor, which contributed to his "fame." Ilyas was part of a network of male converts from California (the Bay Area, L.A., and San Diego) for whom hip hop and *tasawwuf* (Sufism) were critical aspects of narratives and growth as Muslims. It was hip hop that had sparked their interest in Islam and established Muslim Cool as their epistemological orientation, and it was through tasawwuf that they had connected themselves to the Sunni Islamic tradition and cultivated certain aesthetic practices that lent themselves to dandyism—they were connoisseurs of coffee and of *oud*, a high-quality wood used to make perfumes and incense. Although I conducted the bulk of my fieldwork in the Chicago area, I also visited the San Francisco Bay Area; in addition, folks from this California network were often in Chicago, invited there by Rami Nashashibi because they shared IMAN's interest in hip hop and in cultivating arts and culture among U.S. American Muslims.

Ilyas was a devout Muslim and a tastemaker. I identify the dandies I interviewed as tastemakers because they tended to take the initiative in community life and to be leaders at the local and national levels. Ilyas's personality was that of a "go-getter," but all his endeavors seemed to be guided by a sense of and a commitment to Islam in the United States as a community- and institution-building project. Accordingly, one of my first interactions with him was through a religious studies summer program that he was leading. He reached out to me for recommendations of female Muslim scholars to be included on the program. In the epistemology of Muslim Cool, he was not just content to be Muslim but also motivated to action as a Muslim.

As I began to explore questions of Muslim Cool and masculinity, I reached out to him to conduct a formal interview. We met up at a major Muslim convention and, as per his legend, he was dressed to impress—actually, he was impeccable. He wore a cream-colored two-button suit, a light blue dress shirt, a maroon tie, and brown dress shoes, and given the way he sauntered I could imagine him having a Slick Rick-like conversation with his own mirror. Ilyas is Filipino, and he located himself within the 'hood and the hip hop generation because of his life experiences. He grew up in an urban Black community and carried himself with the iconic male Black cool described at the outset of this chapter.

Ilyas described his parents as liking to dress well and as placing a high value on formal etiquette and social graces. This fostered in him a kind of fashion habitus, a disposition learned from his parents, which guided all his sartorial choices. However, his habitus was temporarily disrupted upon his conversion. Like most of the Muslim dandies I encountered, Ilyas had spent some time abroad to study Islam. He had left the United States propelled by a desire to be a pious Muslim. Initially, he had envisioned his journey as a move, potentially permanent, to the Islamic East in order to learn "the Tradition"—religion unadulterated. Critically, his decision had been paired with a particular sense of piety that had sartorial implications: "I was refusing the world, moved to Yemen, put on a thobe, and wait[ed] for the Mahdi."

As we have seen, the politics of pious respectability is a performative landscape that conflates particular sets of cultural specificities from the Islamic East with normative notions of Muslim piety. This conflation, which privileges certain culturally contingent practices, repudiates Blackness. Thus claims made to religious authenticity and belonging are made by moving toward the Islamic East (which as described in chapter 2 excludes Africa beyond Egypt, Mauritania, and Morocco) as the archive of tradition, and away from Blackness, which is defined as outside the tradition. It is noteworthy that Ilyas had planned on waiting for the Mahdi in a thobe. Mirroring the debates we have discussed around music, dress too serves as a site for the politics of pious respectability. Norms of Islamic authenticity and religious authority privilege certain forms of male dress—specifically "traditional" Middle Eastern and South Asian garments—over others.[9]

Dress operated as a particular maker of piety for Ilyas *within* the United States; but when he actually left the United States and encountered the Islamic East and the "tradition" that he had been searching for, he found that being a good Muslim and being pious were not contingent upon a particular outfit. In fact, the way Ilyas came to see it, "the Tradition" encompassed a tradition of dressing well as a form of piety.

Su'ad: How do people respond to the way you dress?

Ilyas: Thing about me, I am in the business of fashion, so it's like "Oh, he's the fashion guy."

Su'ad: So people expect it.

Ilyas: So people expect it, they know me as the guy who is in fashion. So do I get flack from it? No. I think people who don't know me and see this guy walking around, it's like . . . I can't front; it shows a little bit of narcissism, it shows a little bit of, like, I wouldn't say it's unmasculine, but it's not *as* masculine as a guy who just doesn't care, you know. Because just the stereotypes of what our [U.S. American] culture has been about, this is what we have been presented as what is appropriate male behavior. It's like [other men say], "You not a girl, man. Stop being in front of the mirror, man." But people fail to remember within our tradition, especially the Maliki *madhhab* [school of religious law], Imam Malik and others, they were big on *izar an-ni'mah*, they were big on "showing the blessings of your Lord." Our scholars were *always* dressed well, Maliki scholars were *always* dressed well. "*Wa amma bi ni'mati rabbi fahaddith*"; "And about the pleasures of your Lord, let it be known." Show it. And there are all these stories of Maliki scholars, Abd al-Karim knows this story, of course he would know it [laughs]:

There are two students of *shuyukh* [plural of *shaykh*, or religious teacher], one is of Imam Malik and there's another student of another shaykh. They walk up to each other, the two students, and he [the other shaykh's student] goes, "My shaykh knows more *tafsir* [Qur'anic exegesis] than your shaykh and he [Imam Malik's student] is like, "Nah, nah, nah, Imam Malik knows more tafsir." Then he goes, "Well, my shaykh knows more *hadith* [prophetic traditions] than your shaykh," and he [Imam Malik's student] goes, "Nah, nah, nah, Imam Malik knows more hadith." Then he goes, "Well, you know, my shaykh knows more *balagha* [linguistic eloquence] than your shaykh," and he [Imam Malik's student] goes, "Nah, Imam Malik [knows more]," and then it got to "My shaykh has more *taqwa* [God-consciousness] than your shaykh" and "No, no, no, Imam Malik has more taqwa," and then he [the other shaykh's student] goes, "Well, my shaykh has more *zuhd* [asceticism] than your shaykh," and he [Imam Malik's student] goes, "Yeah, I think your shaykh might get my shaykh" [we both laugh].

Because Imam Malik was always fly, and it's key when you look at the *Haba'ib*, it just makes them look very noble, you know. [So] do I catch flack? No. But Abd al-Karim, I think, is different, because you have to understand he is in a *particular* position and role and looked upon differently because he is a man of scholarship. The thing is, this monasticism and resenting the world and refusing the world—that's from a certain group of Muslims who have held the banner of this, like, "Because I don't care about the world, I only care about God," you know, which even scholars have refuted; [they say] "You know you can't, don't be like this." You know a true *zahid* [ascetic] is in the world but not of it, he is not attached—not that he doesn't have [nice things].

Ilyas argued that "people fail to remember" that Muslim scholars dressed well, based on the principle of izar an-ni'mah. What he referred to as "a failure to remember" marks how ideas of tradition and piety become codified through the narration and performances of certain practices and the "forgetting" of others. Ilyas also identified an idealized "American" masculinity defined by its complete *inattention* to fashion. This ideal seems to match the critique that Abd al-Karim experienced and Ilyas's own sense that "there is a certain amount of engagement with the self that people regard as being antithetical to the religious calling."

However, as detailed earlier, the desire to look good and to "see and be seen" in Black communities and among the hip hop generation is also characteristic of an ideal manly type. Yet the desire to look good does not seem to translate well when the Muslim dandy enters the Muslim male sartorial landscape. According to Abd al-Karim, "If you were just as scrupulous and exacting about thobes and *bukhoor* [incense], it could be regarded as *ihsan* [spiritual excellence], but when it's this particular aesthetic, it's like you are too into yourself." Although attuned to the expectation described by Abd al-Karim and present in many religious traditions of asceticism as a sign of piety, this asceticism is not innocent. It is not merely the sartorial practice of 'inayah that is at issue but the politics of pious respectability—what sartorial form this attentiveness takes on.

To be "exacting about thobes and bukhoor" is a quality of the Haba'ib whom Ilyas also referenced. The Haba'ib are a priestly family from Yemen who are highly regarded, particularly among Ilyas's California network and within other groups of young Sufis in the United States. The Haba'ib are notable because they claim descent from the Prophet's family and because they are seen as both knowledgeable about the "books" of Islam and spiritually enlightened. Each of my interviewees who mentioned the Haba'ib mentioned their dress. Just like for Imam

Malik in Ilyas's description, for the Haba'ib, in their view, dressing well was part of their spiritual discipline, part of their piety.

The Haba'ib wear clothes that are associated with their locale: *jubbas* (long coats), thobes, pristine white turbans, and embroidered Yemeni scarves worn on the shoulders. They also have a specific set of accessories: a silver ring and a cane or a walking stick, and oud as perfume. These are clothes and accessories that can be costly in terms of time and money. Nevertheless, the Haba'ib are held in high esteem. This esteem is generated by their intellectual and spiritual status among U.S. American Muslims, but this status is legible because their sartorial style is culturally normative of the Islamic East. The 'inayah of the Haba'ib carries the esteem of "tradition" and is interpreted as piety—a possibility that is foreclosed for the styles of the Muslim dandy because the latter were woven in the "West."

Ilyas described himself as getting a pass because he was the "fashion" guy, which, he argued, distinguished him from Abd al-Karim as a "man of scholarship." Again, Abd al-Karim's legitimacy as a religious authority lay in dressing the part. According to the politics of pious respectability, to dress the part is not to draw on a broader U.S. American aesthetic, as the Muslim dandy does. Rather, to be legibly pious, stylish, and religiously authoritative, a Muslim man must dress like the Haba'ib, in a style that is culturally normative of the Islamic East.

Counter-Respectability Politics

The Muslim dandies I interviewed, such as Ilyas and Abd al-Karim, do not dress like the Haba'ib, but the Haba'ib are sartorial inspirations for the Muslim dandy's performance of a counterpolitics of pious respectability—dressing well in "Western" clothes as a practice of piety. I use the term "Western" advisedly, for Abd al-Karim did not identify his style as Western but as African American:

> I think for me it's trying to locate an African American culture. Because sometimes we have these very strange conversations about culture, it seems like it's this kind of reified thing that is out there. And one thing I like to assert with my aesthetic is that we already have something that if we were to do it, people would regard it as identifiably American, at the very least.

Sandal Pin. Courtesy of Evan Brown.

As he described it, Abd al-Karim's aesthetic was an assertion of male Blackness. This gendered racial assertiveness is a self-conscious choice that harkens to the dandyism of W. E. B. Du Bois. Du Bois's dandyism did not lie solely in his personal style (although he had that in spades) but also in what Monica Miller identifies as his rhetorical use of the dandy figure to underscore the critical "importance and necessity" of beauty, the arts, and "self-fashioning and self-re/presentation" to Black liberation in the diaspora (Miller 2009, 153–59). The Black dandy, by way of Du Bois, is not just a style maven but also an "antiracist race man" (Miller 2009). This view aligns with Abd al-Karim's interpretation of his dandyism as well as with my own reading of it. Abd al-Karim's style was an intervention into the way "we talk about culture." The "we" here is U.S. American Muslims, who idealize cultures "over there" in the Islamic elsewhere, thereby leaving U.S. Black Muslims, who have no natal ties to this elsewhere, cultureless.

This is a discourse on culture that Blacks in the United States are quite familiar with—older distinctions made between "high and low" and "civilized and primitive" cultures operate similarly. Thus Abd al-Karim's assertion works both explicitly and implicitly. He uses a suit to confront and challenge a hegemonic aesthetic that renders U.S. Black American Muslim men marginal while marking the thobe and the shalwar kameez as essentially religiously authentic and authoritative. Similarly, in a context in which Black authenticity is bound to an urban aesthetic that is criminalized, parochialized, and powerless, he puts his Black body in a suit as a direct confrontation with white supremacy. Deploying the Black dandy aesthetic, Abd al-Karim too is an "antiracist race man" (Miller 2009). Like Du Bois, he has chosen a stylistic point of view that is cosmopolitan while remaining committed to the project of Black liberation:

> And I am not saying that my aesthetic is the only iteration of [U.S. Black American Muslim style]. There are different iterations of that. . . . Even what I see in Philly, it's deeply influenced by hip hop and deeply consistent with patterns and norms of dress within African American communities, at least here in the States. I am also really intrigued with African American ability to appropriate some of the signs and symbols, signs of status, signs of acquisition of White mainstream culture and to kind of flip them; in that way, of course, the Nation of Islam is very impressive to me.

Mirroring the model he saw in Philadelphia, Abd al-Karim sought to dress in a way that was "deeply consistent with patterns and norms of dress within African American communities." This aim was a conscious effort to resist rather than capitulate to the authoritative aesthetics of Arab and South Asian American hegemonies that continually bracket off Blackness as outside "the Tradition." Abd al-Karim explained to me that when his growing authority was challenged because of his style, he initially chose to try and conform. However, this was deeply unsatisfying to him. Like Ilyas, he too had a fashion habitus—he was raised in a family in which style was a prized possession. In addition, the pressure to conform gradually lost its credibility as Abd al-Karim became a man of scholarship. He received advanced religious training in some of the historic centers of the Islamic intellectual tradition, and in these spaces he encountered "the Tradition" as diverse and dynamic in both textual and lived form.

Importantly, while his style was distinct, he noted that his was not the only or the first sartorial statement made by U.S. Black American men. He cited Philadelphia, which has a large U.S. Black American Muslim community that sets fashion trends for all Black Philadelphians. For example, a beard style popular among Black men in Philadelphia, the "Philly Beard," is also known as the "Sunnah Beard" or the "Sunni Beard" because the cut and style—full, wide, and extending beneath the chin—originated among U.S. Black Muslim men. The beard was initially known as the Sunnah because Muslim men wear facial hair as a form of piety in order to follow the Sunnah, the model of the Prophet Muhammad.[10] In a YouTube video called "The Philly Beard," non-Muslim Black men note that while they wear the beard for stylistic reasons, they are often mistaken for Muslims.

Another Philly trend I recall from the late 1990s and the early twenty-first century is young Black men wearing jeans they had cut at the ankles or right above them. The length of the jeans, again, came from a Muslim male practice of the Sunnah, but the style was worn by both Muslim and non-Muslim men. As Abd al-Karim noted, male Muslim styles in Philadelphia were linked to hip hop fashion but also to styles from the Islamic East. One of the more notable styles that was described to me is the pairing of hip hop staples, a white T-shirt and sneakers, with an *izar*, a male skirt, made of denim. Within U.S. Black American Muslim communities, Philly Muslims are noted for their construction of such creative and hybrid styles, which flip the authoritative aesthetics of multiple "mainstreams"—White U.S. American as well as Arab.[11] U.S. Black Muslim Philly styles, as Abd al-Karim noted, are located in the historic Black tradition of sartorial signifyin'. Importantly, signifyin' for U.S. Black American Muslims is an aesthetic choice that is racially and religiously significant. A denim izar looks "fresh" because it is legible in the 'hood, but it also upholds a particular interpretation of the Sunnah and thus fulfills a particular desire for piety.

Abd al-Karim ended his reflections by identifying the Nation of Islam as a particularly impressive and influential model of signifyin'. Men in the NOI, in the past and today, are distinguished in Black communities for being impeccably dressed, and they have come to be known by the refrain "Suited and Booted!" Whether featuring the uniform of the Fruit of Islam or tailored suits with bow ties and well-shined boots, the arresting image of NOI men has had a profound impact on the sartorial landscape in U.S. Black American communities. Accordingly, "suited and booted" describes not only what men in the NOI wear but also the

Suited and Booted. Courtesy of Evan Brown.

meaning made from their clothes. In his research with former members of the NOI, anthropologist Zain Abdullah's interlocutors recalled being attracted to the Nation because of how its men dressed, in "suits" and "shining boots," projecting an aura of being "clean," "intelligent," and "doing something" (Abdullah 2012). Abdullah's interviewees consistently articulate a relationship between notions of manhood and dress. Abdullah argues that to be suited and booted is to embody an "oppositional masculinity" that advances ideas of "Black beauty, intelligence and fearlessness" that oppose White authority.

To be suited and booted is to oppose White authority by taking recourse to respectability, which continues to be attractive to U.S. Black communities that understand the role of clothes in the presumption of Black inferiority and the perpetuation of racial inequality. However, drawing on the White middle-class aesthetic is not a simple capitulation to White middle-class norms but rather, as Edward Curtis has argued, the appropriation of these norms within an "Islamic matrix" to construct "a new Islamized body" (2002, 127). Hence it is important to see the suits and uniforms of the NOI as a response to ideas of Black inferiority and as a form of Muslim piety.

As I argue throughout this book, Muslim Cool is formed through a loop, which means that it is both an extension and a remix of older discursive and aesthetic traditions. Accordingly, the NOI is both an inspiration and an important precursor to the Muslim dandy. The NOI is a model of signifyin' that links the sartorial and the spiritual and offers an alternative form of pious respectability grounded in Black resistance and Black redemption.

In her work on Black dandyism, Miller identifies the Harlem Renaissance as a key moment at which the Black dandy's insistence on agency through style was actualized. From its politics to its arts to the bodies of the well-known and the unknown, the Harlem Renaissance reflected a striking assertion of Blackness. This was the renaissance of the "New Negro" in a city that no longer stood in awe or (feigned) deference to White authority. Likewise, the Nation of Islam positioned itself as a counterpoint to the politics of the "so-called Negro" who held to the hope that White authority could be reasonable and reasoned with. In contrast, the "Black Muslim" confronted white supremacy head on through the articulation of self-conscious priorities of Black resistance and Black redemption.

Placing the Muslim dandy, through the story of Abd al-Karim, beside Du Bois and the NOI underscores how sartorial questions of piety and respectability are tied to the notion of tradition—Islamic and Muslim, Black, urban, and U.S. American. Abd al-Karim's and Ilyas's stylistic choices are part of a self-conscious process of recovering a lost traditional aesthetic. Du Bois, the NOI, the Haba'ib, and the Maliki tradition form an archive of tradition recovered and remade by the Muslim dandy. Hence, through his sartorial intervention, the Muslim dandy seeks to confront White, Arab, and South Asian U.S. American supremacies by defining his own priorities. These are priorities of resistance and redemption, grounded in Blackness as a pious and respectable Muslim male style.

From a Thobe to a Boss

ILYAS: I look at myself, in terms of wearing suits. . . . I think it's the natural progression for the American man. When they say, "I'm on my grown man now," what does that entail? Like you going to be wearing Ecko and jeans? You know what I mean? If someone tells me, "I'm on my grown man tonight," what are you going to say? "Oh, you must be wearing a suit." You are not going to be chilling in a 3 XL white tee, Levi 501s, and Chuck Taylors [laughs].

As an American, I make this as a clear distinction, when people say, "Oh, where are you from?" I say, "Oh, my family?" I always say that because unlike you I fall under the perpetual foreigner syndrome. I'm just gonna be a perpetual foreigner. [They keep asking,] "No, no, like where are you from?" "I'm from Cali, man!" "Like no, no, like where?" So for me, I make it an effort, to me as an American if I'm "on my grown man" I know what grown men wear, you know what I'm saying? And that's what a professor looks like, what a CEO looks like, a CFO . . . that's what they look like: "I'm on some grown man"; "I run this." What does a boss wear? Don Corleone, they're wearing suits; [in a Godfather voice] "You come to me on my daughter's wedding day. . . ." You know what I mean? That's what bosses do . . . bow ties, ties. . . . So for me it was an evolution. I was naturally going to get here because I'm not going to be dressing "nice" as a twenty-five-year-old when I am fifty-five.

Ilyas used the suit to mark his identity as an American man. He identified part of his motivation for choosing to wear a suit as a response to the ways in which he, as an Asian U.S. American, is rendered perpetually foreign. In her concept of racial triangulation, Claire Jean Kim notes that while Asian U.S. Americans are seen positively as a model minority, they are also negatively triangulated against White and Black "nativeness" as U.S. Americans and viewed as always foreign or as immigrants.[12] Ilyas also wore the suit to mark his identity as a "grown [American] man." He identified being a "grown man" with key sites of intellectual and financial power in the United States, namely, the positions of professors and businessmen. Thus, for him a grown man was also a "boss," which is a hip hop term (also spelled "bawse") for someone who not only runs a business but is powerfully capable in all spheres of life. Ilyas also identified Don Corleone as an example of a grown man.

Don Corleone, the main protagonist in the *Godfather* trilogy, is powerful, but he wields his power through means that transgress mainstream

Americana. Corleone's immigrant background may resonate with Ilyas, whose parents were immigrants. Although Ilyas did not tie his fashion habitus to his Filipinoness beyond his immediate family, scholars of the Philippines and the Filipino diaspora in the United States have documented the ways in which "looking good" was key to Filipino "colonial negotiation and contestation" with the Spanish and later the United States. Filipino men, in particular, wore western dress as a way to mark themselves as civilized and masculine in order to bolster their claims for independence in the Philippines (Steinbock-Pratt 2015). Stateside, the value attached to looking good by Filipino dandies of the early twentieth century, which was a reassertion of middle-class status (Steinbock-Pratt 2015, 199), was read by the White majority as a threat and responded to with violence (Dunn and Shwartz 1984).[13]

Along with the Philippines and the Filipino Diaspora, Ilyas is also a member of the hip hop nation. Accordingly, I also read Ilyas's reference to Coreleone as a marker of the fact that he belongs to the hip hop generation. It is subversive power that has made Hollywood characters such as the Godfather and the role of the Italian mafia in the United States a much used trope of power within hip hop music and culture. Ilyas is not a U.S. Black American, nor is he Arab or South Asian. Moreover, he is a convert to Islam who embodies what most recognize as an urban/Black aesthetic. As such, he parallels the U.S. Black American dandy, who also lacks access to the privilege that comes with ties to the Islamic East. Ilyas identified the suit as the epitome of power, authority, and masculinity in American culture, and Abd al-Karim excavated the suit as a style that is "identifiably American, at least." For converts with no natal ties to the Islamic East, the nation becomes a critical reference point and a counter site of authenticity within the context of intraracial Muslim contestations over authority.

When putting his style into context, Abd al-Karim described the U.S. Muslim community as "growing, changing, and dealing with crisis, particularly crisis of authority." As described earlier, this is a crisis of religious authority (who has the power to decide?) that is intimately tied to notions of authenticity (what does it mean to be a real Muslim in the United States?). For U.S. Muslims, the crisis lies in determining from where authenticity and thus authority are derived. Is the source the Islamic East or an alternative site? Can authenticity and authority stem from natal distance from the Islamic East and natal proximity to the U.S. here and now? To the latter question the Muslim dandy says yes by making a claim to Muslim authenticity through a Black aesthetic and by making a claim on the U.S. nation. The Muslim dandy's invocation of the nation is an important move within the U.S. Muslim community. It is also, I suggest, an important marker of the relationship of Black Muslim maleness to the nation.

Muslim Dandies and the War on Terror

In reading the body of the young Malcolm X during World War II, Robin Kelley argues that Malcolm's wearing of a zoot suit was the embodiment of an oppositional stance to the nation. Kelley notes that the suit, which featured wide-leg pants and an equally voluminous jacket with padded shoulders, was not designed with oppositional intent but that its political content came from the young Black and Latino men who wore it (Kelley 1996). Zoot suits were seen as a "pernicious act of anti-Americanism" because the amount of fabric required to craft a zoot suit transgressed the values of thrift and economy that marked wartime sentiment (Kelley 1996). Zoot suiters were also accused of anti-Americanism because they dodged the draft, a stance taken by a cohort of U.S. Black Americans critical of fighting a White man's war (Kelley 1996).

In contrast to this use of wearing a suit to *counter* the nation, the mainstreaming of hip hop fashion marks a Black masculine *investment in* the nation, as Fleetwood illustrates (2011). She examines the clothing lines of hip hop moguls Russell Simmons (Phat Farm), Sean Combs (Sean John), and Jay-Z (Roca Wear), who have joined the fashion elite by bringing young Black styles—which appropriate the mainstream—into the mainstream. These men are behind the sartorial interventions of "classic American flava" that attempts to write Black and brown bodies into the nation. As a result, "the black male figure of hip-hop" emerges "as a possessor of a new American dream and an inheritor of the legacy of Americana" (Fleetwood 2011, 152). Critically, however, Fleetwood maintains that while such fashions represent a Black masculine investment in a multicultural United States, the new dream of Americana preserves ideals of "American privilege and domination" (Fleetwood 2011, 165).

Ideals of American privilege and domination are closely tied to American ideals of masculinity. As Ilyas's comment illustrates, a "grown man" in the United States is one who has power and who dominates. Qualities of strength, courage, bravery, might, rationality, and valor are highly prized characteristics of a man who acts for the nation, enabling U.S. success and the country's ability to dominate. As feminist scholarship has shown, women stand in for the nation and men are its patriarchs, protectors, and engines for expansion (Moallem 2005; Naber 2012).

American studies scholars have argued that in an interesting reversal, the U.S. Black American man moves from pariah to protector of the nation in early twenty-first-century cultural production (McAlister 2005; Bayoumi 2010; Alsultany 2012; Edwards 2011). Erica Edwards has noted the specific role of the figure of the Black president in Hollywood story lines that depict the United States running head first into the apocalypse. The president's Blackness on screen functions as a form of national redemption and justification for the war on terror offscreen. Edwards argues that "the image of the necessarily black presidency at the end of the world . . . normalizes state-sanctioned and state-enforced terrorism" (Edwards 2011, 48).

Similarly, in his examination of the Hollywood films *The Siege* (1998) and *The Kingdom* (2007), Moustafa Bayoumi (2010) identifies two roles for the Black male protagonist: as a leader who will not compromise democratic values even when other U.S. Americans are willing to cut corners in the name of security, and as a mentor to the newest racialized minority, the Muslim (Bayoumi 2010). By situating U.S. Black American men as protectors, this mediascape becomes a document of American exceptionalism. If those most marginalized can inhabit high office and save the nation from its own destruction, then the offscreen actions of the United States, at home and abroad, are imbued with legitimacy.

This scholarship has contributed some much needed complexity to our understanding of the positioning of the U.S. Black American vis-à-vis the U.S. nation. Yet the Muslimness of the Muslim dandy may preclude his position as the nation's redeemer. Edwards critically notes that the figure of the Black president sanctions U.S. American policing and domination abroad as well as at home, where unexceptional Black

men are still "in crisis." Indeed, the Black Hollywood protagonist reproduces the narrative and consequences of what Jodi Melamed terms neoliberal multiculturalism (2011). Neoliberal multiculturalism celebrates
appropriately enacted racial and ethnic diversity. "Exceptional" citizens
of color are privileged, which enables the negative valuation of "people
of color in the United States who do not fit the category multicultural
American, i.e., who are unassimilated, lack class privilege, or are not
citizens" (Melamed 2011, 153).

For Black Muslim men navigating the nation, their Muslim identity
continues to be a sign of the inability to assimilate. Prior to 9/11, this
failure was tied to narration of the "Black Muslim" as a dangerous sepa-
ratist. Post–9/11, the failure is the same, but it is now tied to the "crisis
of Muslim masculinity." If the crisis of Black masculinity can be encap-
sulated by the question "Why are so many Black men criminals?" the
crisis of Muslim masculinity is underpinned by the question "Why are
so many Muslim men terrorists?"

The Muslim man is an essential terrorist subject: violent, patriarchal,
dogmatic, and illiberal—a depiction that has been reinforced since the
events of 9/11 (Razack 2008; Alsultany 2012; Rana 2011).[14] Jasbir Puar
(2007) argues that dominant policy and scholarly narratives of terrorism treat it as a fundamentally masculine and Muslim domain, defined
by Muslim men's feeling of emasculation because they cannot match the
pace of the modern world. Frustrated because they cannot be properly
heterosexual, they turn to patriarchy and religion (Puar 2007). Racialized and sexualized, "Muslim masculinity is simultaneously patho-
logically excessive yet repressive, perverse yet homophobic, virile yet
emasculated, monstrous yet flaccid" (Puar 2007, xxv). Accordingly, in
the war on terror the terrorist Muslim figure is also a figure of surplus
and lack. Whereas the thug is envisioned as a failed patriarch, the terrorist is seen as a failed heterosexual.

Shantrelle Lewis defines global Black dandyism as a transnational
movement among men of the African diaspora to assert their masculinity, humanity, and Africanity. Lewis identifies this assertion of Africana
masculinity as a specific intervention in the image of the Black man as
a thug (Lewis 2015). In the case of the Black Muslim man, the dandy
aesthetic can be read as a response to his image as a thug and a terrorist.
The thug wears jeans and a T-shirt, but the Muslim dandy is suited and

booted. The terrorist wears a thobe, but the Muslim dandy wears a Dr. J throwback. Since Black dandyism is an act of signifyin', Lewis describes the Africana dandy as a trickster manipulating "clothing and attitude to exert his agency rather than succumb to the limited ideals placed on him by society" (Lewis 2015). This is also a useful reading of the Muslim dandy across race. The Muslim dandy confronts intersecting hegemonies of race, gender, religion, and nation by using style to make his own claim to U.S. American Muslim masculinity.

SCENE 5: RAJOOLAH

(In this scene I play a young Black Muslim dandy. At the start of the scene I am holding a cane, frozen stage right. A Miles Davis track plays and I walk around the stage examining items in a high-end men's boutique.)

(Turning to the imaginary shopkeeper offstage) No, thank you. I'm just browsing. (Music fades off)

(Stops)

Maaaaaaan! These shoes are *nice*!

Looks like something the shaykh was rocking last time I saw him.

(Turns to audience)

No, he's not that kind of shaykh, not a scholar of religion, a scholar of *style*—haha!—but Alhamdulillah, he's good brother, who always be on the set and stays dipped—knows how to be Muslim without losing your *soul* . . . get it?

And that can happen, ironically enough, finding Islam and losing your soul. And one of the first ways you can tell—see your soul receding—is in your style. . . . You see me today, a three-piece tweed Ralph Lauren suit, modern fit; crisp Armani shirt; skinny Jaan J. non-silk tie; sandal pin cuff links; and . . . this Brooks Brothers pocket square—a nice contrast, wouldn't you say? And some of that private reserve Cambodi oud, keeping a brother smelling as good as he looks, nah mean? And a walking stick for good measure. . . . You see me today and you could say I take cues from hustlers and the Haba'ib, but it took me a minute to get back here.

(Sits down on a chair stage left, facing the audience)

You see, I wasn't always a Muslim. I grew up on the South Side, in my grandmama's house, me, my mother, and the twins. We didn't have much but my grandmother, mother, all the women in my family were very stylish people. Grandma in particular set the standard. My grandfather had style, too. . . . He died when I was fairly young but he looms large in my child-hood memories, a towering figure, always, I mean always in a suit! At his funeral, I tugged on my mother and asked, "When is granddaddy gonna get up?" I didn't understand death yet and since he was always in a suit, I just assumed he slept in one, too! So between my grandparents and then my mother I kind of inherited the style gene.

(Gets up and uses the length of the stage)

. . . And then there was the hustlers. It's kind of crazy when you think of it, despite the griminess of their exploits they were always real clean with theirs—style that made a statement. You know, I would say my first impression of Islam was also about style; those NOI brothers, man! suited and booted—though they didn't dress with the flair of the hustlers, their competition for souls, but they made an distinct impression on me. But it wasn't until my senior year in high school that I really considered Islam, Sunni Islam, for myself.

At first, I didn't change anything really, but then as I got to know the "rules" . . . well. Like this one time: I was going to jummah as a Muslim for the first time, it was October, and I was dressed in my Friday best, so to speak. Freshly pressed slacks, olive green corduroy jacket—kind with the el-bow pads, pink oxford shirt, cream Nautica sweater-vest pullover. I thought I looked really good, but when I get there this brother comes up to me, pulls me to the side, and without a hint of laughter in his eyes goes, "You know we don't celebrate Halloween, right?"

Halloween?! Halloween?! Here I am trying to get my grown man—André 3000—on, in my best clothes! And *he* thinks it's a costume?!

So I learned real quick that dressing like that was not gonna earn me my bones with the brothas. And I wanted to earn my bones, these were my people and I wanted to fit in. But when I think about it, I kinda knew my gear would seem bogus to these particular Muslims—at a storefront mas-jid in the 'hood—because as a general rule, it's the pookies of the world that become Muslim, not the Trumps. . . . It always had seemed to me that Islam was kind of a 'hood religion, and as a young man this appealed to me; I wanted to be 'hood. Now I mean I grew up in the 'hood, we Black folk, we live together, the poor among us and those with some pocket change, but I didn't live in the Greens! That's a whole 'nother level of the game . . . and I wanted to live that life, I wanted to be real, be authentic, and be a *man*. . . .

And so to fit in I went between two looks: wearing a turban and an Arab or going straight Deobandi in a turban and shalwar kameez. Neither look really screams Blackness, masculinity, or poverty, except of course that all the really down brothas with the juice wore them—and to my mind, at the time, they also screamed "tradition," and in them I felt authentic and I felt like I belonged.

Yet I later learned that while I belonged I wasn't as authentic as I thought.

(Sits down on a chair stage left, facing the audience)

I actually ended up in Yemen, Tarim, to study the deen. And there I encountered the Haba'ib, they are sort of a priestly family, claim descent from the Prophet, and are known for great knowledge and piety. And those brothers . . . are sharp! If you see one of the Haba'ib you'll see him in a thobe and jubba, which is sort of like a long and light coat, and they are of the finest cottons. And on his shoulder right or left will be a folded Yemeni shawl, And on the heads of the Haba'ib is a turban, white and spotless, layered and folded with such precision and distinction. And on the right hand, silver ring. And they rock canes . . . these brothers are nice with theirs!

Here I am thinking piety equals poverty of style, and the model of the Haba'ib was all about *izar an-ni'mah*, like it says in the Qur'an (recites) *wa amma bi ni'mati rabbika fahaddith!* The bounty of your Lord, let it be known! And this wasn't no prosperity gospel, it was about stylistic dignity and beauty, ihsan, excellence, that reminds the wearer and the one who sees him of Allah's awesomeness.

So I am back home now, and rocking this suit . . .

(Stands)

And yes, brothas still giving me shade. Looking at me like, "Who do you think you are? Putting on airs? Acting like a bint?" But I ain't takin' no shorts from no one, so I meet them, bar for bar, like, "Nigga, please! You on Eighty-Seventh and Stoney dressed like you should be some street peddler in Karachi, and *you* giving *me* the side eye? Pshh! I studied with giants and you don' even know it. I was the shaykh's prized pupil and you don' even know it. I got license to teach *fiqh* [Islamic law] and you don' even know it. I speak the language of the Prophet and you. Don't. Even. Know. It.

Well, no, I don't use those words exactly, that wouldn't be ihsan, but the sentiment is there. And yeah, I'm coming a little hard, but what gives them the right to judge me? To question my Islam? To question my manhood? To question my belonging? All because of what I am wearing? Who said real

On the Corner. Courtesy of Evan Brown.

Islam can only come in a thobe, a turban, and some broken English? Who said in order to be down you had to be down and out? Who said manhood meant being hard all the time? Who? Who said that? I don't know who said it but I'm sure it wasn't the Prophet.

(Turns to imaginary shopkeeper)

Excuse me, do you have these shoes in a 12? (Miles Davis plays and fades)

END SCENE

5

The Limits of Muslim Cool

After settling into my economy-class seat for the long haul flight to London in April 2014, I opened up my iPad to peruse, with a fair bit of chagrin, a recently released 104-page U.S. Department of State digital publication entitled *American Muslims*. The design quality of the color- and photo-filled report was impressive. Beyond its design, one of the first things that struck me about the report was how it represented the racial and ethnic diversity of U.S. American Muslim communities. Specifically, the booklet included U.S. Black Muslim narratives. This jumped out at me from the photos used, including one of Ibtihaj Muhammad, a member of the U.S. national fencing team, to the individuals profiled, such as magazine editor Tayyibah Taylor. Likewise, a U.S. Black American, the Harvard-trained historian Precious Muhammad, had penned one of the reflective autobiographical articles in the publication. Although she was the sole Black Muslim who had written for the booklet (and whose other publications were cited in the "Want to know more?" reference section), this remains a significant inclusion that stands in stark contrast to the many ways in which Blackness is marginalized or rendered invisible in U.S. Muslim communities and the broader U.S. discourse about Muslims.

Another remarkable characteristic of the report—and this was the source of my chagrin—was that it explicitly highlighted Chicago and indirectly appropriated Muslim Cool. While the organizations and individuals profiled in the report came from across the United States, Chicago was the only city that was specifically highlighted as a symbol of American exceptionalism. For example, echoing the celebration of the United States as a multicultural nation, the report quoted a local Chicago Muslim leader heralding the city: "There is no other place where Muslims from different parts of the world have established one community with so much diversity"(2014, 38).[1] The booklet and the four short videos that accompanied it online (U.S. Department of State 2014) also prominently feature IMAN, IMAN's Executive Director, Dr. Rami Na-shashibi, and Muslim hip hop artists, citing their contributions to U.S. American society as symbols of successful Muslim integration in the multicultural fabric of the United States.[2] In this report, then, the figures, institutions, and movements that I had identified as the vanguard of Muslim Cool—because they engage Blackness to offer a counternarrative to hegemonies that produce unequal power relations—were strategically deployed to reinforce the hegemonic power of the state.

This booklet was not designed for domestic consumption but for U.S. embassies abroad, yet I first found out about it through postings on my Facebook timeline. Friends and colleagues, some of whom contributed to the publication, were celebrating the report as a symbol of inclusion and recognition by the U.S. government. The fortuitous timing of my reading of the report, on the eve of my U.K. trip, and its explicit and subtle references to my field sites and to Muslim Cool, gave fresh urgency to the questions that had led me to the United Kingdom. I was on my way to follow a multicity tour of U.S. American artists, six of whom were Muslim, which was sponsored by the U.S. embassy in the United Kingdom. I decided to follow these U.S. American Muslim artists to a different context, that of the United Kingdom, in order to explore how Muslim Cool travels beyond the United States. My interest in the circulation of Muslim Cool outside the United States was sparked by my interactions with non-U.S. Muslim artists who performed and participated in IMAN's arts and culture work while I was in the field. I found that although they were from different contexts, including the United Kingdom, they were still doing Muslim Cool; their identities as Muslims were being forged through the loop of hip hop, Islam, and Blackness.

I also met the U.S. American artists on tour in the United Kingdom through my relationship with IMAN. Each of these artists had an individual music career, but they were on tour as members of the FEW Collective, a group of artists that had expanded in membership since the 2007 ISNA convention mentioned earlier. These artists were politically conscious and had multiple motivations for participating in the tour—none of which was to endorse U.S. foreign policies. The tour was an opportunity to do a gig, to expand their international audiences, and to connect with like-minded artists and activists in the United Kingdom. These were not the first U.S. Muslims to participate in what scholars and

the state call "hip hop diplomacy." The State Department's hip hop ambassador program began in 2005 with a non-Muslim U.S. Black American female activist, Toni Blackman. But over the years these tours have
taken U.S. Muslim hip hop artists, predominantly U.S. Black men, to a
number of Muslim-majority locations such as Turkey, Morocco, Indonesia, Pakistan, and the Occupied Territories. Twenty-first-century hip
hop diplomacy reenacts the jazz diplomacy of the Cold War era. At that
time the U.S. State Department deployed jazz artists as part of a cultural
offensive against the Soviet Union. "Jazz ambassadors," particularly U.S.
Black American artists, were used to counter the perception that the
United States was a racist nation, a perception the Soviets attempted
to use to their advantage (Von Eschen 2004). In the post–civil rights
and post–9/11 era, hip hop has similarly served as a tool of the broader
agenda of cultural diplomacy. It has been deployed by the state to manage the U.S. profile abroad but also to manage young Muslims who are
perceived as potential terrorists (Aidi 2014, 225). Critically, in this management of an imperial relationship with the "Muslim world," U.S. Muslims have become a strategic asset for the state's efforts to "reform" Islam
outside the United States.

This chapter, through a look at IMAN and the Muslim hip hop
tours, examines Muslim Cool's relationship to the state on two scales—
the domestic and the global. It also looks at this relationship temporally; specifically, I question how this post–civil rights and post–9/11
moment creates the possibility for Muslim Cool to tell a counternarrative to anti-Black racial and religious hegemonies while simultaneously telling the hegemonic narrative of the state. As Stuart Hall (1998)
insightfully noted, popular cultural forms are always in a tactical relationship with power. Thus, the utility in investigating the possible limits of Muslim Cool lies not in declaring Muslim Cool, IMAN, or this
cadre of U.S. American Muslim artists complicit with the state—which
would divert attention away from the real holders of power. Rather, it
lies in charting the context that engenders the limits of Muslim Cool's
alterity.

I illustrate how Muslim Cool's claim to alterity hits a stumbling block,
a wall, or a tension in its encounters with the state. The state, and the
power it enacts, is not contained by the various arms of the U.S. government but rather is a "complex formation" (Hall 1996, 429) that "has no

institutional fixity" (Trouillot 2001, 126). Importantly, the state's lack of "fixedness" is not a weakness but the source of its power. Examining Gramsci's formulation as it relates to the modern state, Hall argues that the hegemony of the liberal democratic state is "sustained, not exclusively through the enforced instrumentality of the state [i.e., force and coercion], but rather, it is grounded in the relations and institutions of civil society" (Hall 1996, 428).

Gramsci's formulation also insists on the recognition that hegemony is "historically specific" (Hall 1996, 424). This is important, because the U.S. hegemony that Muslim Cool must contend with is post–civil rights and post–9/11. This periodization is critical because it is a marker of how regimes of surveillance and multiculturalism coexist and complement claims of U.S. exceptionalism, and these are claims made through the incorporation of dissent. Institutions of civil society, nonprofits such as IMAN, are incorporated within the state's technologies of governmentality (Kwon 2013). Likewise, the symbols and signs of marginalized groups such as U.S. Black Americans are incorporated to authenticate the "legitimacy and social completeness" of the United States (Greenhouse 2005, 359). At this historically specific moment, U.S. American Muslims are deployed as a "critical component of the late American empire's cultural repertoire" (Aidi 2014, 257). They symbolize the success of U.S. multicultural inclusion and are evidence of the fitness of the United States as the dominant global power.

In the first half of this chapter I address the limits of Muslim Cool within the United States. I look at the construction of Muslim Cool as an alternative and as resistance through the deployment of the Black radical tradition in the arts activism of IMAN. I show that because of the paradox of the post–civil rights era, IMAN's connection to the Black radical tradition is in tension with IMAN's status as a nonprofit and with its commitment to a rights-based discourse of critical engagement, which results in an alignment with state objectives of subjectification—the cultivation of citizens as subjects who reproduce the state's hegemonic power. In the second part of the chapter, I chart the contested context of U.S. American Muslim participation in cultural diplomacy. I argue that the political realities of the post–civil rights and post–9/11 United States cut a hard bargain to belong for U.S. American Muslims.

The Black Radical Genealogy of the Muslim Hip Hop Generation

On a yellow notepad I quickly jotted down some notes on Imam Talib's talk "Artists of the Hip Hop Generation and Liberation." I was still working at IMAN at this time, and Imam Talib was at the IMAN office for an "artists' brunch." The brunch had been designed by Nashashibi as an intimate conversation between Imam Talib and a select group of about fifteen young Muslims, including Man-O-Wax, Tasleem, and Tyesha. These artists had been invited to the brunch because of their long-standing relationship to IMAN's work and to the Muslim hip hop scenes in Chicago and beyond. For Nashashibi, closeness between scholars such as Imam Talib, artists such as Tasleem, and activists such as himself was the bedrock of IMAN's work. Yet he was not the only one invested in building these relationships. Imam Talib had been working since the 1990s to instruct and support musicians and performers who had converted to Islam and who, as Imam Talib explained, were seeking spiritual balance while working within an industry that was hostile to the moral code they struggled to live by. For the artists in the IMAN conference room that morning, the talk was like a port in a storm, a refuge from the kind of policing described earlier.

The central focus of Imam Talib's presentation was the hip hop generation. He drew on religious and secular texts to impress upon us that we were part of a generation—the hip hop generation—and had to be attentive to the opportunities and responsibilities that came with our generational location. Specifically, he cited the Qur'anic verse 2:141 (trans. Muhammad Asad): "Now those people who have passed away: unto them shall be accounted what they have earned; and unto you, what you have earned; and you will not be judged on the strength of what they did." He amplified the point by referencing Frantz Fanon: "Each generation must, out of relative obscurity, discover its mission, fulfill it or betray it" (Fanon [1963] 2005, 206).

During his lecture Imam Talib suggested that the hip hop generation should take its cues from earlier generations, such as the *Salaf as-Salih* and Black Power activists. The term Salaf as-Salih, "the pious predecessors," is used by Muslims to denote the first three generations of Muslims—those who were companions of the Prophet Muhammad and the two generations that followed, all of whom are widely revered

in Sunni Muslim tradition. Linking the Salaf to the hip hop generation, Imam Talib highlighted the role of the arts and artists among the
Salaf: "The *Rasul* [Prophet] recited poetry at [the battle of] Uhud to lift
the spirits of the troops. . . . Prophet Muhammad loved the poetry of
Umayyah Ibn Abi as-Salt and Ka'b Ibn Malik, and Hasan Ibn Thabit,
whose skills were so sublime the Prophet had another *minbar* [pulpit]
built for him." Likewise, Imam Talib linked the hip hop generation to the
Black Power movement through the arts, specifically citing the poetry
ensemble The Last Poets, established in the late 1960s, and the role it
played as part of the Black Arts Movement.

His lecture was emphatic in its claim that artists play a critical role in
the struggle against injustice. This role, Imam Talib argued, is described
in the Qur'an (22:78, trans. Muhammad Asad): "And strive hard in God's
cause with all the striving that is due to Him: It is He who has elected
you [to carry his message], and has laid no hardship on you in [any-
thing that pertains to] religion, [and made you follow] the creed of your
forefather Abraham." Drawing on this verse and the model provided
by the earlier generations of artist-activists, Imam Talib contended that
the hip hop generation had a specific and momentous role to fulfill. He
maintained that Muslim hip hop artists are a part of a historical "con-
tinuum . . . back through African American history, back to West Africa,
back to the Prophet. There is no reason whatsoever why the young Muslim artists of this day and time, like their ancestors, the Last Poets, and
like their ancestors, the Griots of Muslim West Africa, there is no reason
why they should not be doing the same exact thing."

Imam Talib asserted that Muslim hip hop practice is genealogically
linked to Muslim tradition because it participates in a history of Muslim
artistic production as the work of liberation—*art as activism*. This genealogy of art as activism locates the Muslim hip hop generation within
multiple lines of descent: as descendants of the transnational and tran-
shistorical Islamic tradition by way of the Salaf but also as descendants
of the African diaspora by way of the West African Griots and as inheri-
tors of the Black radical tradition by way of the Last Poets. Imam Talib
claimed this genealogy for Muslim hip hop artists irrespective of their
contemporary racialized position. However, beyond the multiethnic
Salaf, his genealogical narrative privileges Muslim arts rooted in Africa
and the African diaspora.

Imam Talib's genealogy was designed with the Muslim hip hop artist in mind, yet he was not the first to identify a "hip hop generation." In his critical study of hip hop's relationship to politics and culture, Bakari Kitwana defines the hip hop generation as "young African Americans born between 1965 and 1984 who came of age in the eighties and nineties and who share a specific set of values and attitudes" (Kitwana 2002, 4). This definition is useful but, as Jeff Chang (2005) notes, also contested because of who might be excluded from its purview, such as hip hop legends who are Puerto Rican or born before 1965 and those born after 1984, like my younger cohort of teachers who are multiethnic millennials who came of age after hip hop made the commercial mainstream (Clay 2012). Therefore, Chang uses the term "hip hop generation" less in terms of a specific timeline and more in relation to a set of social shifts, "the turn from politics to culture [and] the process of entropy and reconstruction" that define the United States in the post–civil rights era (Chang 2005, 2).

These divergent definitions reflect diversity within the hip hop generation. This diversity is tied to hip hop's ascendance as a popular culture form, encompassing an older hip hop generation that came of age when hip hop was at the periphery of the White U.S. American mainstream and a younger cohort for whom hip hop *is* the mainstream. My teachers came from both groups, and accordingly I use the term the "hip hop generation" in acknowledgment of the similarities and differences that define the hip hop generation across race, class, gender, and age as well as the dialogic relationship between different hip hop generations, especially as I experienced this in the field. Whatever the timeline, like Imam Talib's genealogy, these parallel definitions juxtapose the hip hop generation with the generation that immediately precedes it—namely, the activists of the civil rights era. Scholarly analysis frames hip hop and hip hop activism in relation to these previous generations and the paradox that defines our current moment—the post–civil rights era (Chang 2005; Kitwana 2002; Rose 1994; Neal 2001).

The paradox of the post–civil rights era is rooted primarily in the era's concurrent gains and losses in racial equality. As Kitwana argues, the hip hop generation is the beneficiary of the legal successes of the civil rights movement: "voting rights, affirmative action, rise of black elected officials," and the limited expansion of economic opportunity that has led to the growth of a small Black economic elite (2002, 147–48). This is an elite that comprises, among others, Black American entertainers and athletes whose success is a hallmark of what Cornel West has termed the "AfroAmericanization of White youth": a process through which styles originated by Black American youth "have become disproportionately influential in shaping popular culture" (West 1994, 10). I understand this AfroAmericanization as the instrumentalization of Blackness, described earlier, which extends the historic love and theft of Blackness (Lott 2013) into the twenty-first century so that Blackness becomes, once again, a globally traded commodity as a piece of Americana. Yet these signs of "progress" parallel, and often obscure, continued racial discrimination in the form of disparities in health, housing, education, and employ-ment, punitive laws and policing practices that target Black and Latin@ youth, astronomical rates of Black and Latin@ incarceration (despite a general downward trend in crime rates), and the broader criminaliza-tion of Black youth in the popular imagination of the United States.

This paradox shapes hip hop activism in two specific ways. As a post–civil rights generation, the hip hop generation is unable to accept fully the easy binary of resistance and cooptation that defined the civil rights era (Kitwana 2002).[3] At the same time, hip hop activism is evaluated on the basis of the success—material, imagined, and commodified—of the civil rights and Black Power era activists (Clay 2012).[4] Hip hop activism, then, is located amid the tensions between the desire for a deeply equi-table world, different levels of entanglement with the current political, economic, and social world orders, and nostalgia for a populist radical-ism. This holds true for IMAN as it does for the broader hip hop genera-tion; for them, the civil rights-Black Power era, particularly Black Power activism, is central to the engagement of art as activism.

Muslim Arts Activism and the Black Arts Movement

I see the role of the arts at IMAN and in the work of the Muslim hip hop artists I met in the field as a partial extension of the Black Arts Move-ment, the cultural arm of the Black Power Movement. The Black Power Movement is the late twentieth-century articulation of the Black radi-cal tradition. The Black radical tradition reconfigures the boundaries and institutions of the nation-state through Black consciousness and a political agenda that is transnational and diasporic in scope. My understanding of the Black Radical tradition encompasses the ever-palpable undercurrent of resistance and revolt that informs the Black experience across the Black Atlantic. Thus, the Black radical tradition includes resistance to white supremacy forged by enslaved African Muslims in forms that encompass both the extraordinary and the everyday—from armed revolt in Bahia to the maintenance of *zakat* (almsgiving) traditions in Sapelo Island to the Black Power Movement and related movements today (Robinson 2000; Gomez 2005; Diouf 2013).

The Black Power Movement denotes the activists and organizations that emerged after the assassination of Malcolm X and whose "collective thrust . . . toward racial pride, strength and self-definition" positioned them as his heirs (Van Deburg 1993, 2). The Black Power Movement is often presented as the counterpoint to the civil rights movement. Whereas the civil rights leadership advocated nonviolence, Black Power activists trained for self-defense; whereas civil rights tactics were often mired in respectability politics, Black Power activists took pride in vernacular and Afrocentric aesthetics; and while the civil rights movement demanded rights as citizens, Black Power activists organized for worldwide revolution (Van Deburg 1993).

The art of the Black Arts Movement, whether poetry, music, or literature, was oppositional at its core because it was explicitly designed to raise the consciousness of the masses by disrupting white supremacist narratives about Black people—narratives circulating within as well as outside Black communities. This art was also generative: artists such as Amiri Baraka and Sonia Sanchez created new interpretations of the poetic form and articulated an aesthetic grounded in the U.S. Black experience. The Black Arts Movement targeted "the cultural arena as the primary site of political action" and advocated "a cultural revolution in art and ideas" (Larry Neal, quoted in Ongiri 2009, 90–117). Like their Black Arts predecessors, my U.S. American Muslim arts activist teachers also saw the arts as a critical field of contestation. The arts became a site where hip hop generation Muslims could mount challenges to the interlocking hegemonies of white supremacy and of Arab and South Asian U.S. American Muslims. Likewise, Man-O-Wax's Turntable *dhikr*, described earlier, and the Arabized graffiti that adorns the wall of IMAN's office are just two examples of how their art is also generative. These similarities showed me how Muslim Cool's alterity was constructed through the Black radical tradition.

To illustrate this dynamic I turn to two examples of IMAN's arts activism: Community Café (CC), a recurring performance event, and a summer program, Leaders of the New School (LONS). Community Café, which took place about every other month, was one of IMAN's signature events that showcased Muslim and/or socially conscious artists. Yet CC was always more than a pure performance event; it was designed to be a symbolically powerful space for making meaning and fostering unity among U.S. Muslims—which is why all promotional materials for the event while I was in the field featured "unity" within the word "Community" in bold type. Crucially, this meaning and this unity were forged through symbolic uses of the Black Radical tradition, exemplifying Muslim Cool's alterity.

For example, not too long after I left my first long stint in field, I was asked to cohost IMAN's first CC in New York City.[5] I am sure I was asked because I am a native New Yorker with fairly extensive connections to NYC Muslims thanks to my activist mother. The NYC CC was themed "Living the Legacy," and it was held in 2009 at the site of Malcolm X's assassination, the Audubon Ballroom, newly remodeled and renamed the Malcolm X and Dr. Betty Shabazz Memorial Center. The remodeled theater is a large room with wood flooring and seating for about three hundred (in black plastic and metal chairs—the good kind), though I am sure that the crowd that night was closer to five hundred. On one side of the room are large windows that look out onto Broadway, and along the other side is a 63-inch panoramic mural that depicts scenes from the lives of the center's namesakes, including iconic images of Malcolm X preaching to an outdoor crowd in Harlem and of him in Nigeria wearing a turban and a West African caftan in 1964.

The promotional materials and program for this CC also featured a head shot of Malcolm X along with a collage of head shots of myself and my cohost, Cap D; DJs K-Salaam and Ali Shaheed Muhammad; members of the Afro-Native group Three Generationz; the hip hop legend Popmaster Fabel; and the underground hip hop giant Brother Ali—all of whom, like Malcolm X, are Muslim. Malcolm X's image was above the others, which made it appear as if he was looking down, perhaps pleased, upon the next generation, the hip hop generation. I was not

Flier for 2009 Community Café in New York. Courtesy of IMAN.

Community Café, New York, January 2009. Courtesy of Author.

involved in the planning for this event, but I know that the choice of location was very deliberate. As the site of IMAN's first CC in NYC, which
itself was part of a larger effort to bring IMAN's model to New York,
this venue introduced IMAN by locating it within Malcolm X's legacy of
Black Radical resistance.

Similarly, the Black radical tradition was the centerpiece of a CC in
celebration of Black history month. This CC was held in coordination
with DePaul University at the university's Reskin Theater. The program
for the CC featured a black-and-white collage of iconic images: a laughing Malcolm X and Martin Luther King Jr. at their first and only face-to-
face meeting; Coretta Scott King speaking at an antiwar rally just weeks
after her husband's assassination; a pensive Angela Davis in 1969; the
classic H. Rap Brown donning black shades in 1967; an afroed Arthur
Ashe holding his 1975 Wimbledon trophy; Chuck Berry posing for his
1959 single, "Johnny B. Goode"; an early photo of Afrika Bambaataa
throwing up the P-Funk sign; and MC Lyte in the early 1990s. Deploying
Black U.S. American icons for Black history month has become so com-

Flier for February 2008 Community Café. Courtesy of IMAN.

mon that images like these are used in all corners from big business to the political right in the United States. But whereas some corporations, pundits, and politicians use Black U.S. American figures to reproduce their own economic and political power, I read the aim of this collage as one of alterity—evoking the Black Radical tradition as resistance.

The collage linked the radical Black politics of figures such as Davis, Brown, and Malcolm X to Berry's musical genius, which stands as a counterpoint to histories that write Blackness out of rock and roll. The collage also featured Bambaataa and Lyte, who are hip hop pioneers—a status derived both from their musical consciousness raising and from their activist contributions to hip hop. The inclusion of Bambaataa *and* Lyte departed from the tendency to represent hip hop as a male enterprise. It was also a visual representation of the hip hop genera-tion's genealogical connection to the civil rights and Black Power activ-ists through arts activism, which is key to the construction of Muslim Cool's alterity.

This construction of Muslim Cool as an alternative and as resistance also took place though the deployment of the Black Radical tradition in the work of the artists who performed at CC. These artists were often

THE LIMITS OF MUSLIM COOL | 191

hip hop emcees and poets, known within Muslim circuits but also in underground and conscious hip hop circles. Over the years of my field research and beyond, the roster for Community Café included Amir Sulaiman, The Reminders, members of Jurassic 5, Cap D, MTeam, Brother Ali, Pop Master Fabel, and others. The lineups also included song and storytelling ensembles such as Three Generationz, who performed at the NYC CC, and the theater troupe Progress Theater, who performed at the Black History Month CC and also a year later at a CC honoring "Mothers of the Movement." These U.S. American Muslim artists used their art as a form of activism. Their work is "consciousness raising" because they push their audiences to reconsider the dominant narratives of power. They challenge hegemonies in the footsteps of the Black Arts Movement.

For example, Amir Sulaiman, a spoken-word poet who came to prominence by appearing on Def Poetry Jam and performs frequently at CC and other IMAN events, always delivers work that is hard hitting and boundary-challenging—in both content and cadence. In verses that challenge the contemporary discourse that links acts of terrorism to Islam and Muslims, Sulaiman proclaims:

> From South Street to Central Road, we are shook in a trauma
> Of terrorism that precedes Al Qaeda and Osama
> Forget Bin Laden; Ben Franklin
> Enslaved my great-great-grandmamma, comma
> Great-great-grandfather, comma
> Indigenous nations of reservations, comma (Sulaiman 2007)

Likewise, Maimouna Youssef, who has performed at CC as part of Three Generationz and as a solo artist, offers a stinging critique of culture-of-poverty narratives in her cover of Lorde's Grammy Award-nominated song "Royals." Renaming the track "*We're Already* Royals," Youssef, who has also been nominated for a Grammy, flips Lorde's song on its head. The original song offered a now common critique of commercial hip hop music's preoccupation with money and consumer goods—a critique that is an extension of an older castigation of the Black poor. Youssef gives a withering rejoinder by reminding her listeners who has the "real paper":

> We don't know that old true blue blood slave money
> war heroes take it to their grave money
> cotton money/cane money
> Diamond blood stain money
> . . . .
> what about that tax money
> oil money
> Africa's rich soil money
> so thick you can't fold money
> British East Indian company old money
> Gold money
> Lime stone
> Coal money (Youssef 2014)

The use of the Black Arts Movement's consciousness-raising strategies was also central to IMAN's youth development work while I was in the field. Participating in a national trend (Clay 2012) that uses hip hop and spoken-word poetry to empower and organize young people, this programming linked the arts and community organizing as a means of developing youth as leaders in their communities. At IMAN and some of its partner organizations on the Southwest Side, young people would discover and/or refine their writing and performance skills through free writing workshops, paid writing internships, regularly scheduled open mic events, and special events such as community forums in local schools. Most of these events took place in the neighborhood, but there were also times when my teachers were invited to suburban Muslim communities to perform at small youth-centered activities as well as large formal banquets.

Toward the end of my fieldwork I attended a few of the early group meetings of IMAN's then newly formed Leaders of the New School (LONS). LONS was a summer artist apprenticeship program that was designed to raise the consciousness of participants through a range of arts-based activities that "teach youth how ideology shapes" their lives and their neighborhoods (Clay 2012, 52). LONS was part of revamped youth development programming at IMAN that focused on distinct levels of engagement, from drop-ins to the appointment of a youth member to IMAN's board of directors. These levels of progressive engagement

were designed to keep youth involved in IMAN's work over a long trajectory.[6] LONS brought together a group of mentors and young people
who were interested in various artistic forms that aligned with the elements of hip hop: movement, vocal performance, music, and visual art.
As an artist apprenticeship program, it connected youth with particular
mentors based on their interests; thus a young woman who was a poet
and singer was mentored by two vocal performance instructors, a poet
and an emcee, both of whom had had formal theater training.

While giving youth the opportunity to explore their interests in the
arts was a central organizing aspect of the program, LONS was about
more than "just art." In line with the positive youth development trend
among nonprofits, LONS activities did promote youth self-expression,
yet these activities were also geared toward getting young people to
think collectively. Unity was repeatedly emphasized in the LONS sessions I attended, reflecting the implicit understanding of arts activism
at IMAN as being in line with the Black radical tradition: consciousness
raising for collective action. In this model, as in that of the Last Poets
ensemble, it is not the singular artist who changes the world but rather
the collective—which is not uniform but united like the fingers in a fist.

LONS brought together the older and younger segments of the hip
hop generation, and the first LONS meeting I attended took place in
the same IMAN conference room in which Imam Talib had lectured.
The first exercise, guided by Man-O-Wax, was a mix between charades
and Pictionary: the young people used their bodies and the large paper
notepad on the easel to get the others to guess their nicknames or stage
names. For example, one b-girl apprentice went by the stage name
Steady Rock. It was challenging to give clues for her name pictorially, but
ultimately (and with much hilarity) the group guessed her name. This
activity had all the elements of a standard youth development exercise:
it broke the ice, created a shared experience, and pushed folks to be creative in performing or visually representing their names (or in creating
names for those who had yet to do so).

We then moved outside to the parking lot to do another exercise,
led by one of the vocal performance teachers. I joined Rabia, Latifah,
Naeemah, and the other youth participants, who were a mix of male
and female, Black, Latin@ and South Asian (i.e. Rabia), and Muslim and
non-Muslim. We were instructed to cross our arms and hold hands, take

a deep breath, close our eyes, and count, going around the circle one by one. The youth laughed a lot. We all laughed a lot. We barely got to twenty, and the instructor lightly reprimanded us, saying that a group our size should have gotten to fifty. We did not, he surmised, because we felt insecure and vulnerable holding hands with people we had just met. This exercise also had the hallmarks of positive youth development and consciousness raising in that it pushed participants outside their comfort zones *and* raised the issue of how to build unity—implicitly introducing the challenge of working collectively. Since LONS was an apprenticeship program, many LONS sessions included mentors and mentees only, but at the group sessions that I attended the strategy of promoting collective work was maintained. From free writes to yoga, to a discussion on gender prompted by Steady Rock who wanted to know, "Where are the b-girls?" while the group watched a movie about hip hop dance, LONS was a program to develop artist activists.

Although LONS began toward the end of my time in Chicago, it stands as the culmination of IMAN's youth-focused programming that was being developed while I was in the field. The centrality of consciousness-raising art as a mobilizing precursor to collective action at IMAN is a marker of the imprint of the Black Arts Movement and illustrates how IMAN's arts activism—from its venues and publicity to its programs and performers—evoked the Black radical tradition. The claims made on the Black radical tradition by the Muslim hip hop generation, as exemplified by IMAN, do important discursive work—work that constitutes Muslim Cool as a counterpoint. However, IMAN's arts activism is only a partial extension of the Black Arts Movement and the Black radical tradition more broadly. Its partiality is rooted in a critical shift that defines the post–civil rights era: the domestication of racial politics in the United States.

Limiting Muslim Cool at Home

Looking back at my initial response to the State Department report I described at the beginning of this chapter, I should not have been too surprised to find IMAN featured in such a document. Its inclusion matches the narrative that has already been constructed around IMAN in mainstream media and some academic work—including, to a certain extent, this monograph. This storyline often centers on Rami Nashashibi's biography (much to his chagrin) and focuses primarily on IMAN's work with the arts, youth, and interfaith engagement in a way that positions the organization as a signpost of the coming of a "uniquely diverse, inclusive *American* Islam" (Warren 2010; emphasis mine). Critically, in this telling the conditions of racial inequality that IMAN seeks to impact become just the backdrop to a triumphant American (Muslim) narrative.

Of course, for IMAN the conditions of racial inequality are not a backdrop but the organization's raison d'être. Yet to be fair, this narrative of "the triumph to come" aligns in some ways with the story IMAN tells about itself. Nashashibi, who wrote an article on IMAN for the State Department publication, guides IMAN's work through the prism of what he calls "critical engagement" for U.S. American Muslims (Nashashibi 2005). This theory of engagement is undergirded by the ever-present and urgent reality that Muslim claims to U.S. belonging are contested. Nashashibi argues that in order to solidify their position as U.S. Americans, U.S. Muslims must engage the political process and the institutions of civil society, much as other historically marginalized groups have done and continue to do: "From 19th-century anti-slavery activists to 20th-century social reformers like Dorothy Day, Malcolm X and Martin Luther King, Jr., people of different faith communities have been at the center of such social activism. Today American Muslims are a growing part of this tradition" (U.S. Department of State 2014).

Two of the three references in Nashashibi's genealogy of faith-based activism are iconic leaders of the Black liberation struggle in the United States. This is reflective of his own thinking and the way IMAN's work and Muslim Cool more broadly are inspired by and seek to connect to Black freedom struggles. Nashashibi is, of course, a hip hop head, and so his nod to Malcolm X also reflects the esteemed position of Malcolm X and the Black radical tradition in hip hop and hip hop activism—an esteem that shapes Muslim Cool's alterity. During my time at IMAN it was clear that Martin Luther King Jr. was also a radical Black figure—IMAN's King marched through Chicago's Marquette Park to protest residential segregation and opposed the Vietnam War. Yet Nashashibi also includes the White female founder of the Catholic Worker Movement, Dorothy Day. This inclusion contests claims that U.S. American Muslims do not belong to the nation by locating these Muslims within a multiracial and multifaith U.S. American tradition of social activism. This is a move of conscious U.S. American Muslim self-making that reflects not only the pressures of the exclusion of the post–9/11 context but the post–civil rights domestication of racial politics in the United States as well.

By the domestication of racial politics I am referring to the way the dominance of the rights-based discourse of the civil rights movement narrows the set of concerns of Blacks and other communities of color in the United States to the demand for full citizenship as *Americans*—a term that implies both the extension of the legal rights of citizenship but also affective modes of belonging as citizens. I consider this a narrowed set of concerns because claims to full citizenship by people of color in the United States require moving away from internationalist and trans-national frameworks of belonging. This does not mean that communities of color give up their transnational attachments, but being legitimate citizens in the eyes of the state requires that move. In the specific case of the U.S. Black American political imagination, domestication came by way of the explicit delinking of the domestic Black struggle from the anticolonial movements of the period by the civil rights establishment. This move, which Richard Iton calls "black realpolitik," meant that the civil rights establishment would fall into step with a vision of American exceptionalism as a concession for racial equality at home (Iton 2012).

The domestication of racial politics does not mean that marginal-ized racial communities no longer engage in forms of dissent. The con-cept of "cultural citizenship" as articulated by Renato Rosaldo (1994) is grounded in dissent—objecting to the institutionalized exclusion of Latin@ communities from the nation. Likewise, in her work on South Asian immigrant teenagers, Sunaina Maira defines "dissenting citizen-ship" as a form of cultural citizenship the basis of whose engagement with the state is "a critique of its [the state's] politics" (Maira 2009, 201). Yet as Maira illustrates, dissenting citizens are still seeking belonging *as citizens*. Thus, because citizenship is a site of subject making by citizens as well as by the state (Ong 1996), the post–civil rights era is defined by the ways in which this desire for belonging is taken up by the state, which coopts dissent through its administration of dissent.

In her recent monograph *Uncivil Youth* (2013), Soo Ah Kwon traces how the expansion of the nonprofit sector in the late twentieth century has worked to limit the forms of political resistance available to racialized communities in the United States. Building on Hall's (1996) Gramscian analysis that state power is "grounded in the relations and institutions of civil society," Kwon argues that limits on political mobilization are not the result of violent state repression but of the incorporation of marginalized communities as a category of administration. Nonprofit organizations serve the state's administration through youth development programming that "empowers" young people to self-actualize as individuals and future leaders of their communities, in the process becoming "ideal democratic subjects" (Kwon 2013, 58). Kwon notes that the growth of 501(c)(3)s is a consequence of civil rights-era mobilization and the concurrent rise of neoliberal governance as the dominant form of state power in the late twentieth-century United States. The nonprofitization of activism is a state objective under neoliberalism, enacting what Kwon terms an "affirmative governmentality that stresses neoliberal principles of self-responsibility and community governance" (Kwon 2013, 46). I do not call on Iton, Maira, and Kwon to make the point that the desire for citizenship, the work of nonprofits, and youth engagement are categorically "negative," but rather to critically consider what kinds of political possibilities are foreclosed to Muslim Cool by the post–civil rights commitment to a rights-based discourse and the cultivation of engaged citizens.

On the one hand, like most activist nonprofits whose work and perspective are explicitly concerned with the suffering of racialized communities, IMAN is at odds with the state, which upholds racial suffering. Yet on the other hand, in a departure from the activist models of the Black radical tradition, IMAN is not in direct confrontation with the state. As a post–civil rights era nonprofit organization IMAN has a much more complicated relationship to state power and governance. IMAN uses the critique of the Black radical tradition to shape the contours of the rhetoric of its dissent: how to levy a critique at the state, the importance of levying a critique at the state, and the necessity for U.S. American Muslims to be critical. Yet the organization's theory of "critical engagement," which guides its work on the ground, turns more on the rights-based rhetoric of the civil rights movement.

Nashashibi articulates IMAN's work as critical engagement to set it apart from U.S. American Muslims who engage with the broader U.S.

American society primarily through education and the marketplace but do not "analyze the intimate relationships they have with a broad set of political arrangements," on the one hand, and from U.S. American Muslims who withdraw from broader U.S. American society "as an articulation of deep Islamic principles or an expression of heightened piety . . . often couched in terms of renouncing or rejecting *dunya* [worldly affairs]," on the other hand (Nashashibi 2005, 2–4). By contrast, Nashashibi proposes for U.S. American Muslims an engagement with the political process and with institutions of civil society that is critical of state power. For Nashashibi, this engagement is also attentive to the ways in which race and class position U.S. American Muslims differently in relation to state power. Critical engagement is a form of dissenting cultural citizenship because at stake in Nashashibi's definition of engagement is the recognition of U.S. American Muslims as *Americans*—which again implies both the extension of the legal rights of citizenship and affective modes of belonging as citizens.

IMAN's arts activism is an important part of a larger agenda for social change. Other projects include participation in rallies for immigration reform; Muslim legislative days at the Illinois state capitol and *iftar*s (Ramadan dinners) at the White House; reentry programs that provide jobs for formerly incarcerated Black Muslim men; a free health clinic for the underinsured; and working with Arab grocers to provide fresh food options at local corner stores on the city's Southwest Side. All these projects come out of IMAN's commitment to critical engagement, which relies on a rights-based framework—IMAN dissents from the exclusion or the neglect of the rights of people of color as citizens—and accordingly responds through a series of programs that reflect the constraints of the post–civil rights era prioritization of one's status as a U.S. citizen. This does not mean that IMAN as an organization or the individuals who participate in its work do not have visions of belonging beyond the state; but it means that the articulation of those linkages is often rendered secondary, if engaged in at all.

IMAN's relationship to state power and governance, which illustrates one of the limits of Muslim Cool, is not merely or even primarily about "where the funding comes from" but about how a commitment to social change through the expansion of the rights of a dissenting racialized citizenry can align with state objectives of subjectification. IMAN's arts activism, like all hip hop activism, is located within tensions between nostalgia for a populist radicalism, desires for a deeply equitable world, and uneasy alignments with the dominant political, economic, and social world orders. Again, I do not consider this a reflection of a desired compatibility with all forms of state power; IMAN consistently dissents from the state's practices of racialized inequality. But it does reflect the paradox of the post–civil rights era, a paradox that enables a neoliberal state hegemony—one that is itself flexible—to set limits on Muslim Cool both domestically and abroad.

Imperial Muslim Cool?

As stated earlier, the limits of Muslim Cool are born out of a context that is post–civil rights and post–9/11. The post–civil rights administration of dissent through the institutions of civil society is a technology of a broader, state-generated discourse of U.S. multiculturalism. The narrative of U.S. multiculturalism upholds the racial and ethnic diversity of the U.S. population as the nation's most valuable asset. This asset is an achievement: the discourse configures the U.S. Black American struggle to overcome slavery and Jim/Jane Crow as a testament to U.S. American ideals and culture. Accordingly, multiculturalism, when deployed by the state, is a triumphant narrative of American exceptionalism.

However, in the lived experience of racial minorities, the state administration of dissent through the incorporation Black freedom movements as quintessentially "American" is not a challenge to structural inequality. While the rhetoric of U.S. multiculturalism allows for affective recognition as citizens, it does not displace the racial hierarchies that privilege the White Christian citizen but rather "remains appropriately hierarchal" (McAlister 2005, 259).

Parallel to the post–civil rights multicultural state is the post–9/11 surveillance state. Replicating the COINTELPRO regime of the mid-twentieth century, the current domestic surveillance state legitimizes increased overt and covert monitoring of U.S. citizens with reference to national security. Post–9/11 practices of the surveillance state, conducted by the Federal Bureau of Investigations (FBI), Immigration and Customs Enforcement (ICE), Department of Homeland Security (DHS), and local law enforcement, include unexpected home visits by "friendly" local FBI agents, more intensive questioning and searches of persons and property at borders, selective detention and deportation, covert monitoring of personal communications and movements without prior evidence of criminal activity, and the use of paid informants to "thwart" homegrown terror plots (Khera 2010; Aaronson 2011; Akbar 2013).

In a partial inversion of state multiculturalism in the United States, race is also central to the logic of the surveillance state. Racialization under regimes of surveillance determines who does not belong. As Junaid Rana has shown, the surveillance state "deploys the Muslim body as a concrete objective entity to control and regulate" (Rana 2011, 155). This marks the contemporary "racialization of Muslims," which scholars have noted in a post–9/11 shift of the designation "Muslim" from a religious to a racial category (Rana 2011; Razack 2008; Volpp 2002; Naber 2008). As a racial category, the "Muslim" is known through bodily and behavioral markers, such as "Middle Eastern looks," beards, and headscarves—markers that are signs of suspicion.

U.S. American Muslims disproportionately feel the gaze of the surveillance state in their homes, prayer spaces, charities, schools, and even intimate lives. Importantly, however, the state enforces these policies of detention, deportation, and surveillance that single out Muslim citizens and immigrants while simultaneously holding to its multiculturalist narrative—declaring that the "war on terror" is not a war on Muslims (Maira 2009). Accordingly, surveillance meets multiculturalism in what scholars refer to as the U.S. government's support for "moderate Islam."

In her article "Secularism, Hermeneutics, and Empire: The Politics of Islamic Reformation," Saba Mahmood analyzes U.S. government efforts to "foster what is now broadly called 'moderate Islam' as an antidote and prophylactic to fundamentalist interpretations of Islam" (Mahmood 2006, 331). Drawing on a broader intellectual critique of secularism's "unmarkedness" (Asad 2003), Mahmood argues that these efforts advance U.S. hegemony through "secular normativity," which does not reject but rather reshapes religious subjectivity to fit U.S. imperial aims (Mahmood 2006, 328).[7] This religious subjectivity is that of the "autonomous individual believer [who] is a necessary protagonist in the plot of secular political rationality, one who owes his allegiance to the sovereign rule of the state rather than the structures of traditional authority" (Mahmood 2006, 340). Importantly, Mahmood notes that some

Muslims too seek the goals of this strategy as part of a "secular liberal Muslim agenda" (Mahmood 2006: 329).

Likewise, in his book *Rebel Music: Race, Empire, and the New Muslim Youth Culture*, political scientist Hisham Aidi (2014) traces the ways in which race, music, and diplomacy bring Muslims directly within Euro-American imperial agendas. He argues that music is "a key component of the Sufi counteroffensive" against the "Salafi" or "Islamist" articulations of Islam that, according to U.S. and European policy makers, fuel so-called Islamic extremism (Aidi 2014, 75). Looking at the specific case of the United Kingdom after the London bombings in 2005, Aidi echoes Mahmood's analysis of Euro-American strategy's ideological bent in seeking to win an alleged "battle of ideas" within the global Muslim community (Aidi 2014, 74). In Great Britain, this has led to the establishment of the Preventing Violent Extremism program (Prevent), whose policy directives have channeled millions of pounds in funding to British Muslim organizations that are expected to expound this counternarrative among British Muslims. According to Aidi, this Sufi counteroffensive in the United Kingdom was openly backed by the United States and a host of prominent U.S. scholars such as Hamza Yusuf, who, while not acting at the behest of the U.S. government, preached messages of political and social integration that aligned with U.S. interests. Music, including hip hop, also emerged as a part of the Prevent strategy.[8]

Around the same time that Prevent was taking shape in the United Kingdom, the U.S. government launched its own efforts at the intersection of the arts and counterterrorism. In a Brookings Institution report, "Mightier Than the Sword: Arts and Culture in the U.S.-Muslim World Relationship," former ambassador Cynthia Schneider, one of the architects of the resurgence of arts diplomacy geared specifically toward Muslims outside the United States, cites

the tremendous potential of hip-hop for building connections between the United States and the Muslim world. Like jazz, hip-hop has resonated throughout the world. . . . From the suburbs of Paris to Palestine and to Kyrgyzstan in central Asia, hip-hop music reflects the struggle against authority. Hip-hop originated in African American communities in the inner city; some of its early pioneers were American Muslims. They carry on an African American Muslim tradition of protest against authority, most powerfully represented by Malcolm X. (Schneider and Nelson 2008, 15)

Critically, U.S. foreign policy is here explicitly drawing on the very link between hip hop and Islam that I argue motivates Muslim Cool. I recall first reading this report while in Doha in 2009. The film *New Muslim Cool* had been nominated for (and ended up winning) an award at the Al-Jazeera Film Festival in Doha, and I had come along with the film's director to network and drum up buzz about the film, which was set to be released the following year in the United States. I mention this connection because the film was also cited by Schneider as a kind of exemplar of the kind of cultural production that could help to illuminate the history of hip hop and Islam in America and thus build bridges in U.S.-Muslim relationships (Schneider and Nelson 2008).

Schneider's reading of the film (and of hip hop more broadly) stands in stark contrast to the way the film's directors saw the relationship between Islam and Black protest—as an indictment of the state. As on the home front, the administration of dissent is at play here. In refiguring hip hop as a bridge builder, the United States also refigures itself as a champion of freedom, in this particular case of free speech. Accordingly, the dissent of racialized and marginalized communities becomes of a marker not of where the state has failed but of where it is succeeding. Like the power inequities between the United States and Muslim-majority nations, the power inequities within the United States voiced by hip hop cannot be heard over the roar of the celebration of U.S. American triumph.

The U.S. embassy's interest in the tour that I followed in 2014 came out of the architecture of this kind of thinking. This was a tour that did not travel to a Muslim-majority territory but to the United Kingdom, which, not inconsequentially, has a significant Muslim minority population. It was a multicity tour that began in London and made stops in Nottingham, Birmingham, and Manchester. A concert was held in each city, and in London, Nottingham, and Birmingham the artists also ran youth-oriented workshops. I attended all these events except for the workshop in London and the concert and workshop in Nottingham. These concerts and workshops, while funded by the U.S. embassy in London, were organized by the tour leader, Man-O-Wax, in coordination with local arts organizations. Sometimes the local organization merely provided a host space for the concert or workshop; at other times it was more deeply involved.

At the final concert of the tour at the Z-Arts Center in Manchester, the center staff had very little involvement with the show besides providing directions to the bathrooms and auditoriums, distributing tickets, and controlling the sound. By contrast, the first concert of the tour had been held in a small auditorium at the School of Oriental and African Studies (SOAS) as a part of the "Salaam Café," a series of events put on by the Rabbani Project, a relatively new (at the time) Sufi-oriented collective that hosts a range of activities from lectures on tea cultures and Islamic music to drumming workshops and outings to learn archery as a "sacred art."[9] This particular Salaam Café was also cosponsored by a SOAS student organization, the Spiritual Dialogue Society,[10] by Rumi's Cave, and by the U.S. embassy in London. Excluding the embassy, all the sponsoring organizations were "third spaces"—ecumenical or Muslim intrafaith gatherings. The idea of the third space is gaining prominence in U.S. American Muslim discourse to describe spaces that are neither mosques, which assert a normative spirituality, nor completely secular spaces, which can be devoid of or hostile to religion. Rumi's Cave is an example of such a third space: it is a standing physical location, a small storefront in a London neighborhood, run by multiethnic young British Muslims under the tutelage of a learned and popular Sufi religious leader, Shaykh Babikar.

Accordingly, the Muslim or, more specifically, Sufi orientation of these sponsoring organizations was very much in the foreground. In addition to opening the event with a recitation from the Qur'an, the evening's host, herself part of the Sufi Muslim music ensemble Pearls of Islam, reiterated the Sufi emphasis on (divine) love by explaining that the objective of the Salaam Café was "to occupy space with love." I am referring to these organizations as event sponsors not because they provided funding for the concert but because they sponsored the event in other ways, such as by publicizing it through their networks, providing local legitimacy, and so on. The event flyer, which prominently featured photos of the FEW Collective artists, also contained small images of the logos of each sponsor, including the U.S. embassy in London.

The embassy logo was a small American flag, and its placement put the embassy on par with the other, nonprofit sponsor organizations, belying the unique financial contribution it had made. Moreover, besides a brief thank you, there was no real mention of the embassy's involvement at the event. This would change at other venues, where the embassy official who traveled with the tour actually introduced the concert or was on hand to film the workshop, as one Foreign Service officer did during the workshop in Manchester. I was able to speak with an embassy employee who attended one of the shows and was adamant about not wanting to be identified. I obliged, but at the conclusion of our brief chat I found that he had said little that I could not have easily found in official statements, such as Schneider's report quoted above. I had asked him why the embassy was supporting this tour. He responded quite enthusiastically that the tour was about "showing American diversity" and demonstrating to U.K. audiences "This is what America is!" I then asked whether the embassy ever got pushback for these events:

THOMAS:[11] What do you mean by pushback?
SU'AD: I mean, whether people say to you: "You [the embassy] say this is American but that is not what America really is."
THOMAS: That does not happen at events like the FEW show; you wouldn't even know we were a part of it, necessarily, which is sometimes something we also do [more intentionally], like in Pakistan, because it [publicizing the U.S. embassy's involvement] could endanger people [the traveling artists].

The FEW tour was one of many embassy-sponsored events and thus part of a broader strategy of cultural diplomacy by the U.S. embassy in London. The London programming is not solely Muslim-oriented; in addition to the FEW tour, according to one source, the U.S. embassy had helped to fund a tour of the United Kingdom by critical race studies professor Kimberlé Crenshaw as part of International Women's Day, a visit by Chicago violence interrupter Aminah Matthews, and a performance by the differently abled hip hop dance crew Ill-Abilities. According to the staffer I spoke with, these events were meant to promote "American values," which included "freedom of speech and American diversity." Diversity seemed to be the main emphasis, as he explained:

THOMAS: Once you are an American, you are an American; you belong
and feel a sense of belonging, as a kind of patriotism—but not a blind
patriotism, I am not for that, but a sense of belonging, a nationhood
you don't see here in the U.K.

SU'AD: So how do you know if the event was successful?

THOMAS: That's something we are still working on, we don't have any
formal evaluation system, but we need something—also to tell Congress why they should keep funding this type of programming!

Toward the end of our conversation, Thomas waxed a little reflective and wondered whether maybe he needed to go back home to make
sure that was still the case—that once you are an American, you are
an American—since he had been in the Foreign Service for quite some
time. He also noted, insightfully, that "reverts in the U.K. say they feel
marginalized and undervalued by the 'Asian' Muslim, yet the Asian
Muslims *love* reverts from the States and put them on a pedestal."[12]

In an interview with a local British Muslim leader, A. R. Malik, I was
introduced to another aspect of the U.S. cultural diplomacy strategy,
which some call "direct engagement." Malik explained:

The Americans learned [from] the failures of Prevent. [The Americans
decided,] "We are going to engage with a broad group of actors." This
is [part of the] paradoxes within American policy. . . . There are pro-
tagonists that are trying to do the right thing, within a CT [counterter-
rorism] perspective. The American embassy in London did something
amazing during this period [right after the bombings in 2005]. I went to
the former ambassador's Eid party at his house, and in that room there
was Ikhwan [members of the Muslim Brotherhood], Salafis, those people
the U.K. government would not talk to, they would not be invited to an
Eid party at Downing Street or the Home Office. . . . [So] the American
embassy has more engagement and buy-in from British Muslims.

Malik and others also noted that direct engagement was not only Eid
parties but also "off the record" conversations, where embassy staff went
off talking points.

For the United States, this multipronged approach seemed to be effective. While the U.S. embassy's presence was fairly discreet in the plan-

ning and presentation of the FEW concert, I noted a familiarity and a friendliness between some of the embassy staff on hand in London and the local British Muslims, which seemed to indicate relationships that preceded the tour and were reinforced by it. Therefore, related to the ways in which nonprofits work for racial equality in the United States, civil society is also central to U.S. cultural diplomacy in the United Kingdom and to the articulation and reproduction of U.S. hegemony. And like for U.S. American Muslims, for the British Muslim community too familiarity and friendliness with the state, be it the American or the British one, represent a complicated entanglement.

I met up with Malik right before the SOAS concert at a bookshop not too far from campus. Malik is one of the main organizers of the Radical Middle Way (RMW), and despite being a Canadian transplant he is a well-known figure in the British Muslim community. This is because of the work of RMW, which began in the shadow of the 7/7 bombings. RMW put on a number of multicity concert tours around the United Kingdom that featured Muslim artists such as Amir Sulaiman and Islamic scholars such as Hamza Yusuf. Similar to the work of IMAN in the United States, RMW's tours made arts and music culture central to its overall mission to open "a safe place" for young Muslims "to ask difficult questions and explore challenging issues" (RMW 2014).

The ideological foundation of RMW came from the work of the British Muslim intellectual Fouad Nahdi and the periodical *QNews*, and as such the questions and issues that RMW focused on were those that challenged the broader Muslim status quo in the United Kingdom as well as the specific "Salafi" narrative. This secondary challenge was where the vision of the RMW and the counterterrorism objectives of the U.K. government were in agreement: both wanted to counter the growth of Muslim fundamentalism in the United Kingdom. As a result, Malik explained, "the Radical Middle Way, as a project, was one of those sixty-three recommendations [that came out of the post–7/7 consultation between the U.K. government and British Muslim leaders], and we were one of the first to be funded and supported." While RMW's vision is much older, the fact that RMW as a working organization came about directly through Prevent has been a source of tension and critique:

MALIK: People said, "Oh, they're funded by the government." Our argument was the funding could be funded from Mickey Mouse, Kermit, your father. For us, [the key was to] look at the content. [After the 7/7 bombings] we made a decision of critical engagement. Either we at this point stand by what we have always been saying [at QNews] that there is a pernicious element in Islamic ideology that's supporting violence and that although it doesn't occur in a vacuum, *it is* part of the matrix of the problem. For us, our sense of integrity was [posing the question], "If we did this event without HMG [Her Majesty's Government] funding, would we do this event differently?" *No.* And what happened on that [Breaking Light] tour? Amir [Sulaiman] comes up and performs "Danger" or "Dead Man Walking" and these are incendiary, difficult, some would say violent, poems. Did we censor him? No. Were our [government] funders concerned? Yes. But for us it was clear. Dissent needed to be a part of talking about empire. The stage became a place where you could speak honestly with safety about these issues; at the same time, there was a [Islamic] morality behind it and ethics behind it.

As further proof that Prevent funding "didn't change the way we [RMW] did things," Malik explained that RMW would ultimately decline future Prevent funding. In 2010 the new Conservative government had revamped the Prevent program. An official report issued by the new government claimed, "The Prevent programme we inherited from the last Government was flawed. It confused the delivery of Government policy to promote integration with Government policy to prevent terrorism" (Prevent Strategy 2011). In this new political climate, for RMW "there were too many [new] conditions to meet," Malik explained, "like a values clarification: [a list of] questions where we would have to clarify our British values." According to Malik, the early version of Prevent had been more porous, thus giving RMW more latitude; however, as it became more ideological and "drilled down to de-rad[icalization]," RMW got out of the Prevent game.

Malik and RMW were not the only British Muslims facing this entanglement. I met Rafeek for a conversation near a shopping square in Manchester—or rather, I met and then waited for Rafeek as he concluded what turned out to be a fairly long cell phone conversation with another Afro-Caribbean Muslim man about ways to organize and re-build solidarity among Afro-British Muslims. Rafeek, like most of the folks I met in the United Kingdom, was both an artist (an emcee) and a youth activist. He was fairly gregarious, with a deep knowledge of Muslim and Black British arts and life. He also had strong opinions about Prevent and the U.S. embassy and a strongly pragmatic relationship with both. Echoing complaints of anti-Black racism among Muslims that I had heard repeatedly in the United States and that the embassy staffer also alluded to above, Rafeek was dismissive of the critics: "Yeah, people have gotten criticized for taking Prevent [funding], but all these Muslim organizations that have millions do nothing for Black [British] people." Describing a kind of counterterrorism nonprofit industrial complex, he said that folks, including himself, used the "CT lingo to get the CT money."

Rafeek explained that he had received U.S. embassy funding to bring an international Muslim leader to speak to working-class youth in the United Kingdom. Like many nonprofit workers, he had an idea and the passion to make it happen but no funding until "one brother who had a connect to the embassy told me to pitch the idea" to the embassy. Rafeek called it a "bargain": he needed the money, and in return the embassy asked that its logo be placed on publicity material and that some of its people be able to attend the lectures. Rafeek obliged, but claimed that his embassy contact later complained that the embassy did not get enough exposure. Again, Rafeek was not moved: he had held up his end of the bargain. Yet even with all his aggressive pragmatism, for Rafeek there was an ethical line in the sand. He explained, pointing to the market square where we were sitting, "Say there was a bunch of Muslim kids rioting in the square; they [a specific local organization] would say, 'Yes, we came and put down the riot [so fund us],' even though they wasn't even there." In contrast, Rafeek said he neither lied nor played the role of informant. The organization Rafeek mentioned was held in suspicion by a number of Muslim leaders I spoke with, who believed that this group not only lied about the efficacy of its CT work but would even make money by reporting innocent Muslim youth to the U.K. government as potential terrorists based on conversations the organization itself had incited. Even those who disagreed with Rafeek about how U.K. Muslims should relate to Prevent, agreed that this particular organization was "dodgy." This particular group also had the reputation of being a favorite partner of the U.S. embassy in London.

I have deliberately refrained from naming the organization in question because my intent is not to write an exposé about CT work in the United Kingdom based on hearsay that I am unable to confirm. Rather, I point out the overall controversy surrounding Prevent and the overlapping relationships between the U.S. embassy and a series of British Muslim groups, dodgy and otherwise, in order to highlight the fact that the complicated entanglement faced by U.K. Muslims also confronts American Muslim hip hop artists who travel within the context of U.S. (and British) empire. Yet like Rafeek, these Muslim artists are also making a kind of bargain, a bargain with empire. The question remains as to what it means to make a bargain like this: how do artists manage it, and does Muslim Cool then become a technique of the state's imperial agenda to not only "reform Islam" but extend its own global domination?

Bargaining with Empire, Bargaining to Belong

My interview with Rafeek ended shortly before one of the FEW tour's shows at a local community arts center. Since he too was a hip hop head, I encouraged Rafeek to come to the show with me, but he was highly skeptical. His skepticism was inspired by his past working relationship with government funders. Often artists sponsored by official outfits such as governments or large foundations are unknown and/or not very talented. Rafeek had never heard of any of the artists on the tour and thus assumed that they were amateurs and not really worth seeing. After much prodding I was ultimately able to convince him to attend. About two minutes into the concert, he turned to me and said, "One word: amazing!"

Rafeek's estimation of the FEW tour was not unfounded. Despite never having performed together as group and having had only limited time to practice, the group's performance was very cohesive. This was due to the individual artists' talent and professionalism and to Man-O-Wax's skills as the band leader. It was also due to the fact that their individual genres—hip hop, Nubian pop, and Gnawa—shared the same sonic home: Africa. One of the songs that impressed me was the group's cover of the Police track "Walking on the Moon." I saw them perform the song on several occasions, and each time I was struck by their skilled and moving ensemble.

Their rendition of the song began with a syncopated break beat dropped by Man-O-Wax, and then Brahim, the Gnawa artist, added on an additional percussive layer with his oud (a lutelike instrument). In bluesy raspy tones, Aja Black of The Reminders sang the verses of the song, and Alsarah harmonized at selected movements. Their two voices came together in the chorus, which was a reggae-style yodel-shout that gave the song an almost haunting quality. And in an embodied accompaniment, the group's b-boy, Brave Monk, moonwalked and popped in slow motion across the stage.

As with the performance attended by Rafeek, the quality and intensity of every performance were high, yet they performed to what I found to be unexpectedly small audiences. When I arrived at the MAC Birmingham Art Center for the group's preconcert workshop it was clear that the FEW Collective workshop and show were just one of many events held at the bustling location. The venue was described to me as "the [official] arts center of the Midlands region." The workshop was scheduled for a three-hour block of time and was designed to start with ice-breaking activities, after which the attendees would be split up, much like the format of LONS, to have a more direct learning experience with one of the artists (vocal, dance, DJ, and emcee). The workshop was attended only by a small group of local preteen girls of color. Although they were initially shy, they eventually warmed up to the event and were full of giggles. The teachers who brought the group together seemed really appreciative of the activity and wished they could have stayed longer, but they had to leave after the icebreaker. Their departure left behind one British Asian teenaged Muslim woman, a thirty-something White Canadian transplant called Kathy, and myself. While the teenager went off to work on her singing with the two vocalists on the tour, Kathy and I stayed to work with the b-boy, Brave Monk. During our session, Kathy commented ironically, "They came all this way to teach hip hop to a Canadian and an American!"

The concert was also poorly attended, with an audience of only a small group of about fifteen Black and Asian British teens from a local organization that the U.S. embassy often partners with—but not the "dodgy" one mentioned above. To be fair, what they lacked in numbers the teens definitely made up for in audience participation. Initially they were seated toward the back in the small stadium-style auditorium, but when asked to move closer to the stage they eagerly came forward to the second row of seats. Likewise, once encouraged to clap, they clapped throughout, and one young man even got popped, locked, and tutted on stage.

Despite this enthusiasm, I was disappointed by the small audience turnout, and I was joined in my disappointment by a local Muslim artist and organizer who described the center as "smack dab" in the middle between two communities: "On one side everyone is White and middle class, and on the other everyone is brown." He complained that typical MAC programming is aimed at that "posh, White elite" and that in the summer the park in which the center is located is full of people of color who come inside the center itself only to use its bathroom. A year earlier he himself had put on a program at the center that had attracted many people, primarily non-White Birmingham residents—so many, in fact, that the center had had to turn people away. This, he argued, was due to the aggressive street marketing he and his partners had used to get the word out. He believed that the same should have been done for the FEW show but had not been because the center's leadership did not "really engage with the community despite all the [state] resources they have been given."

I attended all but one of the tour's concerts, and the issue of small audiences plagued the entire tour. In neither London, nor Birmingham, nor Manchester was the hall where the tour performed filled to even 75 percent capacity; rather, each was full of empty seats. I was disappointed for the artists because of all the time and effort they had spent in preparation. But I was also perplexed. The U.S. embassy's stated goal in promoting a tour such as this was to showcase U.S. American diversity; it would seem reasonable, then, that the embassy would do its best to make sure that the venues were packed. Why would they spend money only to have the invited artists perform to very small audiences? The issue of audience size could be chalked up to the typical inconsistencies inherent in running a bureaucracy: the embassy had big ideas but a small staff and limited time. From my limited exposure to the embassy's work through this tour, I believe this was part of the story. However, it seemed to me that the apparent negligence also formed part of a strategy of soft power:

MALIK: What the American Embassy does is they promote American culture and American soft power, and FEW is here because the embassy sees the value of FEW as a representation of American Muslims within a broader culture space. FEW is coming here, they are going to *represent*. What's the impact going to be? On one level it's patronage, plain and simple. I think it's kind of low impact. Bring them over and people [the audience] enjoy a musical experience, they [the embassy] do it all the time. So why Muslims? Because the American embassy wants to engage with Muslim communities. It is important for them. Why? Because London is the Muslim capital of Europe. Here you exert a lot of soft power. The right inputs here will carry to the Muslim world.

Malik's reflection implies that the U.S. embassy's engagement is somewhat run of the mill and low impact by design. Unlike drone attacks or torture, the instrument of state hegemony in this case is not a high-impact spectacle of violence but minute gestures of relationship building through culture and civil society—gaining hearts and minds. Yet the goal is the same as that of drone attacks and torture: extending the power of the state. Muslim populations are geopolitically significant. Power over these populations enables access to significant natural resources and consumer markets, and control over these resources and markets is thus a key state objective for the United States. However, Muslims have their own objectives that may or may not align with those of the state—hence the need for the right input here and the right input there to reach the aggregate impact of U.S. hegemony. This suggests that, as an effect of power, the low-impact cultural diplomacy strategy must be seen in the aggregate. Multiple low-impact events, small inputs, and each tidbit of information are pooled to spin a particular narrative of American exceptionalism in order to justify U.S. empire.

Importantly, this is not the first time the arts and racialized minorities have been central to U.S. global pursuits. In the Cold War face-off between the United States and the Soviet Union, jazz became a critical weapon of U.S. soft power as officials strove to manage the international perception of U.S. racism (Von Eschen 2004). Jazz became critical to the government's strategy "to build cordial relations with new African and Asian states" as a means to shift the global balance of power in favor of the United States (Von Eschen 2004, 3). Officials hoped that endorsing jazz, a form of Black expressive culture, as quintessentially American would undercut beliefs that the U.S. government discriminated against its Black citizens (Von Eschen 2004, 3). Rehearsing earlier U.S. diplomatic history, then, the present, post–9/11 U.S. policy initiative attempts to fashion U.S. American Muslims as cultural ambassadors in a different war—the war on terror (Aidi 2014; Von Eschen 2004).

Like their jazz predecessors, Muslim hip hop artists are presented as examples of the triumph of U.S. multiculturalism and democracy. Yet unlike their jazz predecessors, who, according to Iton (2010), would tactically avoid discussing U.S. foreign policy while on tour, Muslim hip hop artists are not similarly censored (Iton 2010). As Malik noted, "The brothers and sisters in the FEW Collective have [not] been told what to say, what to sing, their scripts haven't been written for them, if they were to criticize drones or not closing Guantanamo or Obama's negligence about Burma or his very strange relationship with American Muslims, I don't think anyone in the State Department would bat an eye."

Based on my observations on the tour and my limited experience as a cultural ambassador, Malik's argument rings true. According to my conversations with Man-O-Wax in the lead-up to the tour, the embassy staff he worked with were much more concerned with budgets than with political statements. Moreover, I had the chance to see the FEW Collective perform the very same set at Community Café in Chicago, one step removed from the cultural diplomacy quagmire of the United Kingdom, and the content of the set as well as quality and energy of the touring artists were the same.

It should also be noted that although no one in the group made any overtly political statements, this did not mean that their music was void of political comment. In London, they chose to cover songs by veteran artists such as Sting and Nina Simone who have well-known political commitments and who have expressed these commitments "on wax," that is, in their recordings. Relatedly, The Reminders performed their original song, "If You Didn't Know," which includes lyrics such as "I'm like Garvey, Ghazali, Gandhi / you scared of Illuminati, I'm drumming with Bobo Shantis, saluting Haile Selassie," and "I'm trying to do the right thing like Radio Rahim / Steal the key from the oppressor, set the caged bird free / and I'm passing to the cadence of Coretta Scott King,

Betty Shabazz, Assata [Shakur], Angela [Davis] and Kathleen [Cleaver]." These musical citations of anti-imperialist heroes, including an activist who is currently at the top of the FBI's most wanted list, demonstrates that the counterpolitics and consciousness raising of Muslim Cool were not reined in by state sponsorship.

In fact, it was this kind of latitude that had encouraged DJ Man-O-Wax to coordinate this tour and others. In 2010 Man-O-Wax traveled to Morocco and Algeria with other U.S. American Muslim hip hop artists on his first trip sponsored by a U.S. embassy. When I asked Man-O-Wax about his trip, he explained that he had initially had reservations about the State Department funding but found that his U.S. American sponsors did not monitor him during his visit. Most important to him were the person-to-person and community-to-community connections that could be made during this kind of exchange. That same year, another hip hop collective, Remarkable Current, toured Indonesia as part of the Performing Arts Initiative of the Department of State. On the Remarkable Current (RC) website, the trip was described in the following way: "RC is honored to travel to Indonesia, at this special time, to promote positivity through music as well as set an example to the world that Islam and Muslims are a part of the fabric and foundation of The United States of America" (Remarkable Current 2010).

Man-O-Wax's account and the RC statement point to the many different motivations that lead artists to participate in this kind of work. There is the pragmatic reason—everybody's got to eat—and the fact that these trips offer an opportunity to expand an artist's audience internationally. These tours also offer an opportunity to build interpersonal connections beyond the state, and it was this opportunity that Man-O-Wax and other artists on the FEW tour were most interested in. This, Penny Von Eschen argues, was also the motivation of their jazz tour predecessors, for whom "the promotion of American culture abroad led just as often to the fostering of collaboration and solidarity throughout the African diaspora" (Von Eschen 2004, 255–57). Muslim hip hop artists' motivation is often tied to commitments to building hip hop community, as artists use the tours to establish mentoring and collaborative relationships with hip hop artists in the countries they visit.

I find compelling Von Eschen's defense of jazz ambassadors against reductive claims of complicity and extend the same defense to my U.S.

American Muslim interlocutors. These individuals were neither walking around with their heads in the sand nor do they bleed red, white, and blue. Yet the specter and the power of the state never disappears. In her study Von Eschen depicts the jazz tours as a victory for the civil rights movement, recording how Louis Armstrong refused to play the role of a jazz ambassador until the Eisenhower administration had enforced desegregation in Little Rock (Von Eschen 2004, 58). Thus, while the jazz ambassadors were not pawns of an omnipotent state, their participation was also influenced by their interest in a civil rights framework—full citizenship as U.S. Americans. In an important way, then, the jazz ambassadors' relationship to the civil rights movement is a marker of the domestication of racial politics that shapes the context of hip hop diplomacy today. In a post–civil rights and post–9/11 era in which Muslim citizenship is contested in the United States, as was the citizenship of Blacks at the time of the jazz tours of the 1950s and 1960s, U.S. American Muslims' participation in hip hop diplomacy abroad has the potential to reap rewards at home. As described by the statement of the RC collective, for U.S. American Muslim hip hop, the bargain made with the state is a bargain to belong.

A Luta Continua

U.S. Muslim hip hop artists are not the only U.S. Muslims dispatched on embassy-sponsored cultural diplomacy tours. About five years before this music tour I traveled to London on a book tour for *Living Islam Out Loud: American Muslim Women Speak* (*LIOL*). *LIOL* is an anthology of first-person narratives by U.S. American Muslim women, and my contribution to it was a series of poems.[13] The tour's audience consisted of London Muslims, except for our first lunch meeting upon arrival. This was a meeting with a U.S. embassy representative, during which I learned that the U.S. embassy in the United Kingdom had funded the trip.[14] For the women on this tour, myself included, the trip represented an opportunity to learn about and network with Muslim communities in the United Kingdom and also to share the U.S. American Muslim experience with U.K. Muslims. It was also particularly important to our group that the U.S. Black American narrative was shared with audiences abroad. Yet after that welcoming lunch a question kept nagging me: Why was this trip important to the U.S. embassy in the United Kingdom in particular and to the U.S. state more broadly?[15]

When I decided to return to London, this time on my university-funded research dime, it was because I continued to be plagued by that question and its implications for my theorization of Muslim Cool. If Muslim Cool, as I have proposed, is a way of thinking about and being a U.S. American Muslim that operates through Blackness as a counterpoint to dominant narratives, how might (or can) that alterity operate in relation to the state?

The geography of this chapter, charted in my movements and in those of my teachers and interlocutors—Chicago, New York City, Doha, London, Morocco—suggests that this relationship to the state is one of limitation; but it is a limitation caused by the circulation of Muslim Cool and of the U.S. American Muslim. The music, artists, and ideas travel, but this circulation does not only or necessarily lead to the proliferation of transgressive practices, as one might hope. Rather, because of the constraints of the post–civil rights and post–9/11 context, as Muslim Cool circulates, its alterity is also constrained by and entangled with the state.

The mentions on my Facebook feed of the State Department report upon its release were celebratory. The U.S. American Muslims who had helped produce the report and the group of consumers I had access to all read the report as a signal of U.S. American Muslim belonging—as a sign that U.S. American Muslims had made the right bargain. Yet this bargain to belong does not come without its costs. In the lead-up to my trip to the United Kingdom, Hisham Aidi's book was released. Although the book dedicates only one out of twelve chapters to the topic of hip hop and cultural diplomacy, a lot of the initial media coverage of the book focused solely on this topic. Aidi is a colleague and a friend of mine, and the selective media attention had an immediate impact on my work. Some participants on the U.K. tour, who are also friends of mine, were no longer comfortable with my following them in the manner I had initially planned. I had hoped to engage in the kind of deep participant observation that would have included not only attending official public events, which I did, but also spending qualitative time with the artists during off-stage periods, which I was not in the end able to do. The tour's artists saw their participation neither as an endorsement of the state nor even as a pragmatic bargain, but rather as an exploratory venture to see whether a tour like this, as Man-O-Wax might put it, could indeed be redeemed. Whereas some U.S. American Muslims might see their participation not just as a bargain but as an extension of their rights and thus of their belonging as U.S. Americans, these politically conscious artists had a more critical view of the United States as a world power. Consequently, they were conflicted about their participation in the tour and concerned about their movements being recorded in ways that might imply a willingness to be complicit with U.S. empire.

Yet alignments with state power, willing or otherwise, are what define the post–civil rights and post–9/11 era, in which claims to rights and belonging are embedded in the state's governing power. Accordingly, as Maira notes, "multicultural belonging becomes laced with questions of complicity and complicates notions of dissent" (Maira 2009, 251). The work of the U.S. embassy in the United Kingdom that I witnessed does appear to fall into step with the "Sufi offensive" that Aidi identifies. The embassy engages Muslim hip hop artists to deploy the symbols of Blackness, cool, and Islam to offer an alternative to the various forms of "immoderate" Islam that are seen as a threat to secular liberal democracy. This is also how I read the State Department report, with its references to "the first Muslim to . . ." engage in a particular activity or reach a particular achievement, the identification of certain prominent hip hop artists as Muslims, and its panegyric for Chicago as the epitome of U.S. American Muslim diversity. Each piece of information was selective and selected, like brush strokes on a canvas, to paint a narrative that promotes U.S. empire. This is a narrative of the United States as embracing diversity and therefore having no actual need to try and censor political perspectives; rather, it administers dissent through nonprofit activism at home and Muslim hip hop abroad.

My focus on the state's administration of dissent is not meant to suggest that Muslim Cool consequently becomes devoid of all potential to resist state hegemony. Rather, I seek to elucidate the very real constraints on the forms of resistance used by a critical racial and religious minority. These constraints accommodate only a narrowed political vision and very particular political options, and divergence from these options is subject to the violence of the surveillance state. In a post–9/11 United States in which the term "radical" has become synonymous with "Muslim terrorist" and where even those U.S. American Muslims who have chosen to cooperate with counterterrorism work are surveilled, what are the alternate choices for resistance and political vision? Indeed, while the hip hop generation is distinct from its civil rights and Black Power predecessors, the intensity of the state's repressive violence directed at Black Power activists—from the surveillance regime of COINTELPRO and its relationship to the assassination of Malcolm X to the police murders of youth activists such as Fred Hampton and of groups such as MOVE and to the ascendance of Assata Shakur to the top of the FBI's most wanted list—seems to stand as a warning that should administration by civil society fail, state repressive violence will follow. This does not mean that Muslim Cool cannot find a way around the state, but it does mean that for it to do so, U.S. American Muslim hip hop activists will continue to have to reconsider what it means to belong. Pa' lante!

Conclusion

#BlackLivesMatter

It is fairly common wisdom that death punctuates life. It causes the living to reevaluate and reconsider just about everything, particularly that deep existential question: *what the hell am I doing with my life?* This question became quite palpable for me in the years since 2012 as the movement for Black lives, popularized by the hashtag #BlackLivesMatter, grew in response to a highly televised spate of state-sanctioned and extrajudicial violence against Black men and women. While in Black communities the problem of state violence is so well known it is almost banal, the broadcast of Black deaths through cell phone-captured video, dash cams, and surveillance tapes gave Black activists the evidence they needed to bring these concerns to the national stage. As young Black activists and their allies took to the streets, faced the police, and suffered the consequences, I had to ask myself how my story of young Muslims and Muslim Cool related to this movement. How did the project, and I myself, respond to the fierce urgency of *now*? The answer to that question is simple: fundamentally, the story of Muslim Cool confirms that yes, Black Lives Matter.

Existence at the Intersection of Power and Inequality

The broad Black Lives Matter movement (now represented, inter alia, by an organization of the same name as well as by events such as the Movement for Black Lives in July 2015) has shaken a mainstream U.S. American assumption about race to its core. Black Lives Matter has undermined the belief that race and racism are things of the past in the United States. This belief became increasingly trenchant after the inauguration of the first Black president of the United States, whose election was interpreted as proof of a postracial America. This utopia is defined by the presumption that the country's institutions and the majority of its citizens "don't see race," and thus when racism does rear its ugly head, it is an anomaly precipitated by the lone-wolf actions of White supremacist outliers, such as grandparents stuck in a pre–civil rights mentality, or of mentally disturbed young White men.

By the summer of 2015, young Black activists had become increasingly effective in pushing back against this narrative. They marshaled citizen journalism and community-based research to document the reality of state violence. For example, young Black activism made the finding of the report *Operation Ghetto Storm*, namely, that a Black person is killed by state-sanctioned violence every 28 hours, an oft-quoted statistic.[1] Although their work gained momentum from this particular form of state violence, the focus of young Black activists was ultimately on articulating the multiple ways in which Black life does not matter in the United States. These include disproportional incarceration rates: more than half of the two million persons in U.S. prisons are Black and Latin@, which, according to legal scholar Michelle Alexander (2012), has resulted in another startling statistic: there are more Blacks in the prison system today than were enslaved in 1860. The devaluing of Black lives is also reflected in income and wealth: Black unemployment levels are twice the national average, and the number of Black children in poverty is more than three times that of White poor children. Thus, while the emergence of crowdfunding campaigns for White men accused of killing Black men and crusades in support of the confederate flag (which inspired its own hashtag, #HeritageNotHate) provided further evidence of the insidiousness of anti-Black racism in the United States, Black activists' focus was not on these familiar interpersonal forms of racism but rather on how anti-Black racism lies at the core of social, political, and economic life in the United States.

As the mantra "Black Lives Matter" suggests, Blackness at the intersection of power and inequality is also fundamentally about life— inequality at the level of life and race as a structural condition of U.S. sociality. In his 2014 book *Habeas Viscus*, the African American Studies scholar Alexander Weheliye offered a long-awaited (at least by me) critique of a popular body of social theory. He took to task theorists such as Michel Foucault and Giorgio Agamben for failing to adequately account for race as central to our ideas of the human. In his critique of Agamben, Weheliye points out that while Agamben theorized the concept of "bare life" as a human experience that is prior to racial categorization, the real-life example Agamben cited was the "muselmann"—a prisoner in a Nazi concentration camp who was close to death; severely emaciated, listless, and resigned. As Weheliye notes, the very term Agamben used to describe life prior to racial categorization was in fact a derogatory, racialized label—a German word for "Muslim." Agamben's unintentional admission reiterates that race is a fundamental condition of life—of what it means to be a living human—in the modern world. The identification of race as an existential reality is not meant to reify it as biological truth but rather to highlight how racialization is embedded in the state's management of life (biopolitics, in Foucault's term) and death (necropolitics, in Mbembe's).

Blackness at the intersection of power and inequality is the contextual backdrop from which Muslim Cool emerges. Muslim Cool is an articulation of Islam, as religious belief and practice, through social justice. The collective action in which my teachers engage begins with these questions of life and the work of the self. Race, Blackness, and systemic inequality frame the activism of my teachers and the work of institutions such as IMAN. They learn how to understand systemic inequality through hip hop epistemologies, and this learning motivates them to "do something" *as* Muslims. Hip hop motivates them to be *Muslim* activists, because when they turn to hip hop they are in fact (re)turning to Black Islam. The (re)turn to Black Islam is made by traveling the loop of Muslim Cool, a journey that begins with knowledge of self, an ethic of the self, and action that is fundamental to hip hop epistemologies. Grounded in the belief and practice of U.S. Black Muslims, knowledge of self gave my teachers the tools to locate themselves in time and space, do the interpretive work of understanding their present conditions, and then get to the work of changing the world around them.

Hence, Muslim Cool is about self-making, about identity and subjectivity, about the way in which young Muslims see, experience, and interpret themselves in the world. Muslim Cool constructs and "shores up" social identity as a religious performativity that is raced and gendered. Muslim Cool is the engagement of Blackness as a blueprint for the Muslim self. It thus constitutes a direct challenge and a counterdiscourse to the anti-Blackness of broader U.S. American society as well as the ethnoreligious hegemonies of U.S. American Islam. Moreover, by engaging Blackness as a way of being Muslim, from food choices to scarf styles, suiting, youth organizing, and hip hop performances, Muslim Cool is an embodiment of the notion that Black Life Matters; it is a demonstration that Blackness is invaluable to our collective existence. Yet because our collective existence in the modern world is shaped by race, power, and inequality, Muslim Cool has varying consequences for my multiethnic teachers. A young Pakistani American Muslim woman can look "so 'hood" while interning at an elite educational institution, whereas for the young Black Muslim woman and the Muslim dandy, "looking 'hood" inspires religious incrimination and, in the context of state violence, could result in death.

Dressing the Part: Gender, Style, and Performance

I was invited to participate on a panel about U.S. American Muslim culture at the ISNA convention in 2014.[2] It was the first main session of the weekend, and the other panelists were Dr. Sherman Jackson and Imam Zaid Shakir, well-known religious scholars in the Muslim community; Alexander Kronemer, the founder of Unity Productions Foundation, an independent company that specializes in films centered on the Muslim experience; and Brother Ali, an acclaimed hip hop artist. The event took place a little more than two years after the death of Trayvon Martin, the unarmed Florida teenager whose murder initiated mobilization around the #BlackLivesMatter hashtag; and less than a month after the Ferguson, Missouri, police officer Darren Wilson shot and killed Mike Brown, another unarmed Black teenager.

This was my first time speaking at ISNA, and the invitation placed me in front of a fairly large audience.[3] I decided to use that visibility to make a statement through more than my words. I went online, found a T-shirt making service, and ordered a navy T-shirt that read, in simple white script, "Black Lives Matter." Well aware of the circulation of anti-Blackness in Muslim spaces in the United States, I chose to wear the T-shirt during my presentation because I wanted to remind the audience that what was happening to U.S. Black Americans beyond the Detroit convention center mattered and should matter to them as Muslims. It is precisely because I was aware of the prevalence of anti-Blackness in U.S.

Muslim communities that my decision, as a Black woman, to wear such a casual clothing item as a T-shirt on a panel with community luminaries was a risky proposition. To assuage that concern I paired the T-shirt with a navy suit jacket and a lime green headscarf, tied to the side in an Afrodiasporic style, and matching pleated palazzo pants. I made these other fashion choices just as intentionally as I had chosen the T-shirt. I chose a scarf style and a color that followed a Black aesthetic that is often unwelcome in spaces such as the ISNA convention. Taking cues from the Muslim dandy, I used dress as a means to push back on white supremacy *and* on Arab and South Asian U.S. American Muslim hegemonies.

While many consider dress to be fluff, "mere husk, the wrapping, the sugar-coating on the pill," in Black expressive cultures style is in fact the "stuff" or, as Stuart Hall (1998, 28) more eloquently put it, "itself the subject of what is going on." As "the subject of what is going on," dress is a site at which we can map not only policies but ways of thinking and being in the world that devalue Black life. The hoodie worn by Trayvon Martin is a prime example of this. Martin's killer, George Zimmerman, defended his actions by claiming that Martin looked "suspicious." Geraldo Rivera, the talk show host turned pundit, famously cosigned this claim by declaring that Trayvon Martin was "wearing thug wear," which made him as responsible for his own death as Zimmerman was (Rivera 2012). In contrast, many others, from churchgoers and state senators to the entire Miami Heat basketball team, donned hoodies as a public act to reject the idea that an article of clothing could justify the murder of an unarmed teen.

The debate over Martin's hoodie highlights the problem of the criminalization of Black people in the United States. Criminalization binds race to crime by advancing the false idea that Black people commit more crime than do other racial and ethnic groups. Black crime is seen to reflect a predisposition to criminality as a result of biology or culture. Criminalization sees potential for criminal behavior in everything a Black person does. Trayvon Martin wore a hoodie to the store. Renisha McBride knocked on a door for help. Eric Garner verbally challenged harassment. Freddie Gray made eye contact with a police officer. Aiyana Stanley-Jones was sleeping.[4]

Young Black men like Trayvon Martin are prime targets of the discourse of criminalization, which has ramifications for the gendered performances of Muslim Cool. In U.S. Muslim circles, Muslim dandies use suiting as a form of resistance and redemption. They counter the politics of pious respectability by articulating alternative notions of piety through styles whose value comes from their roots not in the Islamic East, but in U.S. Black and U.S. Black Muslim sartorial traditions—advancing a redemptive value of Blackness. The Muslim dandy is a gendered performance of an explicitly heterosexual Muslim masculinity that resists broader white supremacist tropes of Blackness as surplus, excess, and lack—the Black man as the Uncle Tom, the Buck, the Old Man, and the Thug. Hence, Muslim dandies' competing politics of pious respectability reflect broader class tensions in U.S. Black American communities that are gendered and sexualized.

While Black men have been specific targets, Black women are also victims of state violence and the attendant discourse on Black criminality. Likewise, the female performance of Muslim Cool also reflects the intersections of race and class. Specifically, the 'hood in the 'hoodjab can conjure the "über-'hood," in which the Black experience is reduced to a mythical and one-dimensional narrative of ruin and pleasure. The 'hood in the 'hoodjab can also be a form of erasure, making the authorial agency of Black women invisible and reifying a female politics of pious respectability in which the sole acceptable type of headscarf for a Muslim woman is the hijab, worn in one non-Black, hegemonic form.

Black criminality and related tropes of Black underclassness and hypersexuality have become facts of Blackness, and these facts animate the disavowal of Blackness within U.S. Muslim communities, as described in this book. As we have seen, forms of policing that repudiate an unadulterated Blackness are undergirded by broader ummah-wide anti-Black sentiments. These facts are institutionalized and endow ethnoreligious hegemony with the power to push Black music in particular and Blackness in general outside the realm of "tradition" and "proper" Muslim practice.

Yet as we have also seen throughout this book, Blackness is polysemous—it carries multiple meanings simultaneously. Accordingly, the 'hood and the 'hoodjab can be part of an architecture of the Muslim self that is not an authenticated performance but a racially sincere embodiment through which Black Muslims can reaffirm the value of Black life, most particularly their own. Indeed, one of the main arguments of this book is that Muslim Cool underscores how critical Blackness is to the self-making of U.S. American Muslims. The U.S. American Muslim's choice to engage or disavow or instrumentalize Blackness in the construction of the self is fundamentally shaped by the politics of race, class, and gender in the performance of identity in the United States. Those Muslims who do Muslim Cool seek to counter prevailing ideas within and outside the U.S. Muslim community that devalue Black life. Their suits and headwraps are embodied forms of resistance that, like my T-shirt, defiantly declare: Black Life Matters.

The Question of Appropriation

In mainstream U.S. American society, Black expressive cultures are the epitome of cool. However, this fact of Blackness—that it is essentially *cool*—is the outcome of a process of objectification. Black styles and Black bodies are rendered into objects—stand-alone signifiers of transgression with style—appropriated for the use and the profit of others. In April 2015 Amandla Stenberg, a young U.S. Black American actress famous from *The Hunger Games* movie, released a video called *Don't Cash Crop My Cornrows*. The video, a high school project Stenberg created with a friend, details these processes of objectification and appropriation. She cites the use of stand-alone signifiers—watermelons, gold teeth, cornrows, and Black women themselves—in music videos, movies, and the personal styles of White actors and musicians.[5]

Stenberg argues that while the line between cultural exchange and cultural appropriation can be blurry, what many members of the White U.S. American cultural elite do is undoubtedly cultural appropriation, because the cultural forms chosen are typically drawn from entrenched racialized stereotypes, such as cornrows as a sign of Black underclassness (Stenberg 2015). These styles are transferred out of Black communities and donned to be cool, for parody, for profit, or for all of the above. The connection to racial myth is not eliminated in this move; rather, it is punctuated—racial stereotype is what makes the appropriated cultural form or artifact valuable in its new context. I do not know whether Ms. Stenberg has read Fanon, but her analysis echoes Fanon's theorization of the transformation of Black people from subjects into objects based on myths woven by "the White man . . . out of a thousand details, anecdotes, stories" (Fanon 1967, 111). As an object, Black life does not matter—it is disavowed—or it matters only when it can be instrumentalized—made useful for non-Black life. Accordingly, Ms. Stenberg ends her video with a haunting question: what would America be like if we loved Black people as much as we love Black culture?

The manner in which Blackness is policed in U.S. American Muslim communities begs the same question: what would U.S. American Muslim communities be like if they loved Black people as much as they love Black culture? The performative context of U.S. American Islam is an echo of the broader society in which Blackness, in its fullest expressions, is disavowed, leaving as the only sanctioned Blackness that which is objectified—turned into an instrument. Disavowal and instrumentalization are extensions of Fanon's early analysis: the Muslim Negro is bad (religiously suspect) as well as *badd* (cool). Black expressive cultures are bracketed out of Islamic practices or, when included, they and the bodies that perform them are policed in such a manner that, as the poet Amir Sulaiman put it, "what makes you Black and American is haram." This kind of engagement with Blackness is grounded in a U.S. context in which unequal power relations among U.S. American Muslims are tied to racialized claims of proximity to the "tradition." However, the move to disavow and instrumentalize Blackness also takes its cues from a longer history of ummah-wide anti-Blackness, which renders claims to the Islamic tradition that are tied to Africa tenuous at best and fully negated at worst. These facts of Blackness, namely, disavowal and instrumentalization, are different techniques that do the same work, the opposite of Muslim Cool, by declaring that Black lives don't matter.

It is in this fraught context that Muslim Cool intervenes. Muslim Cool does not see Blackness as a break with the Islamic tradition that needs to be policed into conformity. Instead, Muslim Cool identifies the interconnections and intersections between the "Black" and the "Muslim" as a pathway to connect to the Islamic tradition. Critically, in this identification Blackness is embraced on its own terms—unpoliced and uncoded. Muslim Cool is a powerful intervention by young Muslims across race and class who are moving toward Blackness by using hip hop to form their Muslim identities in a U.S. American Muslim community whose perspective is colored by the lenses of anti-Blackness. Therefore, to answer my rephrasing of Ms. Stenberg's question: if we, U.S. American Muslims, loved Black people as we love Black culture, we would look a lot like my teachers. We would look like a community that binds itself to the Islamic tradition by binding itself to Blackness. We would look like Muslim Cool.

The Challenges and Potentials of Solidarity

In July 2015 the Movement for Black Lives held its first national convening. Event organizers invited "all Black people invested in this movement to join the convening to shape our present and chart our future" (Movement 2015). For the conveners, the creation of a space by Black people for Black people was critical for mobilization as well as for healing and recharging in order to organize against the many forms of violence that specifically target Black people. But their decision was not without controversy. One Palestinian journalist tweeted "Segregated organizing?" as she questioned the wisdom of "organizing along racial lines" (Rania Khalek, @RaniaKhalek, July 22, 2015). Detailing that debate is beyond the scope of this discussion, but the event is pertinent here because the choice to create a space that privileges Black people is directly related to the aforementioned problem of cultural appropriation. If the pattern in society is to objectify Blackness in order to appropriate it, then it makes sense that Blacks would want spaces where their self-determination is not compromised. Moreover, the creation of this kind of space is also a practice of racial sincerity, in which race is not about authenticity but about sincere bonds between people that enable collective liberation.[6]

Muslim Cool and its techniques of Blackness also reiterate race's sincerity; it is unsettled and unsettling and it is a tie that binds. Highlighting the links between race, gender, and religious subjectivity in the United States, Muslim Cool illustrates that while religion may seek the Divine, religious identity is not transcendent but rather is produced through intersubjective relationships charged by the complexities of race. Critically, these complexities can challenge cross-racial solidarity. While Muslim Cool seeks to intervene in the facts of Blackness at play in wider American society and in the specific contexts of many ethnic Muslim spaces in the United States, the practice of Muslim Cool is not completely disentangled from the quagmire of appropriation. In the field, engagements with Blackness were always trailed by the specter of minstrelsy—for the non-Black Muslim, is Muslim Cool just a means to be edgy?

As we have seen, when Muslim Cool is done across race, it is informed by the racial politics of Black cool as youthful rebellion. On some level, what makes Blackness attractive to young non-Black Muslims is that it diverges from the hegemonic Muslim Desiness and Arabness of their home communities. However, for my teachers, practitioners of Muslim Cool, the relationship to Blackness does not begin and end there, as is often the case with the appropriation of Blackness, particularly through hip hop. Whereas hip hop's rebelliousness has now become mainstream, for my teachers hip hop remains an alternative to mainstream popular culture, whose values they see as the antithesis of who they should be as Muslims. Moreover, their relationships to Blackness are not only constructed through the adoption of styles initiated by Black Muslims but also through interactions with real-life Black people through activism that directly confronts the violence of racism. As Esperanza remarked (quoted in the Introduction to this book), Muslim Cool consciousness is something my non-Black teachers "had to fight for" and continue to fight to maintain, because while the ghost of minstrelsy does not determine the meanings of Muslim Cool, it is nonetheless ever-present.

Just as important, however, racial complexity can provide the elements that make cross-racial solidarity possible. Accordingly, Muslim Cool is also a way of being Muslim that extends the legacy of cross-racial solidarities in the United States. Specifically for my non-Black teachers, the ways in which they see and align their own experiences as racialized minorities mimic earlier traditions of Afro-Asian and Arab-Black U.S. American solidarity. In particular, hip hop's reiteration of the Black radical tradition enabled my teachers to reject notions of race and ethnicity that mark immigrant U.S. Americans as model minorities and Black U.S. Americans as the "anti-model" minority. Muslim Cool thus offers a way to disrupt narratives of division among Arab, Asian and Black U.S. Americans.

My non-Black teachers extend these legacies of solidarity through their activism but also in the way they challenge the boundaries of Muslimness within their ethnic Muslim communities. When they travel the loop of Muslim Cool and (re)turn to Black Islam, they take on knowledge of self as an ethical epistemology as *Muslims*. When they undo narratives of anti-Blackness in the way they think about and perform their Muslimness and encourage others to do likewise, they open up a new space for solidarity between differently racialized Muslims. For them, Muslim Cool is, then, both a means to critique their position as racial minorities in the United States and a means of intervention in interminority relations among U.S. Muslims.

We Have Nothing to Lose but Our Chains . . .
We Gon' Be Alright

One organizational aspect that has come to define the Black Lives Matter movement is its leadership style. The civil rights and Black Power movements had many leaders, whose biographies we continue to learn, yet the period, or more specifically our memory of it, is defined by the singular and charismatic leadership of individuals such as Dr. Martin Luther King Jr. and Malcolm X. In a compelling contrast, while many people around the United States could easily recognize the hashtag #BlackLivesMatter and were mobilizing around it, it was unlikely, for better or worse, that those same people would recognize the names of the three Black women, Alicia Garza, Patrisse Cullors, and Opal Tometi, who started it.[7]

The movement, like its civil rights predecessor, also took to marching in the streets and, like the uprisings of the past, also resulted in the destruction of private property—the kind of resistance that polite company likes to call rioting. The stance of the old guard civil rights establishment toward this form of rebellion has been to call for calm and to reassert the necessity for demonstrators to protest peacefully. The diverse body of young Black leaders at the helm of the Black Lives Matter movement has taken a different position. Although they did not call for rioting, they did call for the disruption of business as usual, for example, during "die-ins" at a mall in St. Louis, by the Water Tower in Chicago on Black Friday, and in the lobby of the Marriott Hotel during the annual meeting of the American Anthropological Association, along with many other locations.[8] They also called for the valuing of "people over profit," pointing to the irony that outrage over damage to private property often outweighed outrage at the loss of Black life from state violence.

I read the style of the Black Lives Matter movement and its divergence from that of the older civil rights tradition as a creative effort to subvert a state that has become adept at administering dissent. The domestication of racial politics is a hallmark of the post–civil rights and post–9/11 United States. Domesticated racial politics narrow the concerns of U.S. communities of color to their rights to legal and affective citizenship. This is a move away from internationalist and transnational frameworks of belonging to a right that only the state can endorse. Therefore, the very demand for rights reinforces the authority of the state. The post–civil rights and post–9/11 era is defined by the ways in which this desire for belonging is taken up by the state, which coopts dissent through its administration of dissent. To put it more plainly, the state and the Black political establishment would like the movement for Black lives to protest through approved channels, but the movement has chosen to resist on its own, Black terms.

The contours of this debate map the limits of Muslim Cool. Throughout this book I have argued for Muslim Cool's bona fides as a counterdiscourse and a counter-performativity of Muslimness in which, in contrast to dominant paradigms, Blackness is central. Yet in the present context Muslim Cool's alterity is also constrained by and entangled with the state. Entanglements with the state are particularly pertinent to Muslim Cool, because as Muslims my teachers are subject to both the post–civil rights multicultural state and the parallel post–9/11 surveillance state. On the one hand, the state seeks to "include" U.S. American Muslims as a multiracial U.S. minority group like the African Americans (to use the official term) as proof of American exceptionalism. On the other hand, the category "Muslim" stands as a signifier of a threat to the state, and Muslims are thus frequently questioned as to their belonging. These parallel state discourses create a political landscape in which U.S. American Muslims, in order to contest claims that they do not belong to the nation, must cut a hard bargain with the state. Accordingly, Muslim Cool is also a timely illustration of the very real constraints on the political imaginaries of a critical racial and religious minority. These constraints are significant but as the movement for Black lives has demonstrated, they are not insurmountable.

At the Black Lives Matter protests I attended while preparing this manuscript, it was common for organizers to lead demonstrators in chanting a mantra composed by the U.S. Black woman revolutionary activist Assata Shakur: "It is our duty to fight for our freedom. It is our duty to win. We must love each other and support each other. We have nothing to lose but our chains." It was reported on social media that in a confrontation with the police at the conclusion of the Movement for Black Lives convening (which I did not attend), demonstrators also chanted "We Gon' Be Alright," the chorus of a song with the same name by the hip hop artist Kendrick Lamar. I think these verses, Shakur's and Lamar's, point to what the future may hold for Muslim Cool. The future of Muslim Cool, and of Muslims in the United States more broadly, lies in its investment in its alterity—the ability to imagine, articulate, and participate in alternate choices for resistance and political vision. This is a prospect that comes at high risk; but we have nothing to lose but our chains . . . we gon' be alright.

NOTES

INTRODUCTION

1 In acknowledgment that the United States is part of the Americas and hence only one among many American nations, I use the phrase "U.S. American" rather than "American" (on its own) to describe residents of the United States.

2 Quotation marks are used here in recognition of the fact that my use of the term teachers to describe my interlocutors might be unfamiliar to readers—they are not used to suggest that my interlocutors are not *really* my teachers. Accordingly, subsequent use of the term, when describing my interlocutors, appears without quotation marks.

3 My expression, Muslim Cool, is inspired by the term *New Muslim Cool* coined by the independent documentary filmmaker Jennifer Maytorena Taylor. *New Muslim Cool* is the title of Taylor's documentary, for which I was a senior project advisor. Taylor's invocation of the term New Muslim Cool is a riff off of Miles Davis's "Birth of the Cool," and her film follows Hamza Perez, a Puerto Rican American Muslim and hip hop artist. The documentary looks intimately at not only Perez's music but also his transitions as a family man and community leader who is targeted by post–9/11 government surveillance.

4 Englewood is a neighborhood located on the South Side of Chicago. Its residents are predominately U.S. Black American and the neighborhood is most popularly known because of a series of negative indicators including high rates of unemployment and violent crime and low incomes. These negative indicators are the results of decades of disinvestment in the neighborhood by the city government and business elites.

5 My rendering of Blackness is deeply informed by the work of Stuart Hall, particularly his theorization of Afrodiasporic identities within the framework of similarity and difference. Similarity underscores what is shared—the broad and specific spatiotemporal realities that link Afrodiasporic peoples—whereas difference emphasizes the diversity of Afrodiasporic experiences and identities (Hall 1990). Hall's formulation of Blackness is true to my own theoretical orientation and also reflects the ways in which Blackness functioned in my field sites. Likewise, Kelley's notion of polyculturalism, that cultures are never pure but in fact come into being through cultural exchange, is also key to my work, particularly in the way he identifies the multiple cultural flows that comprise the category marked "Black." For more engagement with polyculturalism, see Prashad 2001; Maira 2009; Sharma 2010; Daulatzai 2012.

6 I use the term "Black" as a modifier in this Diasporic sense and "U.S. Black," "U.S. Black American," or "Black U.S. American" when identifying the specific contours of Blackness in the United States as well as those Black individuals who live in the United States. This designation would include Black individuals who are recent immigrants from Africa; however, the majority of my Black teachers were not of recent immigrant origin, whether from the continent of Africa or from other parts of the Americas.

7 In his recent monograph *The Hip Hop Underground* James Peterson deploys "root" and "route" as "figuratively emblematic of an individual's connections to his/her history and culture," and "rhizome" as a "conceptual understanding" of how Blackness "achieves its many meanings and manifestations" (2014, 1–2). Scholars have also used roots, routes, and rhizomes to deterritorialize the African diaspora itself in order to attend to the being and becoming of Diasporic Black- ness (Hall 1990; Moore 1994; West 1994).

8 In a cypher, hip hop heads "battle" each other to establish who has the best dance moves or lyrical skills. The cypher is also a place in which knowledge and cultural practices are exchanged and through which community is built among hip hop folk.

9 This bias is reflective of anthropology's area studies fetish, which is a remnant of anthropology's colonial past as well as a focus motivated by disciplinary anxiet- ies around "objectivity," which ties research validity to the distance between the researcher and her data. This focus is symptomatic of the current U.S. cultural milieu, in which intellectual production is valuable only if it is "objective," that is, "scientific." If objectivity can arise only through distance from research subjects, then U.S. American anthropology must be conceived of as the study of the "other" outside the United States.

10 These differences are geographic (e.g., Senegalese versus Syrians) as well as based on class and timing (e.g., the waves of highly educated immigrants in the 1960s and 1970s versus the less-skilled immigrants in subsequent decades).

11 Other examples of this approach include Alim 2006a; Sharma 2010; Hill 2009; Clay 2012; and Love 2012.

12 The East-West University study reported slightly higher income and education rates among U.S. Black American Muslims compared with the overall Black population of Chicago as recorded in the 2000 census. The class position of U.S. Black American Muslims indicated by the 1997 report was reflected in the lifestyles of many of the Black U.S. American Muslims I encountered at IMAN. A number of my Black teachers lived in communities on the edges of the city or in adjacent southern suburbs. These are the locations to which the general population of middle-class Blacks have relocated in an effort to find better quality housing than was available in traditional urban Black Chicago neigh- borhoods.

13 Ummah is an Arabic term used to describe the Muslims as a community, imply- ing mutual obligation, solidarity, and shared experience.

14 Some have estimated that up to 30 percent of the enslaved Africans who were settled in the United States were Muslims. For more on this history, see Austin 1997; Curtis 2009; Diouf 2013.

15 For example, a Bosnian Muslim community has been living in the Chicago area since the 1950s. However, it was a phenotypically "White" community that did not carry any of the signs such has headscarves that would have made it visibly "Muslim" during this period.

16 The Islamic Family Reunion was a weekend conference in Orlando, Florida, held in 2003. It culminated in a hip hop concert.

17 I will address definitions of the term "'hood" in chapter 3. Here I am using the term in the way it was used at IMAN. For example, in 2010 IMAN held a "Heal the 'Hood" fund-raising campaign during Ramadan, the Islamic month of fasting. The short video that accompanied this campaign included images of boarded-up buildings and trash-strewn streets along with local Black, Mexican, and Palestinian U.S. American youth engaged in IMAN programming. It also featured Black men rebuilding local housing. These images suggest that the 'hood, according to IMAN, is economically poor but resource-rich in its residents of color.

18 Some of the young people also participated in youth organizing activities at other youth-oriented community organizations on the Southwest Side.

19 I can say that I rarely encountered any open hesitation to interact with me after my IMAN credentials had been established. However, I would like to acknowledge the possibility that I was still viewed with skepticism by some.

CHAPTER 1. THE LOOP OF MUSLIM COOL

1 Community Café is a regular event held by IMAN that showcases Muslim artists.

2 The Five Percent Nation of Gods and Earths is a spiritual movement that emerged in the late 1960s under the teaching of Clarence 13X, later known by the title Father Allah. Before leading his own movement, Father Allah was a youth minister in the Nation of Islam. Father Allah used the "Lost-Found Muslim Lessons," which make up what scholars refer to as the NOI catechism (Swedenburg 1997; Miyakawa 2005), in the expansion of his own spiritual teachings. Thus, Five Percenters "learn the same history, geography, origin stories, and eschatology of the Nation of Islam" (Miyakawa 2005, 25) but also draw on "Kemetic symbolism, Masonic mysticism, and Gnostic spirituality" (Miyakawa 2005, 5).

3 This network is international and includes artists such as The Narcycist, based in Toronto, and Poetic Pilgrimage and Mohammad Yahya, both from the United Kingdom.

4 This, like most of the other names that appear in this book, is a pseudonym.

5 After the death of Elijah Muhammad, the leadership of the NOI passed on to his seventh child, Wallace Mohammed, who later became known as Warith Deen Mohammed, Imam Mohammed, or "the Imam" in community circles. Although raised in the household of "the Messenger," as his father was known, Imam W. D. Mohammed grew to hold beliefs that diverged from his father's and moved

toward orthodox Sunni Islam. Therefore, when he became leader of the NOI, he guided his community toward Sunni Islam. Scholars consider his effort "a remarkable transformation": "in less than a decade, Wallace Muhammad debunked the myth of Yacub, became an advocate of American patriotism, and aligned the NOI with Sunni Islamic teachings and the Arab Islamic world" (Curtis 2002, 107).

6 In 2000, Black residents made up 52 percent of the population of the south suburbs, which comprise "thirty communities directly south of Chicago from the Indiana border on the east, to approximately Interstate 57 on the west, and Will County on the south" (SSHC 2008, 2). By contrast, the southwest suburbs, the twenty-three communities west of the south suburbs and the location of the village of Bridgeview, are an area "traditionally perceived to be 'closed' to African-Americans who comprised at the [2000] census, only 3.4% of the population" (SSHC 2008, 3).

7 The RZA is a hip hop artist and producer and one of the founding members of the group, the Wu Tang Clan.

8 Bambaataa is a "generative and promethean" hip hop figure (Chang 2005). One of hip hop's Godfathers, Bambaataa has made signature musical contributions, such as creating break-beat DJing along with Kool Herc and Grandmaster Flash, and developed the Electro Funk Sound.

9 In an interview with Troy L. Smith, Se'Divine stated that "The World's Famous Supreme Team Show" followed Mr. Magic's show on WHBI 105.9. See www. oldschoolhiphop.com.

10 For example, "Thou art but [sent] to warn those who stand in awe of it [the day of judgment]." Qur'an 79:45 (trans. Muhammad Asad).

11 It is unknown whether any of the artists Pabon mentioned were indeed Muslims.

12 A hadith is a narration of the Prophet Muhammad's words and deeds. Within the Five Percenter community, some consider themselves Muslim while others do not.

13 A jilbab is a long, loose, long-sleeved garment that originated as a form of dress for Muslim women in the Middle East.

14 For example, Lauryn Hill (1996) mentions Khalid Muhammad in the song "How Many Mics." More recently, D'Angelo, the R&B artist, included an excerpt of a Khalid Muhammad speech on his latest album (2014).

15 This is a community of Black U.S. American Jews who claim descent from the original tribe of Israel and practice vegetarianism. They were founded in Chicago but have communities all over the world, including in Dimona, Israel.

16 Hip hop heads and academics alike debate the actual time frame of the golden era. However, for the purposes of contextualizing Tasleem's comments, William Jelani Cobb's demarcation, 1984–1992, is particularly useful. Cobb identifies 1992, which saw the release of the album *The Chronic* by the California-based hip hop producer Dr. Dre, as the year in which the ascendancy of West Coast artists and the genre of Gangsta rap commenced. See Cobb (2007).

17 For earlier analysis of this video, see Roberts 1994; and Keyes 2004, 213.

18 Within the historiography of Black Islam, Islam has been identified as the "natural" religion for African-descended peoples and thus the most suitable means
toward true liberation. Intellectuals such as Edward Blyden and Duse Muhammad Ali have espoused this idea since the nineteenth century. Blyden, a Diasporic
Black intellectual, ardent Black Nationalist, and statesman, is most famously
known for his treatise *Christianity, Islam and the Negro Race*. Although he was
an ordained Christian minister, Blyden championed the link between Islam and
Black liberation, arguing that "Islam created an authentically black civilization
[and] encouraged a type of progress that also created dignity and self-respect"
(Curtis 2002, 29). This link was also espoused by Muslims such as Ali, who
integrated Pan-Africanism, Islam, and anti-imperialist politics as the editor and
publisher of the Pan-African and anticolonialist periodical *The African Times and
Orient Review* and as the teacher of Marcus Garvey (GhaneaBassiri 2010).

19 Because of her name, Latifah, there has always been unconfirmed speculation
that the Queen is in fact a Muslim. There are two official narratives—that she was
nicknamed Latifah by her cousin who was a Muslim, and that she chose the name
Latifah following a trend in her New Jersey neighborhood of taking on Arabic
names. Most online biographies, including that on biography.com, narrate the
first naming story, which is the one I have always been told and read about. However, there are also mainstream media outlets such as ABC News that have cited
Queen Latifah as saying she named herself.

20 However, there are also U.S. Black Americans who see Islam as a colonial force on
the continent of Africa.

21 Furthermore, the military discipline of PE's security team, S1W (Security of the
First World), is reminiscent of the NOI paramilitary regiment, the Fruit of Islam,
and the security team's name is reportedly based on the idea that Africans are
First World people as the first inhabitants on earth, an idea that is taken from
NOI beliefs.

22 In Supreme Mathematics and the Supreme Alphabet, meanings found in the Lost-
Found Lessons of the Nation of Islam are assigned to the Roman numerals zero
through nine and the letters A through Z, respectively.

23 "Breaking down" is also a creative process in which meanings may emerge
that are not directly derived from the Lost-Found Lessons but reflect the same
worldview (Miyakawa 2005). One example of breaking down is the Five Percenter
redefinition of the word Allah. By "breaking down" the word according to its
form in English transliteration, "Arm Leg Leg Arm Head," Five Percenters believe
it reveals the godhood of Black men.

24 The greeting "What up God" comes from the Five Percenter belief in the divin-
ity of the Black man, "dropping science" reflects the Five Percenter emphasis on
learning and sharing knowledge, and "word is bond" represents the value the Five
Percenter community places on an ethic of trustworthiness in word and deed
(Floyd-Thomas 2003; Miyakawa 2005). As Miyakawa explains, "word is bond" is a
reference to Lost-Found Lesson no. 1, question 11: "Have you not learned that your

word shall be Bond regardless of whom or what? Yes. My word is Bond and Bond is life, and I will give my life before my word shall fail" (Miyakawa 2005, 49).

25 These values are taken from a longer list featured in the "Zulu Beliefs" section of the official website of the Zulu Nation, which states, "The Zulu Nation stands for: knowledge, wisdom, understanding, freedom, justice, equality, peace, unity, love, respect, work, fun, overcoming the negative to the positive, economics, mathematics, science, life, truth, facts, faith and the oneness of God." See www. zulunation.com. This is an extensive and deliberate list, which also draws on the Five Percenters. It is illustrative of the holistic awareness of the self and the social world that Bambaataa and the Zulu Nation seek to promote.

26 Cobb (2007) notes that for some hip hop artists, unlike Malcolm, rebirth leads to social and economic integration into the dominant culture.

27 Elijah Muhammad referred to Black U.S. Americans as "so-called Negroes" because he believed that neither "Negro" nor "colored" was a "proper name" for the descendants of the Asiatic Black tribe of Shabazz (Muhammad 1965, 34).

28 See al-Ghazali (1997). The potential links between al-Ghazali and the Nation of Islam are beyond the purview of the present project, but they do suggest that knowledge of self is an ethic that has a long history in the Islamic intellectual tradition.

29 Rabia, like many others, reads Richie as White.

30 Marijuana smoking is a common activity in the hip hop community, "commercial" and "conscious" alike.

31 That is, give the Muslim greeting "As Salaamu Alaikum" ("Peace be upon you").

32 "O Mankind! Partake of what is lawful and good (*tayyib*) on earth and follow not in Satan's footsteps for, verily he is your open foe." Qur'an 2:168 (trans. Muhammad Asad).

33 The Hanafi school is one of the four major schools of Sunni jurisprudence.

34 Except for one crew member who responds, "Yeah, all the time."

35 Other practices, such as Stic.Man's marijuana use, cannot. The same song, "Be Healthy," also includes the lyrics "No fish though, no candy bars, no cigarettes / only ganja [marijuana] and fresh squeezed juice from oranges" (Dead Prez 2000). However, the Dead Prez 2010 mixtape *Revolutionary but Gangsta Grillz* warns against the potential dangers of recreational drug use, including marijuana and alcohol, in the tracks "Don't Waste It" and "Overdose."

36 The current director of youth programming at IMAN is also a vegetarian. This is not a coincidence but speaks to the kinds of ideologies present at IMAN.

37 Race is not an explicit category in this body of work, although it should be.

CHAPTER 2. POLICING MUSIC AND THE FACTS OF BLACKNESS

1 "From among my followers there will be some people who will consider illegal sexual intercourse, the wearing of silk (clothes), the drinking of alcoholic drinks, and the use of musical instruments lawful" (*Sahih Bukhari*, Volume 7, Book 69, Number 494, trans. Muhsin Khan).

2 Yusuf al-Qaradawi, a prominent Muslim scholar, states: "Although this hadith is in Sahih Al-Bukhari [the most respected collection of hadith] its chain of transmission is not connected to Prophet Muhammad (peace and blessings be upon him) and this invalidates its authenticity" (Qaradawi 2010).

3 "Good Blackness" and "bad Blackness" recall Mahmood Mamdani's (2005) "good Muslim-bad Muslim" binary. Tracing shifts in the U.S. government's engagements with Muslim populations beyond its borders, Mamdani argues that these shifts are determined by a culture talk that constructs two Muslim types based on essentialist notions of culture and behavior. Good Muslims are those whose Muslim identity is appropriately different, defined by their alleged commitments to freedom and democracy, "progressive" interpretations of religion, and full incorporation in the neoliberal marketplace. In contrast, bad Muslims are inappropriately different, noted for their alleged cultural parochialism, religious fundamentalism, and tendency toward violence. I use the word "alleged" here because good Muslim and bad Muslim, like good and bad Blackness, do not describe real people but strategically deployed ideal types. Similar to the deployment of a Black president, official state and media recognition of the good Muslim is marshaled as evidence that the U.S.-led war on terror is not unfairly singling out Muslims. Yet Evelyn Alsultany (2012) has shown that representations of the good Muslim in popular media reinforce rather than disrupt the narrative of the bad Muslim. The good Muslim makes an appearance, but only as the staunch and sacrificial patriot always juxtaposed with the bad Muslim bent on terrorizing the nation. Alsultany argues that while these parallel depictions could imply a greater complexity of representation because they are constructed around the simple good/bad opposition, they actually work to legitimize racist policies and practices (Alsultany 2012, 22).

4 The Taqwa Tour, a touring group of five Taqwacore or Muslim punk bands, took the stage at the ISNA open mic. I was not in attendance, but according to what I was told and later online reports, the performances included lyrics with expletives and female singing to a mixed-gender audience, both of which were prohibited by ISNA's guidelines. Poetry recital by women was generally considered acceptable at ISNA at this point, but singing was still deemed inappropriate. Eventually, ISNA's staff interrupted the performance of the all-female group Secret Trial Five, which led to a standoff between the Taqwacore bands, which wanted to continue the show, and ISNA representatives, who insisted that they leave. In the end, the Taqwa Tour left under police escort, and the entire open mic event was shut down.

5 This later changed. Poetry performances by women are now included at ISNA events, and there was even a Qur'anic recitation by a woman, Tahera Ahmad, in 2013—a first for ISNA.

6 This is one of hip hop's great ironies. Despite the central role of the DJ in hip hop, the art of turntablism, the skilled use of the turntable as an instrument, can be virtually unknown among young people who consume hip hop as a form of mainstream popular culture.

7 Many debates among lay Muslims, in part a result of the discursive influence of the literal textuality of U.S. American salafism, are often won or lost by one's ability to instantly cite daleel (evidence).

8 Analogy is a tool used within the Islamic jurisprudential tradition.

9 One recent example of such critique was prompted by ISNA's press release in the wake of the Baltimore Uprising of 2015: in the release, the organization declared it was "disturbed by the escalation of violence in Baltimore" (ISNA 2015). Critics held that ISNA should have been more disturbed by the rate of the loss of U.S. Black life at the hands of the police and identified the press release as another example of tone deafness in matters of race and Blackness among Arab and South Asian U.S. American Muslims.

10 For example, notions of Black criminality were institutionalized through the enforcement of official Black codes. Adjustments to penal codes (such as making the theft of a pig a felony), convict leasing, unfair sharecropping practices, and official and unofficial laws that governed the use of public space by Black people (White and White 1998) regulated Black life—fueling Black death, Black incarceration, and White profit.

11 My point here is not that these scholars render Africa invisible themselves but that their popularity among U.S. Muslims is tied to the places where they studied, which are outside the continent or only in select countries in Africa.

12 According to the MAS website, the organization has no affiliation with revivalist groups such as the Egyptian Muslim Brotherhood. However, Brotherhood ideology had some influence on the group in its early days. MAS has critically reevaluated the relevance of Brotherhood authors such as Hasan al-Banna and Sayyid Qutb to its work in the United States (MAS 2014).

13 I used the term *dawah-pop* to describe an emerging genre of Muslim music that is stylistically pop music yet motivated to spread the message of Islam.

14 Material in this section is revised and expanded from my article "American Muslims and the Facts of Blackness," in the *Islamic Monthly* (Spring/Summer 2014).

15 In Black Muslim spaces the prominence of men is often due to the persistence of patriarchal assumptions that equate masculinity with authority—assumptions that are not particular to Black Muslims.

CHAPTER 3. BLACKNESS AS A BLUEPRINT FOR THE MUSLIM SELF

1 *Hijabi* is a colloquial term popular among young American Muslims to describe Muslim women who wear headscarves. Hijabi is a play on "hijab," an Arabic term used by many Muslims to describe the Muslim woman's headscarf.

2 Forman's citation of Eazy-E is not meant to imply that he created the term, but to identify hip hop's role in the term's popularization in mainstream society.

3 "The 'hood involves an intentional, engaged process of cultural recuperation of African American and Latino-dominated space enacted primarily by contemporary urban youth. . . . The 'hood accommodates the general spatial images of the ghetto but the term also allows greater flexibility. . . . Where the ghetto has been

culturally shackled to a negative symbolic configuration of images and ideas, the 'hood offers a new terminology and discursive frame that can simultaneously address conditions in all 'hoods everywhere, to individuated places, or to particular sites of significance" (Forman 2002, 65).

4 Forman also conceives of the distinction between the ghetto and the 'hood as a movement from abstract notions of space to localized ones. The distinction becomes useful or apparent when considering how the 'hood, through hip hop's commercial power, becomes accessible in ways the "ghetto" is not. Some examples of redeployments of the 'hood include "Coming Soon to a 'Hood Near You: Street Sweeping"—the title of a blog post about street sweeping in Salem, Massachusetts, a city whose population is over 80 percent White and middle class (Guerrirero 2010); "Adopt-a-Street in Your 'Hood"—the title of an educational curriculum for middle school students developed by the Environmental Protection Agency; and "Meetro Eases Hookups in Your Hood"—an ad on the technology site wired.com for social networking technology used mainly by 18- to 30-year-olds and recent transplants to New York City and Chicago (Singel 2005). It is hard to imagine similar headlines so far removed from Black and Latin@ communities using the word "ghetto." In fact "ghetto" has become commonly used as a colloquialism, "That's so ghetto," in mainstream U.S. pop culture to describe things that are undesirable.

5 A remix is a revised version of a song; usually the revision includes the addition of other rappers and/or singers and beats to the song. The remix is a long tradition in hip hop. The original 2005 song is by Chicago native and internationally renowned emcee Common.

6 As a place, the city has been identified since antiquity. Yet it is the rapid growth of cities in Western Europe and the United States in the eighteenth and nineteenth centuries that has captured the imagination of intellectuals. The explosion of industrial centers and massive human migrations prompted scholars to take up the city as a subject of theoretical inquiry; approaches to the city range from the administrative to the philosophical (Simmel 1971; Benjamin 2008; Wirth 1995; Jacobs 1961; Hannerz 1983; Low 1999). Like Common, Scarface, and Yasiin Bey, what these intellectual inquiries into the city and urban life struggle to capture is the central paradox of the modern city: it is at once a place of progress and marginality, cosmopolitanism and segregation, physical density and psychic alienation—the city is simultaneously a place of life and one of death.

7 The term *khimar* is derived from the Qur'anic verse 24:31 that speaks directly to the issue of modesty and female dress. According to Hans Wehr's dictionary the term can be translated as cover, headscarf, or face veil. I have found that the term "hijab" is predominant in non-Black U.S. American Muslim communities and has only recently come to be used by U.S. Blacks, who tended to refer to headscarves using the term khimar or English equivalents.

8 For other examples of this, see Curtis (2002); Rouse (2004); and Karim (2008).

9 A similar erasure is happening with the rising popularity of turban-style headscarves among non-Black Muslim women in the United States. This stylistic

choice has become a media favorite in telling tales of stylish Muslim women, as if Muslim women only recently discovered a love of fashion—a love that is tied to how "Western" they are. In these stories, the turban's origins have been linked to a Malaysian pop star. However, the turban is, of course, a very old head wrapping practice that, as the headdress of Muslim women in the United States, neither just began in the twenty-first century nor was initiated by a Malaysian artist. Rather, Black Muslim women have covered their heads in this way in the United States for at least a century, if not longer.

CHAPTER 4. COOL MUSLIM DANDIES

1 "Al-Fatiha" is the first chapter of the Qur'an and the chapter first learned by Muslims, as it is required for all prayers and many other devotional activities.

2 For example, Carolyn Rouse (2004) describes how U.S. Black American women embraced divisions of labor that allowed them to stay out of the workforce, because the option to join it was never afforded to Black women.

3 As Cedric Robinson (2007) notes, some of these ideas predate transatlantic slavery. Specifically, he cites Othello as "the buck" in Shakespeare's eponymous play (2007, 86).

4 This symbolic figure goes back to the controversial radio turned television comedy *Amos 'n' Andy*. Sapphire was a loud and sassy character who incessantly nagged her "no good" husband, Kingfish. Kingfish was a "coon," a buffoon figure who was always cooking up "fast money" and other schemes to shirk responsibility, particularly responsibilities tied to White normative masculine ideals. The all-Black world of *Amos 'n' Andy* was originally played by White actors, until the show moved to television and many Black U.S. Americans protested, arguing that it trafficked in stereotypical images. The NAACP also waged a campaign against the televised version of the show. There have been a number of later biographical accounts of Black viewers who felt that there were redeemable aspects to the show. See Lipsitz (1990).

5 The 1965 report penned by then-senator Daniel Patrick Moynihan proclaimed the end of legalized racial discrimination but warned that Black disadvantage would continue, not because of White racism but because of Black pathology.

6 Martin was a 17-year-old U.S. Black American who was shot by George Zimmerman in Miami, Florida. Zimmerman, who was patrolling the neighborhood, claimed that Martin looked dangerous. Martin was visiting his father and returning from a local candy store when he was killed.

7 Diawara theorizes strolls in the Village as "enjoying the black good life" by conquering White-dominated spaces (Diawara 1998). Juxtaposing the movement of youth of color with the civil rights tradition, the "good life" for Diawara is distinct from the respectable good of an earlier generation, which privileged thrift and the delay of pleasure. The Black good life "rejects the imprisoning and policing of black bodies by a racist and capitalist system" while signifyin' on that very same system. The hip hop mogul not only dominates public city streets in his $4,000

Tom Ford suit but also "strolls" down White-controlled spaces, from music label boardrooms to Paris fashion week.

8 The Fruit of Islam is a group that trains males in the Nation of Islam to be men, within the context of the NOI definition of manhood. The FOI or "Fruit" are also responsible for security within the community

9 Although not from the geographical Middle East, the Moroccan *jallaba* can sometimes wield this kind of authenticity, but my observations indicate that its adoption among mainstream Muslim male leaders in the United States has been restricted to a particular cohort of neotraditionalists such as Hamza Yusuf.

10 The Sunni/Philly Beard has become such a symbol of the city that in 2014 the city's tourism board collaborated with Curran J. Swint, a local business owner who is a U.S. Black American Muslim man, in the production of a video entitled "The Bearded Bunch." The video features eight different men, some Muslim and others non-Muslim, mostly Black and young (in their twenties and thirties), who would all easily be characterized as dandies. In the video they discuss the meaning of the beard to Philly and the beard as a sign of mature masculinity. See https://vimeo.com.

11 I imagine they are also creatively using dress from South Asia; however, I have no data on that point to date.

12 Dorinne Kondo notes that in addition to being seen as perpetually foreign, Asian U.S. American men also argue that they are "emasculated and desexualized" in Euro-American culture (Kondo 1997, 165). Although Ilyas never referred to sexuality, his choice of an iconically masculine outfit that is tied to dominant and subversive forms of male power in the United States may also index this concern.

13 As documented in *Dollar a Day, Ten Cents a Dance*, Filipino farmworkers in California, through the 1930s, were subjected to intense racial discrimination and violence. Filipino men, seen as "dashing, good looking, good dressers and sauve with the women," were popular at taxi dance halls, where men paid ten cents per dance with a woman, all of whom were White. This was determined a threat by their White male counterparts and accusations of sexual contact with White women led to the Watsonville Riot of 1930, in which a Filipino man, Fermin Tobera, was killed.

14 This depiction and the context that gave rise to it are being examined by a small but growing body of scholarship on Muslim masculinity. This body of work looks at Muslim men as men and investigates the forms of masculinity accessible for, generated by, and relevant to the construction of Muslim masculinity. The majority of this literature, like most academic work on Muslim life, makes generalized claims about Muslim men based on communities of Muslims in North Africa and the Middle East. One significant departure is Amanullah De Sondy's work (2015), which explores these issues in the intellectual and practical context of South Asia. Abdullah's (2012) recent work on masculinity in the NOI can be counted among this literature, as can that of Curtis (2002).

CHAPTER 5. THE LIMITS OF MUSLIM COOL

1   This narrative of Chicago began with immigration and ended with immigration, with only a casual reference to native-born converts and without any mention of the Nation of Islam. It thus differs from Muslim Cool's and IMAN's narrative of Islam in Chicago.

2   Like the chapters of the booklet, the four videos are organized around the following questions: Who are American Muslims? Where are American Muslims? How do American Muslims live their religion? What do American Muslims do?

3   I use the term "civil rights era" to refer to the period from the 1950s through the 1970s, not the activism specific to the civil rights movement.

4   Kitwana argues that this paradox blurs the boundaries of political action, which fundamentally shapes the form of contemporary hip hop activism. He contends that the easy binary of "nationalist versus integrationist" that shaped Black politics during the civil rights era does not have currency for the hip hop generation, for whom the enemy "is not simply white supremacy [or even] capitalism," especially "when financial success and the righteousness of the free market have become synonymous with patriotism" (Kitwana 2002, 149). However, as Adreanna Clay points out in her study of hip hop activism, as much as the hip hop generation diverges from the binaries of the civil rights era, "today's youth activists are also expected to organize in the *shadow* of previous social movement activists [and] this organizing happens in the midst of the mass commodification of activist images and documentary (and fictional) retellings of these movements" (emphasis in original; Clay 2012, 7).

5   I had done enough reading on fieldwork to know that my "departure" was tenuous because the interests and relationships I had built in the field would be ongoing.

6   These various levels spanned the drop-in level, which engaged young people through one-time events such as block parties; the program level, which connected youth to the organization through activities such as the "Kids and Docs" summer program on filmmaking; the rites of passage level, in which young people worked in small intimate groups over an extended period of time on holistic personal development though IMAN's PILLARS program; and the "leader" level, which included participation in Leaders of the New School and/or membership in IMAN Youth Council. Although all these levels were driven by a broader youth leadership development goal, the fourth, "leader" level was specifically designed to prepare youth for the fifth level of engagement, in which young people would take on specific positions within the leadership of IMAN, for example, as a member of the organization's board of directors.

7   Her conclusions are drawn from an examination of "Muslim world outreach" efforts under the Bush administration (which have continued under Obama) whose "pedagogical strategy is to convince Muslims that they must learn to historicize the Quran." By seeing the Qur'an as embedded in a certain time, Muslims can

follow the spirit of the Qur'an while abandoning practices that do not jibe with "a certain modality of liberal political rule" (Mahmood 2006, 335).

8 As described in chapter 3, music, because of the religious debates that surround it, is a contentious issue in the U.S. Muslim community and a flash point of distinction. Similarly, in the U.K. context music is a sonic line in the sand—Salafism's British Muslim critics use music to mark their difference from the Salafis (Aidi 2014, 75).

9 Archery was known to be encouraged by the Prophet Muhammad.

10 The group's Facebook page describes it as "a student society based at SOAS for the promotion of spirituality"; www.facebook.com (2014).

11 Like most of my teachers' and interlocutors' names in the book, "Thomas" is a pseudonym.

12 "Revert" is a term used within U.S. and U.K. Muslim communities as an alternative to "convert." Describing conversion to Islam as a reversion is linked to the theological belief that each human is born Muslim. "Asian" in the U.K. context refers primarily to individuals of South Asian descent.

13 Other poets featured in the collection included Suheir Hammad and Dr. Mohja Kahf.

14 Until that point, I had assumed the trip was sponsored either by the book's publisher or by the Muslim-run interfaith-oriented organization that had handled all the logistics of the trip. I had made these assumptions and not asked too many questions. I probably should have but as a poor, struggling graduate student I was simply excited to be able to travel!

15 It was because of this nagging concern that I declined an invitation to travel to Bahrain for the film I advised, *New Muslim Cool*.

CONCLUSION

1 According to the 2012 report released by the Malcolm X Grassroots Movement, every 28 hours a Black person is killed by either the police, security guards, or citizen vigilantes.

2 Material in this section is revised and expanded from "Fuck Tha Police: A Rumination on Black Life and Death," an article I wrote for the *Islamic Monthly* (Spring/Summer 2015).

3 The true size of which I did not know at the time—the panel was recorded by CSPAN and shown on its network.

4 Renisha McBride, unarmed, was shot through a screen door in Dearborn Heights, Michigan, when looking for help after crashing her car. Eric Garner, unarmed, was approached by New York police officers in Staten Island for allegedly selling loose cigarettes. Garner verbally argued with police about what he saw as harassment and was subsequently killed by a police choke hold. Freddie Gray, unarmed, was shot by Baltimore Police after making eye contact with an officer. Aiyana Stanley-Jones, unarmed, was killed by a SWAT team officer in pursuit of suspected killers who entered the wrong house; this police action was being shot for Reality TV.

5 She specifically notes the discovery of cornrows by White high end fashion designers and pop culture figures, the use of Black cultural styles to "be edgy" and "get attention," and the use of Black women as "props" in the video of Miley Cyrus's 2013 pop song "We Can't Stop."

6 Authenticity was off the table at the convening. Organizers were very intentional that the conference would show solidarity across Black difference.

7 On the one hand this anonymity was for the better, because the move away from hierarchical leadership models was seen by young Black activists to empower everyday people to organize their communities. On the other hand, however, one of the problems with the way we remember the civil rights and Black Power eras is that we tend to recall only the singular leaders and consequently fail to acknowledge and celebrate the leadership of the less famous leaders, many of whom, like Ella Baker, were Black women. Accordingly, the fact that the general public did not know the names of the #BlackLivesMatter founders was for the worse, insomuch as it aligns with the trend of the invisibility of Black women's leadership in the United States.

8 I had the privilege of participating in the die-ins in Chicago and at the AAA meeting.

DISCOGRAPHY

Amandla Stenberg. 2015. *Don't Cash Crop My Cornrows*. YouTube video. www.youtube. com. Accessed August 27.

Amir Sulaiman. "Danger." *Like a Thief in the Night*. Released 2007. Uprising Records. Audio CD.

Boogie Down Productions. "Beef." Produced by KRS-One, D-Nice, and Pal Joey. *Edutainment*. Released 1990. Jive/RCA Records. Audio CD.

Brand Nubian. "Allah and Justice." Produced by Lord Jamar, DJ Sincere, and Sadat X. *In God We Trust*. Released 1993. Electra/Arista BMG Records. Audio CD.

Common. "The Corner (Remix)." Single. Produced by Kanye West. Featuring Scarface and Mos Def. Released 2005. Geffen Records. YouTube recording. www.youtube.com.

D'Angelo and the Vanguard. 2014. *Black Messiah*. RCA. Digital Download.

dead prez. "Be Healthy." Produced by Headrush and dead prez. Featuring Prodigy. *Lets Get Free*. Released 2000. Loud/Columbia/Relativity Records. Audio CD.

D-Nick Da Microphone Misfit. "Abnormality." Produced by Dominique Stockman. *Graphic Novel*. Released 2010. Independent release. YouTube recording. www. youtube.com.

———. "99 Names of Jah/God/Allah." Unreleased. Private recording.

Doug E. Fresh and MC Ricky D. "La Di Da Di." Single. Released 1985. Reality Records. YouTube recording. www.youtube.com.

Geoffrey Dunn and Mark Schwartz. 1984. *Dollar a Day, Ten Cents a Dance* (documentary). Center for Asian American Media

Grace Lee. 2013 *American Revolutionary: The Evolution of Grace Lee Boggs* (documentary). LeeLee Films.

Jennifer Maytorena Taylor. 2009. *New Muslim Cool* (documentary). Specific Pictures.

Kendrick Lamar. "i." Produced by Rahki. *To Pimp a Butterfly*. Released 2014. Top Dawg Entertainment/Aftermath/Interscope. Mp3 file.

Lauryn Hill. "Doo Wop (That Thing)." Produced by Lauryn Hill. *The Miseducation of Lauryn Hill*. Released 1998. Ruffhouse/Columbia Records. Audio CD.

Maimouna Youssef. "We're Already Royal." Produced by Maimouna Youssef and DJ Dummy. *The Reintroduction of Mumu Fresh*. Released 2014. Independent Release. YouTube recording. www.youtube.com.

Mos Def and Talib Kweli. "K.O.S. (Determination)." Produced by Hi-Tek. Featuring Vinia Mojica. *Mos Def & Talib Kweli Are Black Star*. Released 1998. Rawkus Records. Audio CD.

Mustafa Davis. 2010. *Deen Tight* (documentary). Cinemotion Media.

Nicki Minaj. "Itty Bitty Piggy." Produced by DJ Holiday and Trapaholics. *Beam Me Up Scotty*. Mixtape. Released 2009. Youtube recording. www.youtube.com.

Public Enemy. "Bring the Noise." Produced by Chuck D, Rick Rubin, and Hank Shocklee. *It Takes a Nation of Millions to Hold Us Back*. Released 1988. Def Jam. Audio CD.

———. "Don't Believe the Hype." Produced by Chuck D, Rick Rubin, and Hank Shocklee. *It Takes a Nation of Millions to Hold Us Back*. Released 1988. Def Jam. Audio CD.

Queen Latifah. "Ladies First." Music video. Featuring Monie Love. Directed by Fab Five Freddy. *All Hail the Queen*. Released 1989. Tommy Boy Records. YouTube video. www.youtube.com.

The Reminders. "If You Didn't Know." Produced by The Reminders. *Born Champions*. Released 2007. The Reminders Music LLC. Audio CD.

Tupac Shakur. "I Ain't Mad at Cha." Produced by Daz. *All Eyez on Me*. Released 1996. Death Row/Interscope Records. Audio CD.

A Tribe Called Quest. "Ham n' Eggs." Produced by A Tribe Called Quest. *People's Instinctive Travels and Paths of Rhythm*. Released 1990. Jive/RCA Records. Audio CD.

BIBLIOGRAPHY

Aaronson, Trevor. 2011. "The Informants." *Mother Jones*. September/October. www. motherjones.com.

Abdullah, Zain. 2012. "Narrating Muslim Masculinities: The Fruit of Islam and the Quest for Black Redemption." *Spectrum: A Journal on Black Men* 1 (1): 141–77.

Abdul-Matin, Ibrahim. 2010. *Green Deen: What Islam Teaches about Protecting the Planet*. San Francisco, Calif.: Berrett-Koehler Publishers.

Adorno, Theodor. 1991. *The Culture Industry: Selected Essays on Mass Culture*. New York: Routledge.

Aidi, Hisham. 2004. "Verily, There Is Only One Hip-Hop Umma: Islam, Cultural Protest and Urban Marginality." *Socialism and Democracy* 19 (36): 107–26.

———[Hishaam]. 2009. "Jihadis in the Hood: Race, Urban Islam and the War on Terror." In *Black Routes to Islam*. Edited by Manning Marable and Hishaam D. Aidi, 283–98. New York: Palgrave Macmillan.

———. 2014. *Rebel Music: Race, Empire, and the New Muslim Youth Culture*. New York: Vintage Books.

Akbar, Amna A. 2013. "Policing 'Radicalization.'" SSRN Scholarly Paper ID 2282659, Social Science Research Network, Rochester, N.Y. http://papers.ssrn.com.

Alexander, Bryant Keith. 2005. "Performance Ethnography: The Reenacting and Inciting of Culture." In *The Sage Handbook of Qualitative Research*. Edited by Norman K. Denzin and Yvonne S. Lincoln, 411–42. Thousand Oaks, Calif.: Sage.

Alexander, Michelle. 2012. *The New Jim Crow: Mass Incarceration in the Age of Colorblindness*. New York: New Press.

Alim, H. Samy. 2005. "A New Research Agenda: Exploring the Transglobal Hip Hop Umma." In *Muslim Networks from Hajj to Hip Hop*. Edited by miriam cooke and Bruce Lawrence, 264–74. Chapel Hill: University of North Carolina Press.

———. 2006a. "Re-Inventing Islam with Unique Modern Tones: Hip Hop Artists as Verbal Mujahidin." *Souls: A Critical Journal of Black Politics, Culture and Society* 8 (4): 45–58.

———. 2006b. *Roc the Mic Right: The Language of Hip Hop Culture*. London: Routledge.

Alsultany, Evelyn. 2012. *The Arabs and Muslims in the Media: Race and Representation after 9/11*. New York: NYU Press.

Asad, Muhammad, trans. 2012. *The Message of the Qur'an*. London: Book Foundation.

Asad, Talal. 1986. "The Idea of an Anthropology of Islam." In *Occasional Papers Series*. Center for Contemporary Arab Studies, Georgetown University.

———. 1993. *Genealogies of Religion: Discipline and Reasons of Power in Christianity and Islam*. Baltimore: Johns Hopkins University Press.

———. 2003. *Formations of the Secular: Christianity, Islam, Modernity*. Stanford, Calif.: Stanford University Press.

Austin, Allan. 1997. *African Muslims in Antebellum America: Transatlantic Stories and Spiritual Struggles*. New York: Routledge.

Banjoko, Adisa. 2004. *Lyrical Swords: Hip Hop and Politics in the Mix*. San Jose: Yin-Sumi Press.

Batiste, Stephanie. 2005. "Stacks of Obits: A Performance Piece." *Women & Performance: A Journal of Feminist Theory* 15 (1): 105–25.

Bayoumi, Moustafa. 2010. "The Race Is On: Muslims and Arabs in the American Imagination." *Middle East Report Online*. March. www.merip.org.

Ba-Yunus, Ilyas. 1997. "Muslims of Illinois: A Demographic Report." Special issue. *East-West Review* Summer: 1–28.

Benjamin, Walter. 2006. *The Writer of Modern Life: Essays on Charles Baudelaire*. Edited by Michael W. Jennings. Translated by Howard Eiland. Cambridge, Mass.: Harvard University Press.

———. 2008. *The Work of Art in the Age of Its Technological Reproducibility and Other Writings on Media*. Edited by Michael W. Jennings, Bridget Doherty, and Thomas Y. Levin. Cambridge, Mass.: Belknap Press.

Bogira, Steve. 2011. "Separate, Unequal and Ignored." *Chicago Reader* February 10: 13–17.

Bourdieu, Pierre. 1990. *The Logic of Practice*. Stanford: Stanford University Press.

Brookings Institution Center on Urban and Metropolitan Policy. 2003. *Chicago in Focus: A Profile from Census 2000*. Washington, D.C.: Brookings Institution.

Bukhari, Muhammad ibn Ismail al-. 2007. *Translation of Sahih Bukhari*. Translated by M. Muhsin Khan. www.usc.edu.

Butler, Judith. 1989. *Gender Trouble: Feminism and the Subversion of Identity*. New York: Routledge.

———. 2004. *Undoing Gender*. New York: Routledge.

Cainkar, Louise. 2005. "Space and Place in the Metropolis: Arabs and Muslims Seeking Safety." *City and Society* 17 (2): 181–209.

———. 2011. *Homeland Insecurity: The Arab American and Muslim American Experience after 9/11*. New York: Russell Sage Foundation.

Chang, Jeff. 2005. *Can't Stop Won't Stop: A History of the Hip Hop Generation*. New York: Picador.

Chan-Malik, Sylvia. 2011. "'Common Cause': On the Black-Immigrant Debate and Constructing the Muslim American." *Journal of Race, Ethnicity, and Religion* 2 (8): 1–39.

Chicago Public Art Group. 2010. *What We Do*. www.cpag.net. Accessed December 2.

Chin, Elizabeth, ed. 2014. *Katherine Dunham: Recovering an Anthropological Legacy, Choreographing Ethnographic Futures*. Santa Fe: SAR Press.

Clay, Andreana. 2012. *The Hip-Hop Generation Fights Back: Youth, Activism and Post-Civil Rights Politics*. New York: NYU Press.

Cobb, William Jelani. 2007. *To the Break of Dawn: A Freestyle on the Hip Hop Aesthetic.* New York: NYU Press.

———. 2008. "The Genius of Cool: The 25 Coolest Brothers of All Time." *Ebony Magazine* August: 68–69.

Curtis, Edward E, IV. 2002. *Islam in Black America: Identity, Liberation and Difference in African-American Islamic Thought.* Albany: SUNY Press.

———. 2006. *Black Muslim Religion and the Nation of Islam, 1960–1975.* Chapel Hill: University of North Carolina Press.

———. 2009. *Muslims in America: A Short History.* Oxford: Oxford University Press.

———. 2014. *The Call of Bilal: Islam in the African Diaspora.* Chapel Hill: University of North Carolina Press.

Daulatzai, Sohail. 2012. *Black Star, Crescent Moon: The Muslim International and Black Freedom beyond America.* Minneapolis: University of Minnesota Press.

Dawson, Michael. 2003. *Black Visions: The Roots of Contemporary African-American Political Ideologies.* Chicago: University of Chicago Press.

De Certeau, Michel. 2002. *The Practice of Everyday Life.* Berkeley: University of California Press.

Deeb, Lara. 2006. *An Enchanted Modern: Gender and Public Piety in Shiʻi Lebanon.* Princeton: Princeton University Press.

———. 2009. "Piety Politics and the Role of a Transnational Feminist Analysis." *Journal of the Royal Anthropological Institute* 15 (May): S112–S126.

De Genova, Nicholas, and Ana Yolanda Ramos-Zayas. 2003. *Latino Crossings: Mexicans, Puerto Ricans, and the Politics of Race and Citizenship.* New York: Routledge.

De Sondy, Amanullah. 2015. *The Crisis of Islamic Masculinities.* London: Bloomsbury Academic.

Diawara, Manthia. 1998. *In Search of Africa.* Cambridge: Harvard University Press.

Dimitriadis, Greg. 2009. *Performing Identity/Performing Culture: Hip Hop as Text, Pedagogy, and Lived Practice.* New York: Peter Lang.

Diouf, Sylviane. 2013. *Servants of Allah: African Muslims Enslaved in the Americas.* New York: NYU Press.

Drake, St. Clair, and Horace Cayton. 1993. *Black Metropolis: A Study of Negro Life in a Northern City.* Chicago: University of Chicago Press.

Dyson, Michael Eric, and Sohail Daulatzai. 2009. *Born to Use Mics: Reading Nas's Illmatic.* New York: Basic Civitas Books.

Edwards, Erica R. 2011. "The Black President Hokum." *American Quarterly* 63 (1): 33–59. doi:10.1353/aq.2011.0013.

Fanon, Frantz. 1967. *Black Skins, White Masks.* New York: Grove Press.

———. 2005. *The Wretched of the Earth.* Translated by Richard Philcox. Introductions by Jean-Paul Sartre and Homi K. Bhabha. New York: Grove Press.

Fleetwood, Nicole R. 2011. *Troubling Vision: Performance, Visuality, and Blackness.* Chicago: University of Chicago Press.

Flores, Juan. 2000. *From Bomba to Hip-Hop: Puerto Rican Culture and Latino Identity.* New York: Columbia University Press.

Floyd-Thomas, Juan M. 2003. "A Jihad of Words: The Evolution of African American Islam and Contemporary Hip-Hop." In *Noise and Spirit: The Religious and Spiritual Sensibilities of Rap Music.* Edited by Anthony Pinn, 49–70. New York: NYU Press.

Forman, Murray. 2002. *The 'Hood Comes First: Race, Space and Place in Rap and Hip Hop.* Middletown, Conn.: Wesleyan University Press.

Foucault, Michel. 1990. *The History of Sexuality, Vol. 1: An Introduction.* Translated by Robert Hurley. New York: Vintage.

Gates, Henry Louis. 1989. *The Signifying Monkey: A Theory of African-American Literary Criticism.* New York: Oxford University Press.

GhaneaBassiri, Kambiz. 2010. *A History of Islam in America: From the New World to the New World Order.* New York: Cambridge University Press.

Ghazali, Abu Hamid al-. 1997. *The Alchemy of Happiness.* Translated by Claud Field. Chicago: Kazi Publications.

Gilroy, Paul. 1993. *Black Atlantic: Modernity and Double Consciousness.* Cambridge, Mass.: Harvard University Press.

Goffman, Erving. 1959. *The Presentation of Self in Everyday Life.* New York: Anchor Books.

Gomez, Michael. 2005. *Black Crescent: The Experience and Legacy of African Muslims in the Americas.* Cambridge: Cambridge University Press.

Greenhouse, Carol J. 2005. "Hegemony and Hidden Transcripts: The Discursive Arts of Neoliberal Legitimation." *American Anthropologist* 107 (3): 356–68. doi:10.1525.

Gregory, Steven. 1999. *Black Corona: Race and the Politics of Place in an Urban Community.* Princeton: Princeton University Press.

Grewal, Zareena. 2013. *Islam Is a Foreign Country: American Muslims and the Global Crisis of Authority.* New York: NYU Press.

Griebel, Helen Bradley. 1995. "The African American Woman's Headwrap: Unwinding the Symbols." In *Dress and Identity.* Edited by Mary Ellen Roach-Higgins, Joanne B. Eicher, and Kim K. P. Johnson, 445–60. New York: Fairchild.

Guerrirero, Lisa. 2010. "Coming to a 'Hood Near You: Street Sweeping." *Salem Blog* April 24. http://blogs.wickedlocal.com.

Haddad, Yvonne Yazbeck. 2007. "The Post-9/11 Hijab as Icon." *Sociology of Religion* 68 (3): 253–67.

Haddad, Yvonne Yazbeck, and John L. Esposito, eds. 2000. *Muslims on the Americanization Path?* New York: Oxford University Press.

Hage, Ghassan. 2009. "Hating Israel in the Field on Ethnography and Political Emotions."
Anthropological Theory 9 (1): 59–79.

Hall, Stuart. 1990. "Cultural Identity and Diaspora." In *Identity: Community, Culture, Difference.* Edited by John Rutherford, 223–37. London: Lawrence and Wishart.

———. 1996. "Gramsci's Relevance for the Study of Race and Ethnicity." In *Stuart Hall: Critical Dialogues in Cultural Studies.* Edited by Kuan-Hsing Chen and David Morley, 411–41. New York: Routledge.

————. 1998. "What Is This 'Black' in Black Popular Culture?" In *Black Popular Culture*. Edited by Gina Dent, 21–33. New York: New Press.

Hannerz, Ulf. 1970. "The Significance of Soul." In *Soul*. Edited by Lee Rainwater, 15–30. Chicago: Aldine.

————. 1983. *Exploring the City*. New York: Columbia University Press.

Harris-Lacewell, Melissa. 2006. *Barbershops, Bibles, and BET: Everyday Talk and Black Political Thought*. Princeton: Princeton University Press.

Harris-Perry, Melissa V. 2013. *Sister Citizen: Shame, Stereotypes, and Black Women in America*. New Haven: Yale University Press.

Harrison, Faye. 1997. *Decolonizing Anthropology: Moving Further Toward an Anthropology for Liberation*. Arlington, Va.: American Anthropological Association.

Hartigan, John. 2005. *Odd Tribes: Toward a Cultural Analysis of White People*. Durham, N.C.: Duke University Press.

Hartman, Saidiya V. 1997. *Scenes of Subjection: Terror, Slavery, and Self-Making in Nineteenth-Century America*. New York: Oxford University Press.

Higginbotham, Evelyn Brooks. 1994. *Righteous Discontent: The Women's Movement in the Black Baptist Church, 1880–1920*. Cambridge, Mass.: Harvard University Press.

Hill, Marc Lamont. 2009. *Beats, Rhymes, and Classroom Life: Hip-Hop Pedagogy and the Politics of Identity*. New York: Teachers College Press.

Hirschkind, Charles. 2009. *The Ethical Soundscape: Cassette Sermons and Islamic Counterpublics*. New York: Columbia University Press.

Ho, Fred, and Bill Mullen, eds. 2008. *Afro Asia: Revolutionary Political and Cultural Connections between African Americans and Asian Americans*. Durham, N.C.: Duke University Press.

hooks, bell. 2003. *We Real Cool: Black Men and Masculinity*. New York: Routledge.

Hopkinson, Natalie, and Natalie Y. Moore. 2006. *Deconstructing Tyrone: A New Look at Black Masculinity in the Hip-Hop Generation*. San Francisco: Cleis Press.

Huntington, Samuel L. 1993. "The Clash of Civilizations?" *Foreign Affairs* Summer. www.foreignaffairs.com.

Inskeep, Steve. 2006. "Between Faith and Country: Muslims in America." National Public Radio. September 11. www.npr.org.

Islamic Society of North America. 2015. "ISNA Disturbed by Escalation of Violence in Baltimore." www.isna.net. Accessed February 26, 2016.

Iton, Richard. 2010. *In Search of the Black Fantastic: Politics and Popular Culture in the Post–Civil Rights Era*. Kindle edition. New York: Oxford University Press.

Jackson, John, Jr. 2003. *Harlemworld: Doing Race and Class in Contemporary Black America*. Chicago: University of Chicago Press.

————. 2005. *Real Black: Adventures in Racial Sincerity*. Chicago: University of Chicago Press.

Jackson, Sherman. 2005. *Islam and the Blackamerican: Looking Toward the Third Resurrection*. New York: Oxford University Press.

Jacobs, Jane. 1961. *The Death and Life of Great American Cities*. New York: Random House.

Jamal, Amaney, and Nadine Naber, eds. 2008. *Race and Arab Americans before and after 9/11: From Invisible Citizens to Visible Subjects.* Syracuse, N.Y.: Syracuse University Press.

James, Frank. 1966. "Martin Luther King, Jr. in Chicago." *Chicago Tribune* August 5.

Jeffries, John. 1998. "Toward the Redefinition of the Urban: The Collision of Culture." In *Black Popular Culture*, edited by Gina Dent, 153–63. New York: New Press.

Kapchan, Deborah. 1996. "Performance." *Journal of American Folklore* 108 (430): 479–508.

Karim, Jamillah. 2008. *Amerian Muslim Women: Negotiating Race, Class and Gender within the Ummah.* New York: NYU Press.

Kelley, Robin D. G. 1996. *Race Rebels: Culture, Politics, and the Black Working Class.* Kindle edition. New York: Free Press.

———. 1997. *Yo' Mama's Disfunktional! Fighting the Culture Wars in Urban America.* Boston: Beacon Press.

———.1999. "Polycultural Me." *Utne Reader.* October. www.utne.com.

———. 2003. *Freedom Dreams: The Black Radical Imagination.* Boston: Beacon Press.

Kelley, Robin D. G., and Betsy Esch. 1999. "Black Like Mao: Red China and Black Revolution." *Souls* 1 (4): 6–41.

Keyes, Cheryl. 2004. *Rap Music and Street Consciousness.* Urbana: University of Illinois Press.

———. 2012. "Empowering Self, Making Choices, Creating Spaces: Black Female Identity via Rap Music Performance." In *That's the Joint: The Hip-Hop Studies Reader.* Edited by Murray Forman and Mark Anthony Neal, 400–12. New York: Routledge.

Khabeer, Su'ad Abdul. 2007. "Rep That Islam1: The Rhyme and Reason of American Islamic Hip Hop." *Muslim World* 97 (1): 125–41.

———. 2009. "Black Arabic: Some Notes on African American Muslims and the Arabic Language." In *Black Routes to Islam.* Edited by Manning Marable and Hishaam Aidi, 167–90. New York: Palgrave Macmillan.

———. 2014. "American Muslims and the 'Facts of Blackness.'" *Islamic Monthly* 7 (Spring/Summer).

———. 2015. "Fuck da Police: A Rumination on Black Life and Death." *Islamic Monthly* (Spring/Summer).

Khera, Farhana. 2010. "Witness Testimony at Hearing on Racial Profiling and the Use of Suspect Classifications in Law Enforcement Policy." Subcommittee on the Constitution, Civil Rights, and Civil Liberties of the Committee on the Judiciary, U.S. House of Representatives, June 17. Serial no. 111–131. Washington, D.C.: U.S. Government Printing Office. http://judiciary.house.gov.

Kim, Claire Jean. 1999. "The Racial Triangulation of Asian Americans." *Politics and Society* 27 (1): 105–38.

Kitwana, Bakari. 2002. *The Hip Hop Generation: Young Blacks and the Crisis in African-American Culture.* New York: Basic Civitas Books.

———. 2006. *Why White Kids Love Hip Hop: Wankstas, Wiggers, Wannabes, and the New Reality of Race in America.* New York: Basic Civitas Books.

Knight, Michael Muhammad. 2008. *The Five Percenters: Islam, Hip-Hop and the Gods of New York*. Oxford: Oneworld.

Kondo, Dorinne. 1997. *About Face: Performing Race in Fashion and Theater*. New York: Routledge.

———. 2000. "(Re)visions of Race: Contemporary Race Theory and the Cultural Politics of Racial Crossover in Documentary Theater." *Theatre Journal* 52 (1): 81–107.

Kundnani, Arun. 2015. *The Muslims Are Coming: Islamophobia, Extremism, and the Domestic War on Terror*. London: Verso.

Kwon, Soo Ah. 2013. *Uncivil Youth: Race, Activism, and Affirmative Governmentality*. Durham, N.C.: Duke University Press.

Lewis, Shantrelle P. 2015. "The Dandy Lion Project." http://shantrelleplewis.com. Accessed August 26.

Lipsitz, George. 2001. *Time Passages: Collective Memory and American Popular Culture*. Minneapolis: University of Minnesota Press.

———. 2006. *The Possessive Investment in Whiteness: How White People Profit from Identity Politics*. Philadelphia: Temple University Press.

Lopez, Ian Haney. 2015. *Dog Whistle Politics: How Coded Racial Appeals Have Reinvented Racism and Wrecked the Middle Class*. Oxford: Oxford University Press.

Lott, Eric. 2013. *Love & Theft: Blackface Minstrelsy and the American Working Class*. New York: Oxford University Press.

Love, Bettina. 2012. *Hip Hop's Li'l Sistas Speak: Negotiating Hip Hop Identities and Politics in the New South*. New York: Peter Lang.

Low, Setha, ed. 1999. *Theorizing the City: The New Urban Anthropology Reader*. New Brunswick, N.J.: Rutgers University Press.

Lubin, Alex. 2009. "Locating Palestine in Pre-1938: Black Internationalism." In *Black Routes to Islam*. Edited by Manning Marable and Hishaam Aidi, 17–32. New York: Palgrave Macmillan.

Madison, D. Soyini. 2005. *Critical Ethnography: Method, Ethics and Performance*. Thousand Oaks, Calif.: Sage.

Mahmood, Saba. 2005. *Politics of Piety: The Islamic Revival and the Feminist Subject*. Princeton: Princeton University Press.

———. 2006. "Secularism, Hermeneutics, and Empire: The Politics of Islamic Reformation." *Public Culture* 18 (2): 323–47.

Mailer, Norman. 1961. *Advertisements for Myself*. London: A. Deutsch.

Maira, Sunaina. 2008. "B-Boys and Bass Girls: Sex, Style and Mobility in Indian American Youth Culture." In *Desi Rap: Hip-Hop and South Asian America*. Edited by Ajay Nair and Murali Balaji, 41–70. Lanham, Md.: Lexington Books.

———. 2009. *Missing: Youth, Citizenship, and Empire after 9/11*. Durham, N.C.: Duke University Press.

Majors, Richard, and Janet Mancini Billson. 1992. *Cool Pose: The Dilemmas of Black Manhood in America*. New York: Lexington Books.

Mamdani, Mahmood. 2005. *Good Muslim, Bad Muslim: America, the Cold War, and the Roots of Terror*. New York: Harmony.

Massey, Douglas, and Nancy Denton. 1998. *American Apartheid: Segregation and the Making of the Underclass*. Cambridge, Mass.: Harvard University Press.

Mbembe, Achille. 2003. "Necropolitics." *Public Culture* 15 (1): 11–40.

McAlister, Melanie. 2005. *Epic Encounters: Culture, Media, and U.S. Interests in the Middle East since 1945*. Updated edition with a post–9/11 chapter. Berkeley: University of California Press.

McClaurin, Irma. 2001. *Black Feminist Anthropology: Theory, Politics, Praxis, and Poetics*. New Brunswick, N.J.: Rutgers University Press.

McCloud, Aminah Beverly. 1995. *African American Islam*. New York: Routledge.

Melamed, Jodi. 2011. *Represent and Destroy: Rationalizing Violence in the New Racial Capitalism*. Minneapolis: University of Minnesota Press.

Miller, Monica L. 2009. *Slaves to Fashion: Black Dandyism and the Styling of Black Diasporic Identity*. Durham, N.C.: Duke University Press.

Miller, Monica R. 2012. *Religion and Hip Hop*. New York: Routledge.

Miller, Monica R., Anthony B. Pinn, and Bernard "Bun B" Freeman, eds. 2015. *Religion in Hip Hop: Mapping the New Terrain in the U.S.* London: Bloomsbury Academic.

Mir, Shabana. 2014. *Muslim American Women on Campus: Undergraduate Social Life and Identity*. Chapel Hill: University of North Carolina Press.

Miyakawa, Felicia M. 2005. *Five Percenter Rap*. Bloomington: Indiana University Press.

Moallem, Minoo. 2005. *Between Warrior Brother and Veiled Sister: Islamic Fundamentalism and the Politics of Patriarchy in Iran*. Berkeley: University of California Press.

Monson, Ingrid. 1995. "The Problem with White Hipness: Race, Gender, and Cultural Conceptions in Jazz Historical Discourse." *Journal of the American Musicological Society* 48 (3): 396–422.

Moore, David Chioni. 1994. "Routes: Alex Haley's Roots and the Rhetoric of Genealogy." *Transition* 64: 4–21.

Morgan, Joan. 2000. *When Chickenheads Come Home to Roost: A Hip Hop Feminist Breaks It Down*. New York: Simon and Schuster.

Morgan, Marcyliena. 1999. "No Woman No Cry: Claiming African American Women's Place." In *Reinventing Identities: The Gendered Self in Discourse*. Edited by Mary Bucholtz, A. C. Liang, and Laurel A. Sutton, 27–45. New York: Oxford University Press.

———. 2009. *The Real Hip Hop: Battling for Knowledge, Power, and Respect in the LA Underground*. Durham, N.C.: Duke University Press.

Moten, Fred. 2003. *In the Break: The Aesthetics of the Black Radical Tradition*. Minneapolis: University of Minnesota Press.

Moynihan, Daniel Patrick. 1965. "The Negro Family: The Case for National Action." Office of Policy Planning and Research, U.S. Department of Labor. www.dol.gov.

Muhammad, Elijah. 1965. *Message to the Blackman in America*. Chicago: Muhammad's Temple No. 2.

Mukherjee, Roopali. 2006. "The Ghetto Fabulous Aesthetic in Contemporary Black Culture." *Cultural Studies* 20 (6): 599–629. doi:10.1080/09502380600973978.

Muslim American Society. 2014. "About the Muslim American Society." March 8. www.
muslimamericansociety.org.

Naber, Nadine. 2008. "Look, Mohammed the Terrorist Is Coming: Cultural Racism,
Nation-Based Racism and the Intersectionality of Oppressions after 9/11." In *Race
and Arab Americans before and after 9/11: From Invisible Citizens to Visible Subjects*.
Edited by Amaney Jamal and Nadine Naber, 276–304. Syracuse: Syracuse University Press.

———. 2012. *Arab America: Gender, Cultural Politics, and Activism*. New York: NYU
Press.

Najam, Haroon. 2011. "Third Biennial Arts and Culture Retreat." *Inner-City Muslim
Action Network*. www.imancentral.org. Accessed February 25, 2016.

Narayan, Kirin. 1993. "How 'Native' Is a Native Anthropologist?" *American Anthropologist* 95 (3): 671–86.

Nashashibi, Rami. 2005. "IMAN & Critical Engagement." Unpublished document.
Photocopy.

———. 2009. "The Black Stone Legacy: Islam and the Rise of Ghetto Cosmopolitanism." In *Black Routes to Islam*. Edited by Manning Marable and Hishaam Aidi,
271–82. New York: Palgrave Macmillan.

Neal, Mark Anthony. 2001. *Soul Babies: Black Popular Culture and the Post-Soul Aesthetic*. New York: Routledge.

———. 2013. *Looking for Leroy: Illegible Black Masculinities*. New York: NYU Press.

Neal, Mark Anthony, and Murray Forman, eds. 2012. *That's the Joint! The Hip-Hop
Studies Reader*. New York: Routledge.

Noble, Denise. 2005. "Remembering Bodies, Healing Histories: The Emotional Politics
of Everyday Freedom." In *Making Race Matter: Bodies, Space and Identity*. Edited by
Claire Alexander and Caroline Knowles, 133–52. New York: Palgrave Macmillan.

Nuruddin, Yusuf. 1998. "African-American Muslims and the Question of Identity: Between Traditional Islam, African Heritage and the American Way." In *Muslims on
the Americanization Path?* Edited by Yvonne Yazbeck Haddad and John L. Esposito,
267–330. Atlanta: Scholars Press.

Nyang, Sulayman. 1999. *Islam in the United States*. Chicago: Kazi Publications.

Omi, Michael, and Howard Winant. 1994. *Racial Formation in the United States: From
the 1960s to the 1990s*. New York: Routledge.

Ong, Aihwa. 1996. "Cultural Citizenship as Subject-Making: Immigrants Negotiate
Race and Cultural Boundaries in the United States." *Current Anthropology* 37 (5):
737–62.

Ongiri, Amy Abugo. 2009. *Spectacular Blackness: The Cultural Politics of the Black
Power Movement and the Search for a Black Aesthetic*. Charlottesville: University of
Virginia Press.

Oyewole, Abiodun. 2003. "Witness to Faith." *This Far by Faith*. January 1. www.pbs.org.

Oyewole, Abiodun, and Umar Bin Hassan. 1996. *On a Mission: Selected Poems and a
History of the Last Poets*. Edited by Kim Green. New York: Henry Holt.

Pattillo, Mary. 2008. *Black on the Block: The Politics of Race and Class in the City*. Chicago: University of Chicago Press.

Pattillo-McCoy, Mary. 2000. *Black Picket Fences: Privilege and Peril among the Black Middle Class*. Chicago: University of Chicago Press.

Perry, Imani. 2004. *Prophets of the Hood: Politics and Poetics in Hip Hop*. Durham, N.C.: Duke University Press.

Peterson, James Braxton. 2014. *The Hip-Hop Underground and African American Culture: Beneath the Surface*. New York: Palgrave Macmillan.

PEW Research Center. 2007. *Muslim Americans: Middle Class and Mostly Mainstream*. Washington, D.C.: PEW.

Pinn, Anthony. 1999. "'How Ya Livin'?' Notes on Rap Music and Social Transformation." *Western Journal of Black Studies* 23 (1): 10–21.

———. 2003. *Noise and Spirit: The Religious and Spiritual Sensibilities of Rap Music*. New York: NYU Press.

Pinn, Anthony B., and Monica R. Miller. 2009. "Introduction: Intersections of Culture and Religion in African-American Communities." *Culture and Religion* 10 (1): 1–9.

Prashad, Vijay. 2001. *The Karma of Brown Folk*. Minneapolis: University of Minnesota Press.

———. 2005. "Second-Hand Dreams." *Social Analysis* 49 (2): 191–98.

"Prevent Strategy." 2011. Presented to Parliament by the Secretary of State for the Home Department by Command of Her Majesty. June. London.

Puar, Jasbir K. 2007. *Terrorist Assemblages: Homonationalism in Queer Times*. Durham, N.C.: Duke University Press.

"Radical Middle Way." 2014. www.facebook.com.

Rainwater, Lee, ed. 1970. *Soul*. Chicago: Aldine.

Rana, Junaid. 2011. *Terrifying Muslims: Race and Labor in the South Asian Diaspora*. Durham, N.C.: Duke University Press.

Razack, Sherene H. 2008. *Casting Out: The Eviction of Muslims from Western Law and Politics*. Toronto: University of Toronto Press.

Remarkable Current. 2010. "Remarkable Current Indonesian Hip Hop Tour." www.remarkablecurrent.com. Accessed March 1.

Rivera, Geraldo. 2012. "Trayvon Martin Would Be Alive but for His Hoodie." *Fox News Latino*. March 23. http://latino.foxnews.com.

Rivera, Raquel Z. 2003. *New York Ricans from the Hip Hop Zone*. New York: Palgrave Macmillan.

Roberts, Robin. 1994. "'Ladies First': Queen Latifah's Afrocentric Feminist Music Video." *African American Review* 28 (2): 245–57.

Robinson, Cedric. 2000. *Black Marxism: The Making of the Black Radical Tradition*. Chapel Hill: University of North Carolina Press.

———. 2007. *Forgeries of Memory and Meaning: Blacks and the Regimes of Race in American Theater and Film before World War II*. Chapel Hill: University of North Carolina Press.

Roediger, David. 1998. "What to Make of *Wiggers*: A Work in Progress." In *Generations of Youth: Youth Cultures and History in Twentieth Century America*. Edited by Joe Austin and Michael Nevin Willard, 358–66. New York: NYU Press.

Rosaldo, Renato. 1994. "Cultural Citizenship in San Jose, California." *PoLAR* 17 (2): 57–63.

Rose, Tricia. 1994. *Black Noise: Rap Music and Black Culture in Contemporary America*. Middletown, Conn.: Wesleyan University Press.

———. 2008. *The Hip Hop Wars: What We Talk about When We Talk about Hip Hop—and Why It Matters*. New York: Basic Civitas Books.

Rosen, Lawrence. 2002. *The Culture of Islam*. Chicago: University of Chicago Press.

Rouse, Carolyn. 2004. *Engaged Surrender: African American Women and Islam*. Berkeley: University of California Press.

Said, Edward W. 1979. *Orientalism*. New York: Vintage Books.

Samuels, David. 2004. "The Rap on Rap: The 'Black Music' That Isn't Either." In *That's the Joint: The Hip Hop Studies Reader*. Edited by Murray Forman and Mark Anthony Neal, 168–76. New York: Routledge.

Schielke, Samuli. 2009. "Being Good in Ramadan: Ambivalence, Fragmentation, and the Moral Self in the Lives of Young Egyptians." *Journal of the Royal Anthropological Institute* 15 (May): S24–S40. doi:10.1111/j.1467–9655.2009.01540.x.

Schloss, Jo. 2009. *Foundation: B-Boys, B-Girls and Hip-Hop Culture in New York*. Oxford: Oxford University Press.

Schmidt, Garbi. 2004. *Islam in Urban America: Sunni Muslims in Chicago*. Philadelphia: Temple University Press.

Schnieder, Cynthia, and Kristina Nelson. 2008. "Mightier than the Sword: Arts and Culture in the U.S.-Muslim World Relationship." Brookings Project on U.S. Relations with the Islamic World. Saban Center for Middle East Policy at Brookings.

Scott, James C. 1990. *Domination and the Arts of Resistance: Hidden Transcripts*. New Haven, Conn.: Yale University Press.

Shakur, Assata, and Angela Davis. 2001. *Assata: An Autobiography*. Chicago: Lawrence Hill.

Sharma, Nitasha. 2010. *Hip Hop Desis: South Asian Americans, Blackness, and a Global Race Consciousness*. Durham, N.C.: Duke University Press.

Simmel, Georg. 1971. *The Metropolis and Mental Life in Individuality and Social Forms*. Edited by Donald Levine. Chicago: University of Chicago Press.

Singel, Ryan. 2005. "Meetro Eases Hookups in Your Hood." *Wired* September 29. www.wired.com.

Smith, Christopher Holmes. 2003. "'I Don't Like to Dream about Getting Paid': Representations of Social Mobility and the Emergence of the Hip-Hop Mogul." *Social Text* 21 (4): 69–97.

South Suburban Housing Center (SSHC). 2008. Written Testimony for the National Commission on Fair Housing and Equal Opportunity. "Still Separate and Unequal: The State of Fair Housing in America." Homewood, Ill.: South Suburban Housing Center.

Spady, James, and Joseph Eure. 1991. *Nation Conscious Rap: The Hip Hop Vision*. Philadelphia: PC International Press.

Spillers, Hortense J. 2003. *Black, White and in Color: Essays on American Literature and Culture*. Chicago: University of Chicago Press.

Steinbock-Pratt, Sarah. 2015. "'It Gave Us Our Nationality': U.S. Education, the Politics of Dress and Transnational Filipino Student Networks, 1901–45." In *Gender, Imperialism and Global Exchanges*. Edited by Stephan F. Miescher, Michele Mitchell, and Naoko Shibusawa, 181–204. Chichester, U.K.: Wiley-Blackwell.

Swedenburg, Ted. 1997. "Islam in the Mix: Lessons of the Five Percent." Paper presented at Anthropology Colloquium. University of Arkansas, Little Rock. February 19.

Tiongson, Antonio, Jr. 2013. *Filipinos Represent: DJs, Racial Authenticity, and the Hip-Hop Nation*. Minneapolis: University of Minnesota Press.

Trouillot, Michel-Rolph. 2001. "The Anthropology of the State in the Age of Globalization: Close Encounters of the Deceptive Kind." *Current Anthropology* 42 (1): 125–38.

Turner, Victor. 1987. *The Anthropology of Performance*. New York: PAJ Publications.

Ulysse, Gina. 2008. *Downtown Ladies: Informal Commercial Importers, a Haitian Anthropologist and Self-Making in Jamaica*. Chicago: University of Chicago Press.

Universal Zulu Nation. 2010. *The Beliefs of the Universal Zulu Nation*. www.zulunation.com. Accessed October 1.

U.S. Department of State. 2014. "American Muslims." http://photos.state.gov.

Utley, Ebony. 2012. *Rap and Religion: Understanding the Gangsta's God*. Santa Barbara, Calif.: Praeger.

Van Deburg, William L. 1993. *New Day in Babylon: The Black Power Movement and American Culture, 1965–1975*. Chicago: University of Chicago Press.

Volpp, Leti. 2002. "The Citizen and the Terrorist." *UCLA Law Review* 49.

Von Eschen, Penny M. 2004. *Satchmo Blows Up the World: Jazz Ambassadors Play the Cold War*. Cambridge, Mass.: Harvard University Press.

Wacquant, Loic. 2004. "Ghetto." In *International Encyclopedia of the Social and Behavioral Sciences*. Edited by Neil Smelser and Paul Baltes, 1–7. London: Pergamon Press.

Warren, James. 2010. "Using an Islamic View to Forge Connections." *New York Times*, April 17. www.nytimes.com.

Weheliye, Alexander G. 2005. *Phonographies: Grooves in Sonic Afro-Modernity*. Durham, N.C.: Duke University Press.

———. 2014. *Habeas Viscus: Racializing Assemblages, Biopolitics, and Black Feminist Theories of the Human*. Durham, N.C.: Duke University Press.

West, Cornel. 2001. *Race Matters*. New York: Vintage Books.

White, Shane, and Graham White. 1998. *Stylin': African American Expressive Culture from Its Beginnings to the Zoot Suit*. Ithaca, N.Y.: Cornell University Press.

Williams, Rhys H., and Gira Vashi. 2007. "Hijab and American Muslim Women: Creating the Space for Autonomous Selves." *Sociology of Religion* 68 (3): 269–87.

Wimsatt, William Upski. 2008. *Bomb the Suburbs: Graffiti, Race, Freight-Hopping and the Search for Hip-Hop's Moral Center*. 15th anniversary edition. Berkeley, Calif.: Soft Skull Press.

Wirth, Louis. 1929. *The Ghetto*. Chicago: University of Chicago Press.

———. 1995. "Urbanism as a Way of Life." In *Metropolis: Center and Symbol of Our Times*. Edited by Philip Kasinitz, 58–82. New York: NYU Press.

Wolfe, George C. 1987. *The Colored Museum*. New York: Methuen.

Woods, Clyde. 2000. *Development Arrested: The Blues and Plantation Power in the Mississippi Delta*. London: Verso.

Woodson, Carter Godwin. 2013. *The Mis-Education of the Negro*. New York: Tribeca Books.

Yancey, George. 2008. *Black Bodies, White Gazes: The Continuing Significance of Race*. Lanham, Md.: Rowman & Littlefield.

Zorbaugh, Harvey Warren. 1976. *Gold Coast and Slum: A Sociological Study of Chicago's Near North Side*. Chicago: University of Chicago Press.

INDEX

415 (emcee), 85, 88, 90

Abdullah, Zain, 167, 243n14
Abdur-Rashid, Imam Al Hajj Talib, 93–95, 182–84
Africa, devalued as locus of Islamic authenticity, 96–97, 226
Afrika Bambaataa, 46, 55–56, 57, 189–90
Afrika Islam, 46–47, 57
Afro-Arab solidarity, 72–73, 228
Afro-Asian solidarity, 73, 228
Afrocentricity: in hip hop, 51–52, 56, 72, 121–22; in the 'hoodjab, 71, 130; and Islam, 53; as social movement, 71, 72, 135
Agamben, Giorgio, 220–21
Ahmadiyya Muslim community, 48
Aidi, Hisham, 201, 216, 217
Ali, Duse Muhammad, 237n18
Ali, Muhammad, 57, 142
Alim, H. Samy, 29
Alsarah, 210
Alsultany, Evelyn, 239n3
America/Islam binary, 8, 24, 136–37
American Islam, 195
American Muslims (State Department), 178–79, 194, 195, 216, 217
Americanness: as identity, 145, 169; as source of authority, 145, 170–71, 224
anthropology of Islam, 8, 74–75
anti-Americanism, zoot suits as markers of, 171
anti-Blackness: in Muslim world, 97; by non-Black U.K. Muslims, 208; by

non-Black U.S. Muslims, 14–15, 41–42, 45, 67–68, 84, 101, 126–27, 222–23, 224, 226; racial logics of, 14–15; as structural condition, 45, 83, 220. *See also* blackness: repudiation of, as un-Islamic
antiracism, official, 82, 92
appropriation: of Black culture by non-Blacks, 1–2, 3–4, 72, 119, 134–35, 225–26, 227; of White clothing styles by Blacks, 153–54, 165, 171
Arabic, as source of status, 21, 42
Arab U.S. American Muslims: anti-Black racism among, 14–15, 43, 126–27; as "immigrants," 12, 15, 84; perceived as non-White, 42; privileged authority of, 12–13, 83–84, 94–95, 100
Architect, 88–89
Armstrong, Louis, 215
Asian U.S. Americans, 73, 132, 169

Babikar, Shaykh, 203
Baraka, Amiri, 186
beards: as identity marker, 24, 166, 200; as source of status, 42, 45
Beatnick, 73
Berry, Chuck, 189–90
Big Daddy Kane, 53, 154–55
Billson, Janet Mancini, 141
bint, 148
Black, Aja, 210
Black Arts Movement, 56, 183, 185, 186, 191–92, 194
Black bodies, objectification of, 102–4, 105–106, 107, 225–26

ABOUT THE AUTHOR

Su'ad Abdul Khabeer is a scholar-artist-activist who uses anthropology and performance to explore the intersections of race and popular culture. She received her Ph.D. in Cultural Anthropology from Princeton University and is a graduate of the School of Foreign Service at Georgetown University. Su'ad is currently Assistant Professor of Anthropology and African American Studies at Purdue University and Founder and Senior Editor of sapelosquare.com.

CPSIA information can be obtained
at www.ICGtesting.com
Printed in the USA
JSHW021214160822
29214JS00009B/2

9 781479 894505